THE GEOPOLITICAL AESTHETIC

Cinema and Space in the World System

THE GEOPOLITICAL AESTHETIC

Cinema and Space in the World System

FREDRIC JAMESON

INDIANA UNIVERSITY PRESS
Bloomington and Indianapolis

BFI PUBLISHING
London

First Paperback Edition 1995

First published in 1992 by
Indiana University Press
601 North Morton Street, Bloomington, Indiana 47404
and the
British Film Institute
21 Stephen Street, London W1P 1PL, England

Library of Congress Cataloging-in-Publication Data
Jameson, Fredric.
   The geopolitical aesthetic: cinema and space in the world system
 / Fredric R. Jameson.
     p.   cm.
   ISBN 0-253-33093-9 (cloth)   ISBN 0-253-20966-8 (pbk.)
   1. Geopolitics in motion pictures.   2. Technology in motion
pictures.   3. Conspiracy in motion pictures.   4. Motion pictures –
Aesthetics. I. Title
PN1995.9.G39J3   1992
791.43′658 – dc20   91–32454

2 3 4 5 00 99 98 97 96 95

British Library Cataloguing in Publication Data
Jameson, Fredric
   The geopolitical aesthetic: cinema and space
   in the world system.
   I. Title
   791.43

   ISBN 0-85170-311-9   ISBN 0-85170-536-7 (pbk.)

For Sam and Harriet Robbins

Contents

Preface

Colin MacCabe

Fredric Jameson is probably the most important cultural critic writing in English today. The range of his analysis, from architecture to science fiction, from the tortuous thought of late Adorno to the *testimonio* novel of the third world, is extraordinary; it can truly be said that nothing cultural is alien to him. He is one of the very few thinkers who genuinely ignores the conventional distinctions between cultural objects: he will as readily bring the same care and attention to the deliberately complex works of high modernism as to the very different complexities of cyberpunk. As importantly he will move between media: the analysis of a text will be followed by a social description of a building, the criticism of a mainstream film will be succeeded by an appreciation of an avant-garde video.

At the same time it must be admitted that his work is particularly difficult, the first encounter with these long and complex sentences in which the sub-clauses beat out complicated theoretical rhythms can be almost vertiginous. At one level this difficulty must simply be encountered – Jameson's style is an integral part of the effort to understand the world as both one and multiple, and if there is difficulty and awkwardness there is also pleasure and grace. But Jameson's work is difficult in another way. He is a systematic thinker, like Sartre and Adorno, his two great masters. That is to say that even the most local and specific analysis finds its place within an overarching theoretical framework. The specific analysis is always related, albeit in dialectical fashion, to an extraordinarily sophisticated and detailed theory of culture and society. That theory, however, provides the underlying assumptions and reference – it is not present explicitly in every text. It is thus the paradoxical case that to read Jameson is always to read the entire oeuvre rather than a single particular text. It is a feature of such systematic thinking that it may very often have a slow start – as the basic premisses are worked out – but once these premisses have been elaborated, more and more material is illuminated by their perspective. Jameson's own bibliography and career follows this pattern as a patient understanding of French and German theory throughout the sixties and seventies then gives way in the eighties to a riot of cultural analysis, starting with *The Political Unconscious* (Cornell University Press, 1981) at the beginning of the decade and working through a whole variety of media in the aftermath of that book.

Although an intense private interest in film had emerged in the seventies with articles on *Zardoz* (*JumpCut* no. 3, Sept./Oct. 1974) and *Dog Day Afternoon* (*Screen Education* no. 30, Spring 1979), Jameson's full theoretical engagement with film is a product of the recent past, with the lectures at the British Film Institute in May 1990 – which form the basis for this book – and the publication in the same year of *Signatures of the Visible* (Routledge, 1990). It is thus possible that readers will be unfamiliar with some of the crucial assumptions of Jameson's thought. A full exposition, which also took account of the way in which the engagement with film feeds back into the theoretical assumptions, would be material for yet another book but it is worth very briefly glossing three terms which are crucial to Jameson's endeavors: the political unconscious, post-modernism and cognitive mapping.

The Political Unconscious

Jameson is a Marxist and traditionally that has meant granting a primacy to the forms of economic activity in an understanding of cultural forms. The most traditional form of Marxist analysis presupposes that an analysis of the economic base will then enable one to read off elements of the cultural superstructure from law to literature. There are two classic theoretical difficulties with this position. The first concentrates on the difficulty in defining the mechanism which leads from base to superstructure. How exactly does economic organization cause effects at levels which cannot be directly related to it? The second, possibly even more serious, questions how one can define the economic base without having recourse to categories which are themselves superstructural – how for example can one describe any set of economic relations without notions of ownership which are legally inscribed?

These two theoretical difficulties are perhaps of less importance to cultural analysts than the practical difficulty that if one adopts a classic Marxist position then all cultural forms end up with the same content. One must resign oneself to endlessly analysing the same messages – in the end, there is simply the endless recoding of property relations which are themselves to be analysed in economic rather than cultural terms.

It is to this practical difficulty that Jameson's theory of the political unconscious responds. Jameson is by training a linguist and a literary analyst – trained to respond to the smallest variations of meaning. For him, it is crucial to develop a form of Marxist analysis which will respect and utilize these differences rather than collapsing them into an undifferentiated reflection. To accomplish this, he makes the radical theoretical move of assuming that the relation to the economic is a fundamental element within the cultural object to be analyzed – not in terms of the economic processes within which the cultural object takes form but in the psychic processes which engage in its production and reception. For Jameson, every text is at its most fundamental level a political fantasy which in contradictory fashion articulates both the actual and potential social relations which constitute individuals within a specific political economy. In postulating this textual level Jameson is fundamentally influenced by the Christian tradition, and its most important recent literary critic Northrop Frye, rather than any of the theorists or critics who have addressed this problem within the Marxist tradition. The religious perspective allows a non-sociological approach to the connection between the individual and the universal.

The great advantage of this solution is that it allows Jameson to respect levels of textual and cultural differentiation. In fact, these differences become a primary element in the development of analyses of new social and economic relations. This advantage is much more striking in *The Geopolitical Aesthetic* than it was in the original *Political Unconscious*. The original theory was elaborated in the context of a reading of nineteenth and early twentieth-century fiction. The political unconscious at work in texts by Balzac or Conrad provides a way of reading a social history and an economic analysis – which are in their outlines very well understood within the Marxist tradition. Balzac and Conrad provide the material to produce a more nuanced account of what is in essence, a well understood story. *The Geopolitical Aesthetic*, on the other hand, addresses contemporary texts and provides readings which suggest radical new ways of formulating both a social history and an economic analysis.

At the same time, Jameson's theoretical originality enables him to maintain an orthodox Marxist position which allows primacy to economic forms or organization, with the nuance that those forms may well need to be understood in the light of analyses produced within cultural texts. Jameson is thus locating himself on very different ground from the various forms of cultural materialism which are currently the dominant academic inheritors of Marxism. For these last emphasize the impossibility of splitting cultural and economic analyses at any theoretical level and thus refuse the primacy to the economic which Jameson still allows. Jameson's position has the advantage of being able to draw fully on the traditions of both literary and cultural criticism as well as classical Marxism. It also provides an original solution to the need to provide some account of a dialectic between economic and cultural categories. However, it falls prey to the most obvious question that has to be asked of any base/

superstructure model: what mechanisms translate social organization into cultural forms? What is novel for a Marxist theory is that what Jameson's account lacks is a psychology rather than a sociology. What Jameson requires is an account of the mechanisms which articulate individual fantasy and social organization.

Post-modernism

If the political unconscious provides the key theoretical term for Jameson's endeavor, the key historical category is that of post-modernism. Post-modernism is a term notorious for its extraordinarily fluid meanings and extremely complicated history. For our current purposes let us simply identify three meanings which contribute to Jameson's use of the term. From the 50s onwards, particularly in America, post-modernism was a term used by literary critics to refer to contemporary works ranging from the Beat movement to campus novels which obviously indicated a new sensibility but, equally obviously, could not simply be linked into the concerns of what was becoming an increasingly institutionalized modernism. As modernism came to dominate the university curriculum, a new term was needed for new literary movements. Some twenty years later in France, and particularly in the work of Lyotard, post-modernism gained increasing currency as a term which would cover both contemporary culture and the new post-industrial economy and society which nourished it. By then it had also gained polemical currency in architectural debates in a devastating attack on modernism and the concerns of the modernist movement, a meaning only hinted at in the previous two uses.

For Jameson the term is crucial as a means of designating a completely new social positioning of art. Post-modernism is not fundamentally a question of subject-matter or themes but of the full entry of art into the world of commodity production. Jameson's definition is thus a fully Marxist one crucially linked to Mandel's analysis of the current stage of global multinational capitalism as marking a new stage in capitalist development. Post-modernism is the cultural form of the current moment of late capitalism just as realism was the privileged artistic form of the first stage of capitalist industrialist development and modernism corresponded to the economic moment of imperialism and monopoly capitalism.

Jameson's analysis, which emphasises the full integration of economics and culture, can thus be understood as both congruent and completely opposed to the modernist perspective of Adorno and the Frankfurt School. For Adorno the commodification of art marked the final abolition of any autonomous perspective from which to criticize the dominant forms of economic development. For Jameson the moment at which cultural production is fully integrated into economic production opens out the possibility of a cultural politics which would fundamentally intervene in the economic.

If the first cultural reaction to capitalism is a realism which attempts to provide forms of representation which will comprehend this new stage of economic development, modernism is the appalled recognition that any such representation is itself subject to social and economic forms which relativize its comprehension in relation to changing audiences. Modernism is the attempt, after a loss of innocence about representation, to invent forms which will determine their own audiences, to project an interiority onto a future unmediated by any form of commodity. It is for this reason that the history of modernism is marked by new forms of sponsorship and above all by an avant-garde ethic which, be it of an aesthetic or political form, looks into the future for an ideal Joycean or proletarian reader. Modernism thus constitutes itself, well before the cultural analyses of an Adorno, as an area of art constitutively opposed to commerce. The effort to project the self onto reality is premissed on a perfected future man who will become the ideal audience for ideal art.

Nowhere are these assumptions more obvious than in modernist architecture and nowhere have their inadequacies been made more apparent. Architecture, which has always been the traditional art most fully integrated with the economy, is the neuralgic point of modernist breakdown as the pretensions of a Corbusier or Frank Lloyd Wright run up against the realities of the post-industrial city. It is for this reason that Jameson's analysis of post-modernism is so firmly anchored in the architectural debates of the late 70s. But if architecture is the traditional art most difficult to dissociate from the economy then film is properly the postmodern art – impossible to understand outside the full development of the first stage of capitalist development. Cinema is a product of the most sophisticated forms of industrial production; it is, in Hollis Frampton's memorable words, the last machine.

One then has to reckon with the historical paradox that this postmodern medium recapitulates the basic realism/modernism/postmodernism aesthetic development, with the classic Hollywood cinema representing realism (and a moment of innocence about the means of representation), the European cinema of the 50s and 60s reliving all the paradoxes of modernism (and Godard is here the exemplary figure) and a fully post-modern cinema having to wait until the early 70s. It is now a cinema in which the distinctions between high and low art (always precarious) have more or less vanished and where culture and economics cross and recross at every level of both fields. It is cinema which still more than any other medium provides – if not the universal form – at least the possibility of combining the most ancient and local artistic traditions with the most modern and global advertising campaigns. It is a cultural form permeated at every level by the practices and paradoxes of marketing – a postmodern practice which oscillates between the passive reproduction and the active remodelling of audiences. If the politics of realism are implicitly reformist (the understanding of society leading directly to its control) and those of modernism vanguardist (in which it is the future tendencies of the system which provide the basis for political action), it is not yet clear what the politics of postmodernism will be, though it is clear that they will articulate the ever-increasing levels of micropolitics with those almost paralyzed stirrings towards global forms which date back to the League of Nations.

If film is the most postmodern of artforms (the discussion about its relation to rock music and television would be a whole separate book) then it will also be one in which the current political unconscious may most fruitfully be analyzed. This is the wager of Jameson's book as he attempts to analyze the geopolitical realities of postmodern cinema. His method, however – the selection of four disconnected moments in current world cinema – depends on a further term: cognitive mapping.

Cognitive Mapping

Cognitive mapping is the least articulated but also the most crucial of the Jamesonian categories. Crucial because it is the missing psychology of the political unconscious, the political edge of the historical analysis of post-modernism and the methodological justification of the Jamesonian undertaking. The term is taken from the geographer Kevin Lynch's *The Image of the City* (MIT Press, 1960) and is used by him to describe the phenomenon by which people make sense of their urban surroundings. Effectively, it works as an intersection of the personal and the social, which enables people to function in the urban spaces through which they move. For Jameson, cognitive mapping is a way of understanding how the individual's representation of his or her social world can escape the traditional critique of representation because the mapping is intimately related to practice – to the individual's successful negotiation of urban space. Cognitive mapping in this sense is the metaphor for the processes of the political unconscious. It is also, however, the model for how we might begin to articulate the local and the global. It provides a way of linking the most intimately local – our particular path through the world – and the most global – the crucial features of our political planet.

Most importantly, however, it provides a justification for Jameson's own cultural analyses of the past decade and of this book in particular. There has been a considerable amount of criticism of Jameson for attempting to generalize about global situations from limited information. Should Jameson ever choose to respond to such criticisms it would have to be in terms of the fact that such generalization is an inevitable cultural process. The point is to make sure that the information (which will always be limited) is nonetheless sufficient to produce a map which will overlap at certain crucial points with other grids of interpretation and which will produce the terms for further political and economic analysis.

Theoretically speaking, cognitive mapping needs more than mere development – it is fundamentally a metaphor which needs to be unpacked into a series of concepts which would link the psychic and the social. At the same time, it proves a very adequate account of Jameson's own personal project. As life in general, and academic life in particular, has become more global there is no figure who has more thoroughly attempted to expand his field of analysis accordingly. There may be more assiduous travellers of the airlines of the world but I know of no-one who more systematically and thoroughly attempts at each new destination to experience both the local cultural forms and their local forms of analysis. In these terms Jameson can be understood as attempting to join the journalistic function of reporting to the intellectual project of cultural analysis. From this perspective, the theoretical underpinnings are beside the point. What those who attended the lectures at the National Film Theatre in May 1990 were privileged to hear and what this book now provides for its readers are a series of cultural reports. What these reports make clear is how crucial it now is to understand film in its global complexity if one is to hope to understand it in its local specificities.

One of the great excitements of this book is the way that the perspective it obtains enables an entirely fresh look at the whole question of film and politics. Ever since the mid-seventies questions of politics within film theory have largely been couched in vanguardist terms. The positions elaborated by *Screen* in the mid-seventies now seem in retrospect to be a terribly belated last gasp of modernism in which a figure like Godard promised to articulate the relation between art and politics prefigured by Mayakovsky and the Formalists in the Soviet 20s or Brecht and Benjamin in the German 30s.

Since the *Screen* of the mid-seventies there really has been no new attempt to theorize the relations between politics and film. While there is always the production of local ideological readings, particularly fuelled by identity politics, these rarely engage with film as form and history. What Jameson suggests is that we must now analyze film comparatively – that we can only understand a film politics when we place it both in its local political context and its global context as film – for any film will inevitably reflect on what one might call its place in the global distribution of cultural power. In this, Jameson's analysis relates very neatly to the massive new importance of festivals as forms of exhibition.

One striking feature of this text is how the analysis advanced in May 1990 has been amply confirmed in the following two years. The fundamental figure of conspiracy and, particularly, the confusion between conspirators, victims and police finds text-book confirmation in films like *Total Recall* and *JFK*. Even more striking is that the fundamental grids that Jameson offers – the encounter of the former Soviet states with capitalism, the resurgence of local realities in the successful economies of the Pacific, the continuing 'under-development' in the 'Third World', the complicated search for a European culture seem ever more pertinent in a world where the political dominance of America is now equal to the cultural dominance that Hollywood achieved over half a century ago. Any future attempt to analyze politics and film will have to take issue with the arguments advanced in this book.

Introduction

Beyond Landscape

The films discussed here have been selected with a view towards an unsystematic mapping or scanning of the world system itself: from what used to be called the superpowers, across that most industrialized zone of a former Third World now called the Pacific Rim, only to conclude with a confrontation between First World or European technology at its most self-conscious (in Godard) and a Third World meditation on that technology at *its* most self-consciously and reflexively *naïf* (in the work of the Philippine film-maker Kidlat Tahimik).[1]

But technology is little more than the outer emblem or symptom by which a systemic variety of concrete situations expresses itself in a specific variety of forms and form-problems. It is not a random variety, and sometimes seems best described in developmental – or better still, in uneven-developmental – language: as when, for example, Edward Yang's film *Terrorizer* seems to raise the question of the belated emergence of a kind of modernism in the modernizing Third World, at a moment when the so-called advanced countries are themselves sinking into full postmodernity. The residues of the modern will then offer one clue or thread for these explorations.

Yet other kinds of relationships also propose convenient figures: the US and Soviet narratives discussed here, as different from each other as the *série noire* from Grimms' fairy tales, both seem to raise the problem of the view from above, and of the invention of new forms of representation for what it is properly impossible to think or represent, and both finally coincide in the logic of conspiracy. But in the North American movies, it is a conspiracy of the espionage-thriller or even paranoid type, while in Alexander Sokurov's stunning *Days of Eclipse* (based on a novel and script by the Strugatsky Brothers) such inverted providentiality becomes on the contrary science-fictional in its resonance.

In fact the theoretical focus of this investigation is modified after the American materials, as the section break indicates. The earlier section sought to document the figuration of conspiracy as an attempt – 'unconscious,' if you follow my loose, figural use of that otherwise

1

individual term – to think a system so vast that it cannot be encompassed by the natural and historically developed categories of perception with which human beings normally orient themselves. Space and demography offer the quickest short-cuts to this perceptual difficulty, provided each is used like a ladder to be kicked away after it has done its work. As far as space is concerned, Bergson's warning about the temptations of spatializing thought remain current in the age of the intercontinental ballistic missile and the new infra-red and laser systems of which we are so proud; it is even more timely in an era of urban dissolution and re-ghettoization, in which we might be tempted to think that the social can be mapped that way, by following across a map insurance red lines and the electrified borders of private police and surveillance forces. Both images are, however, only caricatures of the mode of production itself (most often called late capitalism), whose mechanisms and dynamics are not visible in that sense, cannot be detected on the surfaces scanned by satellites, and therefore stand as a fundamental representational problem – indeed, a problem of a historically new and original type.

All of the terms that lie to hand, indeed, are already figural, already soaked and saturated in ideology: this is why demography won't work either, although it is certain, not merely that the sheer numbers of new people on the globe, but even more surely their unprecedented self-consciousness, play their part in the new representational situation. But for most people, demography projects an immediate and subliminal image of the starving masses abroad and the homeless at home, of birth control and abortion. It thereby fixes the theme permanently at the political level and in a form which – all the more so because of its intrinsic urgency – does not move the viewer or the listener, the reader or 'public opinion' itself on to the underlying systemic reality, the root cause of missiles and permanent underemployment, or birth-rates abroad fully as much as break-ins at home. To make your way from those vivid miseries, which offer no problems of figuration since they can all at once be witnessed on your television set – and indeed somehow offer the example of an idea that includes an image, or an image that comes pre-packaged and already labelled with its ideational slogan – to be able to make your way through that level so as to think it together with its deeper, but non-visual systemic cause – this, if it is possible, is what used to be called self-consciousness about the social totality.

My thesis, however, is not merely that we ought to strive for it, but that we do so all the time anyway without being aware of the process. Critics and theorists have shown enthusiasm for the proposition that figures and narratives can bear many different meanings at the same time, and know distinct, sometimes even contradictory functions. They have been less eager to make an inventory of some of the specific meanings in question, something I try to do here for what

2

may be called the 'conspiratorial text,' which, whatever other messages it emits or implies, may also be taken to constitute an unconscious, collective effort at trying to figure out where we are and what landscapes and forces confront us in a late twentieth century whose abominations are heightened by their concealment and their bureaucratic impersonality. Conspiracy film takes a wild stab at the heart of all that, in a situation in which it is the intent and the gesture that counts. Nothing is gained by having been persuaded of the definitive verisimilitude of this or that conspiratorial hypothesis: but in the intent to hypothesize, in the desire called cognitive mapping – therein lies the beginning of wisdom.

In Part Two, this orientation is reversed; and a series of 'filmic texts' is scanned for a kind of allegorical thinking which is less ultimate than the cartography of the absolute invoked in the preceding paragraphs, although of a piece with it and sharing common mental operations. At a more local level, indeed, what I have called cognitive mapping – and what Althusser described in his classic model of the three fundamental terms of ideology (the individual subject, the real, and the Imaginary projection by the subject of the former's relationship to the latter)[2] – was simplified by a Cold War division for which henceforth traditional class categories could largely serve (business classes and managers, factory workers, fieldworkers, and lumpens or unemployed). Now however we revert to a multiplicity of nation states (and fantasmatic nationalisms), not yet culturally and ideologically organized around the categories of the new triumvirate of superstates (the US, Europe and Japan). In the absence of general categories under which to subsume such particulars, the lapse back into features of the pre-World War I international system is inevitable and convenient (it includes all the national stereotypes which, inevitably racist whether positive or negative, organize our possibility of viewing and confronting the collective Other).[3]

It is also important to stress the fact that these archaic categories will not work for the new world system: it is enough, for example, to reflect on the disappearance of specifically national cultures and their replacement, either by a centralized commercial production for world export or by their own mass-produced neotraditional images, for the lack of fit between the categories of the nineteenth century and the realities of the twenty-first to become apparent. Under these circumstances, the operations of some banal political unconscious clearly continue – we map our fellows in class terms day by day and fantasize our current events in terms of larger mythic narratives, we allegorize our consumption and construction of the object-world in terms of Utopian wishes and commercially programmed habits – but to that must be added what I will now call a geopolitical unconscious. This it is which now attempts to refashion national allegory into a conceptual instrument for grasping our new being-in-the-world. It may

3

henceforth be thought to be at least one of the fundamental allegorical referents or levels of all seemingly abstract philosophical thought: so that a fundamental hypothesis would pose the principle that all thinking today is *also*, whatever else it is, an attempt to think the world system as such. All the more true will this be for narrative figurations, whose very structure encourages a soaking up of whatever ideas in the air are left and a fantasy-solution to all the anxieties that rush to fill our current vacuum. The films analyzed in the second part of this present book may all of them be taken as exhibits in that process, and as examples of the way in which narrative today (or at least narrative outside the superstate, which need not worry about these problems in the same way, as Part One will show) conflates ontology with geography and endlessly processes images of the unmappable system.

The issue is thereby joined of representation itself, or rather (since that word has been associated with polemics it may be distracting to recall in the present context) of representability: a term that raises in its turn the fundamental historical question of the conditions of possibility of such representation in the first place. It is a question which necessarily opens out onto the nature of the social raw material on the one hand (a raw material which necessarily includes the psychic and the subjective within itself) and the state of the form on the other, the aesthetic technologies available for the crystallization of a particular spatial or narrative model of the social totality.

For it is ultimately always of the social totality itself that it is a question in representation, and never more so than in the present age of a multinational global corporate network. It is, indeed, as if the imagination included a sound barrier, undetectable save in those moments in which a representational task or program suddenly collapses. Such a sound barrier (if not the speed of light itself) could be thought of in terms of demography, of the sheer quantities of other people, whose figural categories cease to multiply beyond a certain point. But what is that point, in our time: the mob; the masses in the plaza, seen from above in a literal bird's-eye view; the silent wheeling of great armies on foot, face to face (as in *Spartacus* [Kubrick, 1960] or Bondarchuk's *War and Peace* [1968])? Most wondrous of all, the first appearance, on the strand, in carts and on foot, on horse- or donkey-back, in rags and tattered uniforms, accompanied by family and concubines, of the rag-tag and bobtail army of the people itself in Pontecorvo's *Burn!* (1969)? Under what circumstances can a necessarily individual story with individual characters function to represent collective processes?

Allegory thereby fatally stages its historic reappearance in the postmodern era (after the long domination of the symbol from romanticism to late modernism), and seems to offer the most satisfactory (if varied and heterogeneous) solutions to these form-problems.

4

On the global scale, allegory allows the most random, minute, or isolated landscapes to function as a figurative machinery in which questions about the system and its control over the local ceaselessly rise and fall, with a fluidity that has no equivalent in those older national allegories of which I have spoken elsewhere.[4] On the actantial level, a host of partial subjects, fragmentary or schizoid constellations, can often now stand in allegorically for trends and forces in the world system, in a transitional situation in which genuinely transnational classes, such as a new international proletariat and a new density of global management, have not yet anywhere clearly emerged. These constellated and allegorical subject-positions are, however, as likely to be collective as they are individual-schizophrenic, something which itself poses new form-problems for an individualistic storytelling tradition.

As for commodification, its relationship to allegory can be expected to be polyvalent; but the fact of the commodification of the cultural product itself can illustrate some of the complications, since, in the postmodern, autoreferentiality can be initially detected in the way in which culture acts out its own commodification. From the generic standpoint, what interests us here is the way in which the former genres (thrillers, spy films, social exposés, science fiction, and so on) now conflate in a movement that re-enacts the dedifferentiation of the social levels, and by way of their own allegorization: so that the new post-generic genre films are allegories of each other, and of the impossible representation of the social totality itself.

Space, representability, allegory: such are then the theoretical and analytic instruments that will be mobilized to examine a variety of filmic narratives from that new world-systemic moment which, gradually laid in place since the end of World War II, has been unveiled in discontinuous convulsions – the end of the 60s, the rise of the Third World debt, the emergence first of Japan and then of a soon-to-be-united new Europe as competing superstates, the collapse of the party state in the East, and finally the reassumption by the United States of a refurbished vocation as global policeman – and which can indifferently be called postmodernity or the third (or 'late') stage of capitalism.

But by the same token, it is to be expected that the remarkable films which constitute the present set of exhibits will have their own commentary to make on those new conceptual and analytic instruments and will modify them appropriately, as have a number of gratifying readers and listeners, among whom are to be mentioned Colin MacCabe, Esther Johnson, Ian Christie, and my audiences at the National Film Theater in London, in the spring of 1990. The final product owes an incalculable debt to Roma Gibson, Candice Ward, Tom Whiteside, and Kevin Heller.

Durham, North Carolina – March, 1991

Notes

1. If I have not included discussions of films from other national cinemas or non-Western traditions, the reader will I hope not too quickly conclude that this accident reflects lack of interest. I have in fact written on Latin-American films in my chapter on 'Magic Realism' in *Signatures of the Visible* (New York: Routledge, 1990); and touched too briefly on African film (Ousmane Sembène) in my essay 'Third World Literature in the Era of Multinational Capitalism,' *Social Text* 15, Fall 1986), pp. 65–88.
2. The reference is to the well-known essay on 'Ideological State Apparatuses,' in *Lenin and Philosophy* (New York: Monthly Review, 1971).
3. I discuss the pre-World War I system of national allegory in chapter 5 of *Fables of Aggression*: *Wyndham Lewis, the Modernist as Fascist* (Berkeley: University of California Press, 1979).
4. In the essay referred to in note 1.

Part One

Totality as Conspiracy

Totality as Conspiracy

In the widespread paralysis of the collective or social imaginary, to which 'nothing occurs' (Karl Kraus) when confronted with the ambitious program of fantasizing an economic system on the scale of the globe itself, the older motif of conspiracy knows a fresh lease on life, as a narrative structure capable of reuniting the minimal basic components: a potentially infinite network, along with a plausible explanation of its invisibility; or in other words: the collective and the epistemological.

To put it this way is to understand how this imperfect mediatory and allegorical structure – the conspiracy, not yet even the world system itself – offers the gravest representational dilemmas, since traditional narratives have never been much good at conveying the collective (save in the explosive punctual moments of war or revolution), while the knowledge function as such has never been thought to be particularly compatible with *belles lettres*. Beyond this, the conspiratorial allegory also raises the issue of Value, insofar as it needs to be marked as imperfect in order to serve as a cognitive map (which it would be disastrous to confuse with reality itself, as when Flaubert's Félicité, shown a map of Havana where her sailor nephew has landed, asks to see the house he is staying in).

On the other hand, the cognitive or allegorical investment in this representation will be for the most part an unconscious one, for it is only at that deeper level of our collective fantasy that we think about the social system all the time, a deeper level that also allows us to slip our political thoughts past a liberal and anti-political censorship. But this means, on the one hand, that the cognitive function of the conspiratorial plot must be able to flicker in and out, like some secondary or subliminal after-image; while by the same token the achieved surface of the representation itself must not be allowed to aspire to the monumental status of high art as such (at least until the beginnings of the postmodern, where a new interpenetration of high art and mass culture enables conspiratorial plot-constructions such as those of Pynchon to attain 'artistic' or high-brow standing).

As for the collective dimension of this hermeneutic machine, what clearly trips it into another order of things is the dialectical intensification of information and communication as such, which remains unthematized as long as we are in the realm of the mob, or of Victor Hugo's bird's-eye view of the battle of Waterloo (in *Les Misérables*), but which the hardening into technology problematizes, all the way from that thesis topic called 'the first appearance of the railroad in English (or French) literature' to Proust's embarrassing Vestal Virgins of the telephone. Since the world system of late capitalism (or post-modernity) is however inconceivable without the computerized media technology which eclipses its former spaces and faxes an unheard-of simultaneity across its branches, information technology will become virtually the representational solution as well as the representational problem of this world system's cognitive mapping, whose allegories can now always be expected to include a communicational third term.

We will therefore want to explore the new symptomatic narratives from three general directions: (1) to interrogate them about the ways in which their object-worlds can be allegorically prepared, disposed, and rewired in order to become the bearers of conspiracy, the existential furniture of daily life thereby finding itself slowly transformed into communications technology; (2) to test the incommensurability between an individual witness – the individual character of a still anthropomorphic narrative – and the collective conspiracy which must somehow be exposed or revealed through these individual efforts; (3) the thing itself, namely, how the local items of the present and the here-and-now can be made to express and to designate the absent, unrepresentable totality; how individuals can add up to more than their sum; what a global or world system might look like after the end of cosmology.

If everything means something else, then so does technology. It would be a mistake to reduce the menacing object-world of allegorical conspiracies to that first, fresh fear of spy systems and informants in the 1960s, when right-wingers discovered a whole new generation of just the right gadgets and someone was listening to you, but only to you personally. J. Edgar Hoover would make a most anachronistic mascot for late capitalism; while the anxieties about privacy seem to have diminished, in a situation in which its tendential erosion or even abolition has come to stand for nothing less than the end of civil society itself. It is as though we were training ourselves, in advance, for the stereotypical dystopian rigors of overpopulation in a world in which no one has a room of her own any more, or secrets anybody else cares about in the first place. But the variable that gears the rest, as always, is the more fundamental abstract category of property: here disclosing a fundamental transition from the private to the corporate, the latter unmasking the former and thereby problematizing the very juridical system on which it is itself constructed. How there could be private things, let alone privacy, in a situation in which almost everything around us is functionally inserted into larger institutional schemes and frameworks of all kinds, which nonetheless belong to *somebody* – this is now the nagging question that haunts the camera dollying around our various life-worlds, looking for a lost object the memory of which it cannot quite retain. Older aesthetics guide its fumbling attempts – old-fashioned interiors, and equally old-fashioned nightmare spaces, ancient collectibles, nostalgia for handicrafts – in a situation in which the appropriate new habits have been unable to form and the antique stores (Balzac, *La Peau de chagrin*) have all disappeared. What has happened to the objects of our object-world is neither youth nor age, but their wholesale transformation into instruments of communication; and this now takes the place of the older surrealist metamorphoses, the oneiric city, the domestic space of the incredible shrinking man, or the horror of the organic of so much science fiction, where brushing against an inanimate object suddenly feels like being touched by someone's hand.

Yet in hindsight, and with the appropriate rewriting, all of that might have been an anticipation of this, whose fundamental precondition is the disappearance of nature as such. Once its eclipse is secured, oppositions like those between animate and inanimate are themselves relegated to a historical lumber room that looks less like a museum or a junk-shop than the place information goes when a word-processor is accidentally erased. Once plants have become machines – and even though not a breath of wind has ruffled the selfsame landscape equal to itself – every object changes and becomes a human sign (not unexpectedly drawing all the theories of language and sign systems after it). Now not the magical speaking beasts or the 'flowers that look back at you,' but the marching automata of *Blade Runner*'s last cavernous private apartment (Ridley Scott, 1982): these are anachronisms that overspring the present into the far future of android technology; and now all of our things, of whatever fabric and purpose, are inhabited by the possibility of becoming nasty dolls with needle teeth that bite (*Barbarella* [Roger Vadim, 1968]).

This is the intuition embodied by the new magic realism of Derek Jarman and Raoul Ruiz: that surrealism was both impossible and unnecessary, since in some other sense it was already real (such had been Alejo Carpentier's original formulation of the style in the preface to his *Kingdom of This World*, which he attributed to the uneven development of Latin America, but which now seems to belong to all of us). Even late Buñuel (*The Discreet Charm* [1972], *The Obscure Object* [1977]) is closer to this than to the heroic period of surrealist desire and Wagnerian longing: *L'Age d'or* (1930) remains a breathtaking relic from the age of gods and heroes, but it is no longer for us, since it would be comical to wish the social burden of bourgeois respectability and elaborate moral taboo back into existence merely to re-endow the sex drive with the value of a political act.

Nonsynchronicity was also the condition, in the surrealist Europe of the 20s, for the eruption of archaic moments of Spanish feudality, French medieval romance, or even Rousseau's state of nature itself, into an incompletely modernized present staffed by the grande and the petite bourgeoisie. All that seems to remain of such effects are the simulations of occult film, which accompany the so-called religious revival like its wish-fulfillment. In Jarman and Ruiz, however, the most 'surrealist' moments are those in which modern technological artifacts – a pocket computer, say, or a once mint roadster covered in dust and housed beneath the grand staircase – are inconspicuously planted among the Renaissance splendor of Roman prelates, their costumes and palaces (*Caravaggio*, 1986); but Buñuel's mumbling bishops turned to bones, leaving only their robes behind them on the rocky promontory where the city was to be founded. That flight into deep geological time takes a different direction from this particular future shock: indeed, insisting that his work has nothing in common with surrealism, Ruiz has cherished incongruities of the type exemplified by the shot in *Cleopatra* in which an airliner can be glimpsed in the distant sky above the togaed actors.[1] This is no longer Breton's 'objective chance,' I think, but rather a Nietzschean affirmation that there is no past, and thus, finally, no time at all – something one often feels in Ruiz's films when this or that chance marker abruptly 'situates' their magical events in modern chronology once more.

Communicational and information technologies – the scientific machineries of reproduction rather than of production (which, however, then trail the latter in their wake and turn it inside out, as their misunderstood predecessor) – foreground and dramatize this transformation of the object-world like its material idea. But they themselves become magical only when grasped as the allegories of something else, of the whole unimaginable decentered global network itself. The new ingredients are already registered in the opening credits of *Three Days of the Condor* (Pollack, 1975), elegantly telexed in stylish computer graphics. Indeed, in postmodern film, the credits have become an inconspicuous yet crucial space in which the desired perceptual habits of a viewer are, as in the old musical modes, generically cued towards either techno- or deco-graphics, respectively.

The relationship between this technology and death itself is then inscribed in *Condor*'s opening sequence – the apparently mistaken liquidation of a whole bureau of minor espionage researchers and specialists – by the clacking of the word-processors among the silence of the sprawling corpses as the machines continue to affirm their mechanical existence and to go on producing 'text' in a haunting sonorous surcharge (which it is instructive to juxtapose with the organic menace of vaguely flapping wings and chicken scratches in the attic during the opening scenes of *The Exorcist* [Friedkin, 1973]).

But who says 'media' traditionally includes and encompasses transportation as well. Not the least beautiful and pertinent feature of the Pollack film is its incorporation of the great traffic networks: not merely the outsized bridges and highways of Manhattan, but also the New York–Washington shuttle in flight, and the dialectical extremes of the helicopter and the little truck, along with the residual insertion of the railway system that infers the other end of this spatial map somewhere in the snows of Vermont.

This X-ray of functional mediations in space was completed, as a kind of program, by John Schlesinger's *Marathon Man* (1976), a virtual anthology of types of space and climate, which suggests the totalizing vocation of such a geographical collection, often required as a kind of backing or after-image for those narratives that set out to map the social totality in some more fundamental structural fashion.

It may, however, be convenient to take a masterwork of the older

13

aesthetic, Hitchcock's *North by Northwest*, as a genealogical precursor in this development. As its title suggests, the narrative grid of this film, which propels us from one empty hotel room to another across continental North America, re-enacts that empty outline of the forty-eight states that all good American citizens carry like a logo etched into their mind's eye.[2] From Mies' newly built Seagram Building in Manhattan to a famous cornfield in Illinois, from the CIA headquarters in Washington, DC, to the balding stone crown of the figures of Mount Rushmore and a cantilevered modern house on the Canadian border – indeed on the very edge of the world itself (its planes taking off for the darkest Iron Curtain) – this sequence makes moves in which the various landscapes emit specific but complementary narrative messages, as though in a return at the very end of modernity to the semiotic landscapes of those tribal or oral narratives Lévi-Strauss de-crypted for us in such studies as *The Epic of Asdiwal*.

The frenzy of the pursuit, however – notoriously, in Hitchcock, motivated only in the most perfunctory way by the espionage intrigue, but more basically by the love triangle – lends this displacement something of the passion and the value of the epistemological itself: wanting to grasp the beast itself, as Mailer has said of that desire called The Great American Novel; covering all the ground and all the bases in the distracted feeling that this gigantic *objet petit a* somehow contains the very secrets of Being itself: comparable in that only to the desperate ride, in Philip K. Dick's novel *Ubik* (1969), from a formerly La Guardia Airport in New York City to a Des Moines, Iowa, funeral home, in which historical time is relentlessly disintegrating around the hapless protagonist, jet planes of the future downgraded to small bi-planes, high technology fading away as in a dream, space enlarging ominously as the means of transport become ever more primitive – the most brilliant of all Dick's nightmares, in which each incremental progress back into time enlarges just ever so more slightly your distance from your heart's desire.

Condor, however, deploys such geographical motifs as a mere signal of the 'intent to totalize'. As for its plot in some literary sense, the neatly tied themes (Redford is a 'reader,' the CIA wargames are structurally connected and opposed to the deciphering of codes in printed stories and novels) are trendily inappropriate for its thriller context, and are thereby trivialized. Alongside this ideational window-dressing, the concrete and more genuinely filmic and spatial working through of these themes can be found in the descent into the interior of the telephone central. Redford as informational mechanic and industrial worker is more interesting than as English major and intellectual, and the great banks of switches and synapses recall again the ghostly proletarian content of other contemporary films such as *Alien* (Scott, 1979), if not indeed of the heist genre itself – always in one way or another an inscription of collective non-alienated work

Three Days of the Condor

that passes the censor by way of its rewriting in terms of crime and sub-generic entertainment. Archetypal journeys back beyond the surface appearance of things are also here dimly reawakened, from antiquity and Dante all the way to Goffman's storefront/backroom, with its canonical form in Marx's great invitation to 'leave this noisy sphere, where everything takes place on the surface and in full view of everyone, and follow [the owner of money and the owner of labor-power] into the hidden abode of production, on whose threshold there hangs the notice "No admittance except on business".'[3] This promise of a deeper inside view is the hermeneutic content of the conspiracy thriller in general, although its spatialization in *Condor* seems somehow more alarming than the imaginary networks of the usual suspects: the representational confirmation that telephone cables and lines and their interchanges follow us everywhere, doubling the streets and buildings of the visible social world with a secondary secret underground world, is a vivid, if paranoid, cognitive map, redeemed for once only by the possibility of turning the tables, when the hero is able to tap into the circuits and bug the buggers, abolishing space with his own kind of simultaneity by scrambling all the symptoms and producing his messages from all corners of the map at the same time.

But no matter how systematically reorganized and postmodernized, telephone technology is still marked as relatively old-fashioned or archaic within the new post-industrial landscape (we will find that representation seems to have demanded a similar regression in the technologies of *All the President's Men*). Whether representation can draw directly, in some new way, on the distinctive technology of capitalism's third stage, whose video- and computer-based furniture and object-world are markedly less photogenic than the media and transportation technology of the second (not excluding telephones), remains one of the great open questions of postmodern culture generally. Surely the newer spy novels, with their bewildering multiplication of secret or private espionage operations within public ones, their dizzying paper structures (more philosophically dematerialized and ideal than the stock market) turning on the facile but effective device of the double agent, so that whole teams of villains can be transformed into heroes at the flip of a switch — surely these go a certain way towards declaring at least the intent to construct a narrative which is in some way an *analogon* of and a stand-in for the unimaginable overdetermination of the computer itself. But in representations like these, the operative effect is confusion rather than articulation. It is at the point where we give up and are no longer able to remember which side the characters are on, and how they have been revealed to be hooked up with the other ones, that we have presumably grasped the deeper truth of the world system (certainly no one will have been astonished or enlightened to discover that the head of the CIA, the Vice President, the Secretary of State, or even the President himself, was secretly behind everything in the first place). Such confusions — which evidently have something to do with structural limits of memory — seem to mark a point of no return beyond which the human organism can no longer match the velocities or the demographies of the new world system. That the symptom betrays some deeper incapacity of the postmodern subject to process history itself can be argued from a variety of other, related, but less officially political, phenomena. One noted long ago, for example, in Ross MacDonald's oedipal detective stories, that it was growing harder and harder to keep the parental generation separate from that of the grandparents: the feeling is now endemic in a whole new generation of detective stories that betray the need to incorporate history.

In high literature, Pynchon comes to mind unavoidably as a body of writing which does not avoid the weaknesses in plot construction of the spy novel (although it negotiates them at a greater level of quality and intensity), but which is marked out for our purposes as a matter of a somewhat different kind of interest, as a space in which new cybernetic figures are forged and elaborated: static op-art after-images spun off the bewildering rotation of just such cyberplots. Kenneth Burke's narratological categories, in which *scene* is pressed into service as a form of *agency*, seem extraordinarily apt for those now distant but still hallucinatory 60s California moments in *The Crying of Lot 49* (1966), when the conspiracy of property development suddenly resonates with some well-nigh runic message:

She drove into San Narcisco on a Sunday, in a rented Impala. Nothing was happening. She looked down a slope, needing to squint for the sunlight, onto a vast sprawl of houses which had grown up all together, like a well-tended crop, from the dull brown earth; and she thought of the time she'd opened a transistor radio to replace a battery and seen her first printed circuit. The ordered swirl of houses and streets, from this high angle, sprang at her now with the same unexpected, astonishing clarity as the circuit card had. Though she knew even less about radios than about Southern Californians, there were to both outward patterns a hieroglyphic sense of concealed meaning, of an intent to communicate. There'd seemed no limit to what the printed circuit could have told her (if she had tried to find out); so in her first minute of San Narcisco, a revelation also trembled just past the threshold of her understanding. Smog hung all round the horizon, the sun on the bright beige countryside was painful; she and the Chevy seemed parked at the centre of an odd, religious instant. As if, on some other frequency, or out of the eye of some whirlwind rotating too slow for her heated skin to feel the centrifugal coolness of, words were being spoken.[4]

The representational ingenuity of this novel lies in its identification of the conspiracy with the media itself, here the postal system, in which the contradiction between private ownership and social production is redramatized by way of the enigmatic reappearance of 'private' mail delivery systems. Yet the force of Pynchon's narrative draws not on the advanced or futuristic technology of the contemporary media so much as from their endowment with an archaic past: the pseudo-histories of the various postal systems and postage stamp substitutes, the traces left in old books, the archival remains of what the present imagines itself to have left behind. Indeed, the most ominous doubt inspired by this novella, which wants to contaminate its readers and beyond them to endow the present age itself with an impalpable but omnipresent culture of paranoia, is the conjecture that if the fossil record were complete, we would be likely to find the Thurn-and-Taxis post-horn on hominid artifacts as far back as the Pleistocene. Still, it must be observed that it is not the patterning system of the computer circuits that conveys this remarkable effect, but rather the archeological hermeneutic itself which endows cybernetic objects with a suggestive power they cannot muster on their own.

Later Pynchon, who sinks further back into the 50s and the rather different conspiracies of the McCarthyite period, stages the conspiratorial epiphany in a rather different way, eschewing the mystical for the little repressions of the bureaucratic everyday:

She drove on downtown, being extra careful because she felt like doing harm to somebody, found a liquor store with a big Checks Cashed sign, got the same turndown inside. Running on nerve and anger, she kept on till she reached the next supermarket, and this time she was told to wait while somebody went in back and made a phone call.

It was there, gazing down a long aisle of frozen food, out past the checkout stands, and into the terminal black glow of the front windows, that she found herself entering a moment of undeniable clairvoyance, rare in her life but recognized. She understood that the Reaganomic ax blades were swinging everywhere, that she and Flash were no longer exempt, might easily be abandoned already to the upper world and any unfinished business in it that might now resume . . . as if they'd been kept safe in some time-free zone all these years but now, at the unreadable whim of something in power, must reenter the clockwork of cause and effect. Someplace there would be a real ax, or something just there would be a real ax, or something just as painful, Jasonic, blade-to-meat final – but at the distance she, Flash, and Justin had by now been brought to, it would all be done with keys on alphanumeric keyboards that stood for weightless, invisible chains of electronic presence or absence. If patterns of ones and zeros were 'like' pattens of human lives and deaths, if everything about an individual could be represented in a computer record by a long string of ones and zeros, then what kind of creature would be represented by a long string of lives and deaths? It would have to be up one level at least – an angel, a minor god, something in a UFO. It would take eight human lives and deaths just to form one character in this being's name – its complete dossier might take up a considerable piece of the history of the world. We are digits in God's computer, she not so much thought as hummed to herself to a sort of standard gospel tune. And the only thing we're good for, to be dead or to be living, is the only thing He sees. What we cry, what we contend for, in our world of toil and blood, it all lies beneath the notice of the hacker we call God.

The night manager came back, holding the check as he might a used disposable diaper. 'They stopped payment on this.'

'The banks are closed, how'd they do that?'

He spent his work life here explaining reality to the herds of computer-illiterate who crowded in and out of the store. 'The computer,' he began gently, once again, 'never has to sleep, or even go take a break. It's like it's open 24 hours a day. . . .'[5]

But in this, far and away the most politically radical of Pynchon's texts, and a belatedly 60s anti-authoritarian attack on the Reagan decade, one wonders sometimes whether the stereotypical wiring that

Youji Watanabe, Sky Building no. 3 (Tokyo, 1971)

is the classic Pynchon inner form has not been reversed, so that the moments of fear are derived from what we already know about the Nixon/Reagan years and their internal conspiracies, rather than the other way round, projecting a fresh breath of hitherto unexperienced anxiety onto plots that seem as comically inept as they may be prophetic. It is a question that will have to be posed again when we come to *All the President's Men*.

The structural alternative, then, to a situation in which technological objects are endowed with symbolic power by their narrative contexts, can be expected to lie in objects whose very function itself generates the narrative and produces the conspiracy in their own right, and in such a way that attention is diverted from their visual inadequacy. Those Japanese apartment buildings constructed like stacks of audio-cassettes can now no longer be inserted into the tape player of the macrocosm; but the media in *Blow Out* (de Palma, 1981) do not merely write their own check, they rewrite the world itself – or at least its soundtrack – and release as many alternate histories. The telltale sound of the assassin's rifle shot can be excised or replaced, while the 'true' or documentary soundtrack of a real murder can be spliced into a fictional horror film, so as not to let anything go to waste.

Blow Out

As its overt organizing allusion to Antonioni's *Blow-up* (1966) suggests, films like *Blow Out*, or *The Conversation* (Coppola, 1974), are best grasped as moments in the historical process of postmodernization, in which the decisive modulation from the visual image to the auditory one is as fundamental as it is paradoxical, given the universal affinity of postmodern culture with visibility and spatiality. Perhaps, indeed, the very omnipresence of the visual commodity requires estrangement and the passage through a different sensory register, endowed with a discontinuous temporal logic more apt to frame its events and components. Meanwhile, the deeper tendency of the postmodern towards a separation and a co-existence of levels and sub-systems has everywhere – in film theory fully as much as in film practice – made for a keener sense of the semi-autonomy of sound and the requirement that it counterpoint sight rather than simply underscore it.[6]

At any rate, although both *Blow Out* and *The Conversation* retain the referent around which Antonioni's film turned far more problematically (was there really a murder in the first place?), the shift from the visual to the auditory has the (very postmodern) effect of annulling Antonioni's Heideggerian and metaphysical dimension, since it can no longer offer some bewildering Bazinian field of Being for desperate inspection.[7] Not unsurprisingly, this occultation of the 'question of Being' now leaves the text fungible and open to all the manipulations the corporate world can muster. The artist-photographer of the Antonioni film, who still secured the philosopher's art function although he earned a living by shooting fashion models, here gives way to technicians for sale to the highest bidder.

Significantly, both these newer films (*Blow Out, The Conversation*), share a key episode, which must now be considered auto-referential: namely, the destruction of the apparatus of reproduction itself – the return to the ransacked laboratory in which great spools of tape festoon the work-place in derision, like eviscerated entrails. This destruction, which fills or implodes space, is of a peculiar type, quite unlike some mute savagery visited on a single object or instrument (as at the end of Faulkner's *The Bear*). Here, not the value of the physical object – which it is a pity to see broken to pieces – but rather its literal and essential worthlessness, is foregrounded: the unreproducible work of art, denied its capacity for reproduction, and reduced to blank high-tech waste. It is clearly an obligatory *scène à faire* which emblematically underscores the lack of iconic force in the newer reproductive technology, in that sense quite unlike the great streamlined 'media objects' of high modernist production, such as the ocean liner or the airplane. In *Blow-up* it was the images themselves, the photographic icons, which were silently and tactfully removed; the physical mayhem here aims at the non-visual inessentiality of the vehicles of reproduction – TV console, cassettes, computer print-outs and the like – which sung the dirge for the human dead in *Three Days of the Condor* and which Pynchon tried to tease into some final plastic exceptionality in *The Crying of Lot 49*. Trashing the apparatus thus underscores the gap between form and content in such postmodern representations of totality, where neither the plot nor its

Blow-Up

21

Blow-Up

unique new technological object-world can bear the freight and import of the conspiratorial ideologeme that was to have revealed, not merely this specific political secret, but the very secret of the world system itself.

It is a gap which rebukes the traditional claim of the works of high culture to take their content up into form in a seamless web, thereby showing up on their surface as the flaw in the crystal or the fly in the ointment. By the same token, it blocks out the representational privileges of low culture or trash in this respect, since it is very precisely that gap between form and content that must be the fundamental content – and also the form – of the conspiratorial allegory of late capitalist totality. The value-paradoxes of allegory – indeed of postmodernism itself – are then here endlessly replayed, where structural failure is a new kind of success in its own right, and what is worst about such art-works may also often be better than what is best about them.

These are also the paradoxes that account for the unique status of David Cronenberg's *Videodrome* (1983) within our paradigm, a film which owes its canonical, well-nigh classical position to its triumphant evasion of virtually all high cultural qualities, from technical perfection to the discriminations of taste and the organon of beauty. In it, the owner of a porno television channel in Toronto (James Woods), while exploring the possibility of acquiring genuine snuff films, discovers that the product in question (produced by an outfit called Videodrome) contains a subliminal signal that causes halluci-

Videodrome

nations and eventually fatal brain damage. This turns out to be a right-wing conspiracy against the degeneration of moral values for which pornography and television alike are held responsible. Woods' discovery then brings into view a counter-conspiracy of a more pro-television, religious type, in which the cathode ray is used as therapy and an instrument of regeneration. But by that time, the Philip K. Dick-like reality-loops and hallucinatory after-effects are so complex as to relieve the viewer of any further narrative responsibility, who can only passively witness the manipulation of the hapless James Woods by both sides, as he becomes assassin-avenger, duped suicidal victim and sacrifice all at once.

Here, a Western, commercial version of the Third-World political aesthetic of Cuban 'imperfect cinema' is deployed, and not only in the function of B-film generic signals (the shoestring horror film, and so on). In another place, I argued something pre-eminently relevant here, namely, that the ideologeme of elegance and glossiness, expensive form, in postmodernism, was also dialectically at one with its opposite number in sleaze, punk, trash and garbage art of all kinds.[8] Meanwhile, in the spirit of the return to origins of much contemporary cinema (Godard's hand-held cameras, the quintessential plebeian archetype of the home movie), this production also re-enacts those more humble predecessors, which are, in *Videodrome*, pornography as such and snuff film 'in reality'. Here too, then, authenticity in the grain and in the camera work means a gradual approximation to the palpable grubbiness of the archetypal model, not excluding a wonderfully garish and cheap color; and this deeper formal affinity is distinct from any passionate, ideological or religious, adherence to B-film status. Finally, the positioning of this film and its production in the world system is no mere external accident either; as we shall see, it marks the content and is thematized in its own right. But even in terms of a signal system, the Canadian provenance of *Videodrome* (and of Cronenberg himself) marginalizes the work internally and assigns it a semi-peripheral resonance, particularly since it is not designed to exemplify some national (or at least English-Canadian) cultural production, even though its deeper ideological values (a horror of US pornography, for example) are very Canadian, or at least Torontonian, indeed.

Yet there is another reason why the new conspiratorial film in general cannot aspire to high aesthetic status. This has to do with the breakdown of the opposition between high art and mass culture generally in the postmodern, but more specifically with the waning of the prestige of the literary and of its older structures. We have already seen how in Pynchon the official ideas or intellectual themes were somehow drawn back inside the representation, so that a slogan like 'paranoia' is no longer of the same order as the 'ideas' debated by the characters of Dostoyevsky or Thomas Mann, or the hyperintellectual speculations of Proust or Musil. Rather such words themselves become a media object and a piece of commercial cultural junk which is embedded in the montage and assimilated to the content of the work rather than to its authorial intentions or its ideological messages. This discrediting of the 'literary,' and the assimilation to it of themes and ideas of the older type, is omnipresent in contemporary (Western) film production, which has triumphantly liquidated its high modernist moment – that of the great *auteurs* and their stylistic 'worlds' – and along with them the genuine 'philosophies' to which film-makers like Bergman and Welles, Hitchcock and Kurosawa, could palpably be seen to aspire.

Yet the outer shell of the older form is here preserved; and *Videodrome* carefully explains its 'themes' to us – the social perniciousness of television and mass culture generally, McLuhanite reflections on the physical changes and perceptual mutations involved in prolonged exposure to the new medium, even the old philosophical questions about the Good and whether the masses' cultural appetites automatically lead them to it. These are all serious issues, with long and distinguished traditions of philosophical speculation and debate behind them; but who would wish to argue that *Videodrome* represents a serious contribution to their development? Equally clearly, however, the film does not misrepresent them in any trendy or lowbrow way, although the viewer may sometimes be tempted to think of it as a tribute to one of Canada's greatest thinkers. My sense is that in the new dimensionality of postmodern cultural space, ideas of the older conceptual type have lost their autonomy and become something like by-products and after-images flung up on the screen of the mind and of social production by the culturalization of daily life. The dissolution of philosophy today then reflects this modification in the status of ideas (and ideology), which itself retroactively unmasks any number of traditional philosophical 'concepts' as having been just such consciousness-symptoms all the while, that could not be identified as such in the culturally impoverished, pre-media, and residually 'natural' human societies (or modes of production) of the past. What is today called Theory is of course another sign of this momentous historical development, which, by rendering Culture absolute, has deeply problematized the vocation of any of its individual products, texts or works (if they can no longer 'mean' something or convey ideas or messages, even in the form of the 'theme' or the 'problem,' what new function can they claim?)

It is worth adding that the 'concepts' I have identified above in the text of *Videodrome* are all in one way or another 'media' concepts: perhaps then, it is only the unique family of concepts of that kind that can no longer achieve respectable philosophical abstraction? Or are we to draw the more somber conclusion that all abstract philosophical concepts were always 'media concepts' in some deeper way without our being aware of it? At any rate, the notion of cognitive mapping that underpins the present investigation hints at some new vocation for the postmodern cultural work, at the same time as it specifies the fundamental function of the 'media idea' in any successful act of social triangulation or cognitive mapping, an act which always seems (as in some new postmodern version of high modernist autoreferentiality) to include the representation of its own media system within itself.[9]

But the crisis of an older literary thematics also brings distinct new formal advantages to a henceforth themeless film of this kind, which has of course covered its tracks by way of simple generic affiliation and its identification as a horror film. (*Videodrome* faithfully reproduces the pornographic rhythms of ever greater and more horrifying physical violence that reach their climax with the exploding – now android, *Alien*-type – body, and their characteristic melancholy after satiation in the final suicide.) What happens on the level of meanings, however, is that immense dedifferentiation of the traditional levels which has seemed to characterize so much else in contemporary society and culture and its theories. With the expansion of the former cultural sphere to encompass and include within itself everything else in social life (something that could also be thought of as an immense commodification and commercialization, the virtual completion of the process of the colonization by the commodity form begun in classical capitalism), it becomes impossible to say whether we are here dealing any longer with the specifically political, or with the

bah

25

cultural, or with the social, or with the economic – not to forget the sexual, the historical, the moral, and so on. But this conflation, which surely presents some signal disadvantages in the realm of thought and action, uniquely intensifies the signifying power of this work that, rotated on its axis, can be said to comment on any of the above, virtually inexhaustibly.

Is *Videodrome* not, for example, the story of the classical struggle between a small businessman and entrepreneur and a great faceless corporation? The owner of the small independent television Channel 83 (James Woods) is indeed eventually suborned by the gigantic optical corporation behind Videodrome, which seizes on its competitor and incorporates it into itself. The post-contemporary spin given to this traditional heroic narrative then clearly involves the tendential international monopolization of the media and the various local culture industries (not excluding the publishing houses). So we have here a fairly explicit economic reading of the text as a narrative about business and competition; and it is worth measuring the distance between this overt and explicit commercial content (which most viewers will however take as a secondary pretext for the rest) and that deepest allegorical impulse of all, which insists on grasping this feature as an articulated nightmare vision of how we as individuals feel within the new multinational world system. It is as though the narrowly economic had to be thematized and thereby marginalized, in

Videodrome

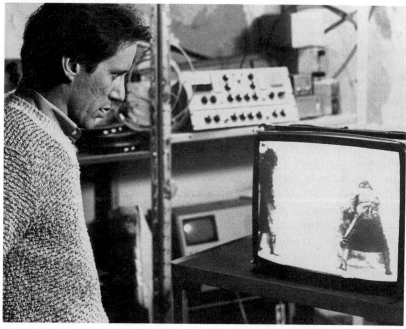

26

order for the deeper socio-economic allegory to pass the censorship.

Meanwhile, a host of political readings also compete for the surface of the text, flickering in and out: the assassination sequence is clearly a topical one, with its manipulation of the hero as a fall guy (shades of Pakula's 1974 *Parallax View*, of which more below). A residual atmosphere of global 60s and 70s politics also shrouds the narrative, with its Third World reaches, its terrorists and infiltrators, its revolutionary puritanism; indeed, the confusion of torture with sex makes it initially unclear whether we have to do with political executions or with S & M pornography in the first emissions of Videodrome, which seem to be coming from somewhere in Malaysia. The unchanging 'set' of the telecast features a clay wall of a most un-Western type, presumably electrified; while, reversing the issue for a moment, the characters observe that pornography as such – if that is what the Videodrome broadcasts are really supposed to be – is a political matter in many Third World countries and punishable by death.

When the correct source of the transmission is identified (it turns out to be Pittsburgh, even then becoming a movie capital), the implications of the revised reading are no less political, but clearly shift their ground. The Canadian undertheme of economic and cultural marginalization is still present in this selection of a non-central, semi-peripheral, formerly industrial US urban area (something like a sister city to Toronto in marginality). Indeed in Pittsburgh, as with the economically stagnant parts of Toronto shown here, the run-down downtown is associated with cultural trash, no doubt by way of peep-shows and x-rated book stores. (It is also worth recalling that Pittsburgh was the setting for George Romero's vampire film, *Martin* [1978], one of the most extraordinary achievements of the recent B- or horror-film revival.)

But the spatial margins also connote a different set of political interests, that might euphemistically be styled 'grass-roots'. These are the vigilante and paramilitary networks that flourish outside the urban centers, powered by narrow-minded moralisms of generally racist and gender varieties. So it is that Videodrome is at length revealed, as has already been said, as a moral-majority conspiracy which, revolted by the permissive immorality everywhere encouraged by the media in our societies, has set forth on an unusual campaign of extermination: a subliminal signal beamed through the pornographic emissions causes an incurable tumor, accompanied by hallucinations and reality-warps worthy of Philip K. Dick, and will eventually be used on the degenerate viewing public of the advanced countries. The political movement here, therefore, cuts across class lines, uniting right-thinking businessmen with mechanics and technicians of a suitably post-Vietnam paramilitary variety. It could conceivably be everywhere, and bide its time, camouflaged comfortably within the familiar social fabric: 'it has something you don't have, Max; it has a

Videodrome

philosophy, and that's what makes it dangerous.' In this particular hermeneutic, the appearance of an end of ideology and a universal instauration of cynical reason (when not the profit motive and the almighty dollar) are stripped away to show the ominous survival of true belief.

Not surprisingly, therefore, this Klan-type-fantasy reading gives way to a somewhat different kind of politics, the religious revival proper: only a new religion – Video New Flesh – can compete with the corporate paramilitary movement. Organized around the doctrines of the dead McLuhanite professor, it offers video therapy to desocialized vagrants and urban delinquents, promising something of an evolutionary leap or mutation to the species by way of its new perceptual prosthesis in the cathode ray. Optimistically, Video New Flesh considers that the Videodrome tumor is merely the way-station towards the development of a new perceptual organ, with functions as yet undreamed of. Here, then, anticipations and premonitions of transfiguration are coded along the recto and verso of a transformation of (technological) culture and a reappearance of religion (Catholicism also played a fundamental role in McLuhan's thinking).

What is finally most interesting about this titanic political struggle between two vast and faceless conspiracies (in which the hapless Max is little more than a pawn) is that they are finally the same, the twin faces of our unconscious meditation on the inevitable mutations a now repressed history has in store for us: fear and hope alike, the loathing for the new beings we ourselves are bound to become in the shedding of the skins of all our current values, intimately intertwined,

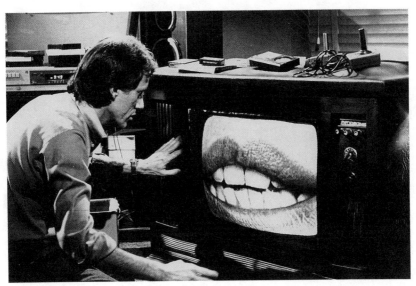

Videodrome

as in some DNA of the collective fantasy, with our quasi-religious longing for social transubstantiation into another flesh and another reality. But they are also the same in the more humdrum changing of the valences on which the conventional narrative mechanism depends. Just as the moral fervor of the conspiratorial enemy (which we cannot altogether share) comes as something of a shock – fanatics or not, these high-tech media wreckers stand for Goodness and Right-eousness in all its traditional senses – so also the seemingly benign or 'white' conspiracy of the New Flesh does not scruple ruthlessly to send James Woods to his death. Certainly this dualism of the flip-a-switch off/on conspiracy is narratively preferable to that proliferation of private surveillance networks and sub-CIAs that has taken place cancerously within the old genre of the spy novel; but it presents its own formal problems, which will be touched on in conclusion.

Yet if *Videodrome* owes its remarkable political polysemousness to the space freed by the end of traditional ideas, concepts and themes, it is thereby also enabled to participate in that reduction to the body everywhere present in the postmodern, here adroitly manipulated by way of those deeper unconscious physical fears and sexual revulsions that persist autonomously and independently in the social body but can occasionally, as in this case, be tapped for the deeper libidinal energy of the work as in a cultural and psychoanalytic ion-exchange. Primary here is no doubt the fear of the subliminal itself; the tele-vision screen as part of the eye; that sense of incorporating unclean or harmful substances that runs all the way from yesterday's phobias about fluorinated water and what it can do to our 'precious bodily

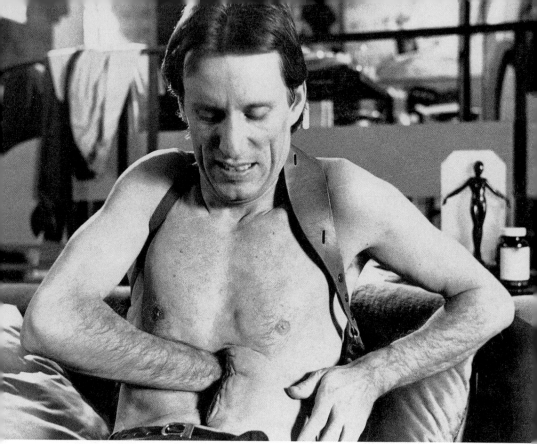

Videodrome

fluids' back into the deep witchcraft and envy of village and tribal societies. The discrepancy between the video monitor and the movie screen, to be sure, wedges a monkey-wrench into any absolute autoreferentiality. Still, the putative subliminal signals of the Videodrome image can be seen to be intensifications of Buñuel's inaugural assault on the viewer's eyeball (with a straight razor), while the deeper fantasy about the lethal properties of commodity consumption runs at least from the legendary coke in Coca-Cola all the way to the first new anxieties of the age of hucksters, dramatized in Pohl and Kornbluth's SF novel *Space Merchants* (1953), with its addictive brand of coffee. The originality of Philip K. Dick was then to have reunited the twin fears of addiction and of schizophrenia (with its reality-loops and hallucinatory alternate worlds) in a lethal combination which Cronenberg's media nightmare transcends, replaces, and intensifies all at once, translating it into the society of the spectacle or image capitalism.

Physiological anxieties are also tapped by the grotesquely sexual nightmare images, in which males are feminized by the insertion of organic cassettes (if not revolvers) into a newly opened dripping slot below the breast bone. Corporeal revulsion of this kind probably has the primary function of expressing fears about activity and passivity in the complexities of late capitalism, and is only secondarily invested with the level of gender itself, which however knows a separate or semi-autonomous figuration elsewhere in the plot. For the three women – the older Greek or Slavic woman, distantly aristocratic, who makes her living as a go-between in semi-pornographic and bohemian spectacles; the intensely sexual radio therapist (Debbie Harry), whose experiments with S & M lead her directly into Videodrome and presumably to her death; the professor's daughter and spiritual heir, who administers the Cathode Ray Chapel and also the white conspiracy of the New Flesh – form a triad that clearly spells out for Max the ancient male fantasy structure of the triple goddess: mother, wife, and daughter. It is a structure which strengthens the film in two distinct ways: first of all by endowing *Videodrome* with an independent kind of closure that overdetermines it and also functions as a kind of secondary generic block in its own right, forestalling embarrassing questions about the contingencies of the plot and its cast of characters. But it also offers up a new register for just those effects of soiling and degradation on which the film depends: the bad mother, whose already illicit sexuality is incestuously directed towards young boys; the insatiable wife, whose drives reinvent, beyond the current permissibility of 'normal' sex relations, the taboo of torture and death; and the chill vestal, who represents the law of another, absent father, and, after deliberately exposing Max to the ray, sends him on into his own manipulated suicide.

Closure is, to be sure, one of the fundamental formal questions one wishes to ask of conspiratorial representations of this type, where its effect is clearly fundamentally related to the problem of totality itself. For the sense of closure here is the sign that somehow all the bases have been touched, and that the galactic dimensions and co-ordinates of the now global social totality have at least been sketched in. It should be obvious that, just as such totalities can never be perceived with the naked eye (where they would remain, in any case, purely contemplative and epistemological images), so also closure in the postmodern, after the end of the (modernist) organic work, has itself become a questionable value, if not a meaningless concept. It will be desirable therefore to speak of a closure-effect, just as we speak of mapping out or triangulating, rather than perceiving or representing, a totality.

What a film like *Videodrome* triumphantly demonstrates is not only the way in which, in much contemporary cultural production, a striking closure-effect is secured by space itself and spatiality, as I have shown above; but also that, in film, and perhaps also in some other arts or media, what used to be called aesthetic value now finds its new locus here, in the realm of a heightened and spatialized per-

Videodrome

ception. For the conspiracy plot of *Videodrome* can now be seen as something like a formal pretext to touch all the bases in the urban landscape itself; and this seems to be something that can only be done laterally, with a genuinely Proustian indirection,[10] as though by way of by-product and supplementary bonus. The city in question must not be an officially central Western metropolis, to which all the stereotypical ideologies of power and centrality distractingly cling; nor must the camera set out intentionally to capture the documentary truth of Toronto, a project that would make the avoidance of the classic Hitchcock picture-postcard identifying shots as conspicuous as their presence.

Here, rather, the plot line leads us from the anonymous bustle of narrow business streets (the plate glass of a set of doors is transported across the streets at one point, as if in distant homage to Cocteau's *vitrier* in *Orphée*), with their generic hostelries (the 'Classical Hotel'), and their redone but still traditional office buildings, to trade shows in modern convention spaces and the inside of radio and television studios, not omitting the roof-tops, the Bowery flophouses and soup kitchens, and finally the abandoned dockyards, in which condemned ships rust away. This yields a splendid, purely filmic essay, which, conjoined with those other co-ordinates of the Third-World clay wall on the one hand, and the placelessness and timelessness of the video-cassette library on the other, goes a long way towards making the invisible tangible and the macrocosm a palpable reality the naked eye can somehow possess.

This spatial closure is formally necessary precisely because the narrative itself cannot know any closure or completion of this kind. Only in the cheapest generic Science Fiction does the revolution triumph, sweeping the conspiratorial present heroically away, or on the contrary bringing to power those very conspiracies, thereby opening up a uniformed dystopia of geological duration. But *Videodrome* is a kind of realism: not only does it let us glimpse the grain of post-modern urban life more vividly than any documentary or social drama (by virtue, as I have argued, of its very laterality); but it also seeks urgently to convince us that on some level, in the superstate, the conspiracies are real and already with us.

But the narrative by which it seeks to achieve this reality-effect remains one in which two incommensurable levels of being impossibly intersect, and in which the individual subject of the protagonist somehow manages to blunder into the collective web of the hidden social order. This intersection, this incommensurability, is the fundamental form-problem of the new globalizing representations. It can be detected most vividly in the area of what A. J. Greimas' narrative semiotics identifies as the actantial function: namely, the transmission of the various narrative developments and reversals across general positions of agency, which, like the subjects of so many narrative verbs, block or impel, assist or fumble, the achievement of an equally abstract or generalized desire or quest. Such articulations of agencies, which can be seen as the gear-boxes of story-telling, are not in Greimas identical with the actual characters on the surface of the narrative. For several 'real' or named characters might conceivably share a single actantial agency (that of the villain, for example), while on the other hand, a given official character on the surface of the narrative text might under certain circumstances move from one actantial position to a wholly different one.

The conspiratorial thriller, at any rate, begins by borrowing the usefully conventional actantial patterns of the sub-genres, such as the detective story, with its rotation around the triangle formed by detective, victim, and murderer. Once this narrative scheme has become reified – which is to say, once it has been recognized and ratified as a genre in its own right – we are generally willing to overlook the formally embarrassing matter of the incommensurability of the detective's narrative and the narrative of the murder and the victim, which, taking place virtually in another world and a different dimension, that of the past, must now be reconstructed within this one. To oversimplify, we may suggest that the detective is individual and the murder itself – as it were a partnership or joint venture between the victim and the perpetrator – is collective. Unless, indeed, it is the other way round, and the detective, incarnating the forces of society and order, stands over against an event of an absolutely unique and disorderly individual kind. At any rate, the conspiratorial plot – as we shall see below in other contexts – must somehow press together these two poles and force them into a common world, something generally done with mirrors and by way of a speed and a rotation such that the viewer can no longer distinguish between the constitutive dimensions.

In the present instance, what is secured is a certain modification of

33

the category of the individual protagonist, in a situation in which what is wanted is as absolute a collectivization of the individual functions as possible: no longer an individual victim, but everybody; no longer an individual villain, but an omnipresent network; no longer an individual detective with a specific brief, but rather someone who blunders into all of this just as anyone might have done. James Woods, as it is perhaps the moment to observe, is something like a privileged and quintessential vehicle for such modifications: as it were the Bogart of the postmodern, who, like his prototype, can be either villain or hero, can be killed off at will just as easily as he can be allowed to take the romantic lead – but above all is able and willing to show fear, to sweat with anxiety, and to embody vulnerability.

The narrative premise and originality of *Videodrome* lies in the coincidence of the three actantial functions identified above: indeed, before our eyes the three positions of detective, victim and villain systematically change place and are, in the momentum of their rotation, slowly conflated with one another. 'Max' is already in some sense the villain, since he is in the business of producing and distributing pornographic films. When 'Videodrome' comes to his attention, he will take on the role of the detective, only to find that it has been prepared for him by the villains themselves and that he is in fact the victim. But it would be equally fair to say that the conspiratorial villains, themselves outpaced by developments, have to become detectives and then victims in their own turn, while the initial 'victim' (the Professor) can reciprocally be reread in all the other positions as his counter-conspiracy becomes slowly visible and in the process makes Max back over into a tool and a murderer in his own right. Perhaps, indeed, it is this deeper narrative structure – rather than any clinical reality or 'state of consciousness' – that defines the ideologeme that currently bears the name of paranoia in the popular mind. Such a structure does not efface the narrative category of the individual character, as seems to have been the intent in many of the high modernist forms, such as the documentary sections of Dos Passos or the bewildering multiplicities of the *roman fleuve*; nor does it eliminate it by degree, as in the postmodern theorization of the death of the subject. Rather it transcends that category by retaining it and yet subjecting it to a momentum of structural displacements whereby the physical actors remain somehow 'the same,' while their actantial functions shift ceaselessly beneath them. At that point, the actors' bodies themselves become part of the new object-world of reproductive technology, and grisly biosyntheses of anatomy and machinery score deeper atavistic anxieties into the text, as with the abdominal VCR referred to above; while the increasingly unidentifiable functions of such formerly traditional narrative characters open up a space through which we gaze, not at people, but at a conspiracy made

Videodrome

into a whole world, in a landscape of media objects now endowed with a delirious life and autonomy of their own.

It is a solution which now poses second-degree narrative problems of a new type: that of the completion or alternatively of the infinite extendability of what we have called narrative 'loops'. Already in the SF time-travel narrative at its most extreme (in Robert F. Heinlein's two classic stories, 'All You Zombies' and 'By Their Bootstraps'), the paradoxes of time travel generated closed loops in which the protagonist became his own son and father simultaneously, and in which this particular alternate world gradually grew away from the real historical one, sealed in an icy solitude that, excluding all difference by virtue of its power to rewrite the past (or future), thereby leaves the protagonist stranded forever in a private monad. Philip K. Dick thematized this peculiarity of the form, transferring it to hallucination and dramatizing the decay and disintegration of whole worlds by way of the fear that those processes might be nothing more than a private nightmare. In *Videodrome* it is the emergence of new conspiracies out of older ones, the white religious conspiracy out of the political one of Videodrome itself, that threatens to become an infinite process, with diminishing returns. Indeed, the plot itself marks the problem with an elegant naïveté, when to Max's final bemusement, 'I don't know where I am now, I'm having trouble . . . finding my way around,' the televised image of the Debbie Harry character replies: 'That's because you've gone just about as far as you can with the way things are.' At that point, so has this particular film, whose viewing day signs off with the blank screen that registers James Woods' salvational suicide.

After this bravura performance, in which virtually all possible permutations on the conspiratorial structure seem to have been rung, it may be desirable more soberly to enumerate the various logical alternate possibilities. The detective story, clearly, seems to offer the most articulated form in which the problems raised by this or that epistemological vocation for representation have been acknowledged. Nowhere, indeed, does the now canonical distinction between *story* and *fable* (narration and narrative, act of enunciation and message, and so on) find more concrete embodiment, since the 'story' of the detective – normally the narration we follow sentence by sentence, by way of a 'point of view' – in no way coincides with that other story that must be reconstructed, and which is tracked like a reified object of a completely different kind, even though it is merely this kind of narration turned back into a finished narrative or *récit*. Nor, in that spirit, is it difficult to imagine more sophisticated or second-degree variants of the form in which it is the 'story' of the detective which is thus unravelled and reconstructed much later on in time by some successor detective: as, for example, in *The Laughing Policeman* (the Sjöwall-Wahlöö novel filmed by Stuart Rosenberg in 1974).

If, however, we start from the premise that a story of knowing is radically distinct, in its very ontology, from a story of doing, then it becomes clear why myth or ideology come to invest the rationalization and naturalization of the detective story at precisely this point: securing the presupposition of some common world shared by the knower and the doer. From the stand-point which is ours here – identifying a form which unconsciously seeks to grasp or represent the social totality as a whole in what must necessarily be a proto-cognitive fashion – it is obvious from the outset that the knower is part of the same social world as the known. What may be less obvious is the way in which this shared narrative world tends to discredit the detective and to undermine the privileged distance of the epistemological point of view. For while the classical or generic detective may be thought to be disinterested, in at least a limited way, and his or her reconstruction of the crime-event personally and ideologically unmotivated, such neutrality and ideology-free objectivity can never obtain in the realm of social knowledge, where every position (including the supposedly objective and ideologically neutral one) is ideological and implies the taking of a political stance and the making of a social judgment.

The social detective, therefore (as we shall now call him), will require a supplement of motivation in order to win narrative plausibility: 'motivation of the device,' as the Formalists pleasantly called it, in which what has to be done artistically (in this case his act of detection) is rationalized after the fact for aesthetic purposes. It is as though the eccentricities with which the Great Detectives were obligatorily endowed (Holmes' violin and cocaine, Nero Wolfe's orchids, Marlowe's chess) now take on some deeper historical and ideological urgency.

This requirement to supply characterological motivation is evidently not unrelated to an even more fundamental distinction we have been presupposing between the criminal detective and the social detective: the fundamental opposition between individual and collective. For in the classical detective story, an individual detective confronts a crime of an individual nature, generally involving an individual criminal and – in the case of the murder story – an individual victim. The motivational requirement that has been touched on rears its head as soon as one of these terms passes from individual to collective status. Should it turn out, for example, that the crime is in reality a collective one, even though the detective remains an individual, then what is in store for us may be the silliness of some of Agatha Christie's more ingenious plots (such as *Murder on the Orient Express*), but it may also present the cold passion of Vadim Abdrashitov's splendid *A Train Has Stopped* (1981), in which a whole town conspires to cover up a railroad accident. But here, as I have suggested, the detective will need a supplementary motivation of a political type: in *A Train Has Stopped* he is *pur et dur* and offers the currently unfashionable picture of orthodox political and civic virtue; not unexpectedly he leaves the town under the hostile stares and silence of a whole collectivity.

Abdrashitov's wonderful film is, however, only the formalization of a much more common generic variant of this structure, in which the instance of the detective tends towards absolute reduction, while the other, collective term – sometimes turning on the meaning of the victim and the crime itself fully as much as that of the murderer – becomes the occasion for the indictment of a whole collectivity. Such representations are most frequently found in that older moment of a still national culture in which the function of literature includes what I have elsewhere called national allegorization, providing individual narrative representations through which the national destiny can be fantasized.[11] The permutation of the detective story into the trial then offers a powerful vehicle whereby this or that defect or weakness in the national character can be problematized and foregrounded, if not stigmatized and indicted. Most Western national literatures in the late nineteenth century offer striking examples of this form: witness *The Brothers Karamazov* or *Le Disciple, An American Tragedy* or *Les Déracinés*, all of which stage crime itself as the emblematic disorder of the national soul and at the moment of emergence of bourgeois society and secular order interrogate the motives of the criminal – but also, as with Papa Karamazov, the offensiveness of the victim – for so many symptoms of the dangers that menace social order when modernity undermines the bases of the old morality. This is to imply, not only that such forms are normally mobilized in the service of conservative culture critiques, but also that they will be less service-able when secularization and modernization have long since become facts of life – not to speak of what obtains when the new multi-national organization of late capitalism problematizes the framework of the nation state along with the national cultural forms specific to it (like this allegorical one). This form, therefore, in which an individual somehow confronts crime and scandal of collective dimensions and consequences, cannot be transferred to the representations of global postmodernity without deep internal and structural modifications.

Oddly enough, the opposite structure – in which a whole collecti-vity plays detective to the solution of what remains an individual crime, with an individual victim and criminal – also occasionally obtains, as we shall see later. Most often, however, the detective will become social, not by the multiplication and refraction of this actan-tial function in a host of separate characters or individuals, but rather by the socialization of the status of this character, who can most often be identified as occupying the space and position of the intellectual as such: that unhappy consciousness, forever suspended between the classes, yet unable to disengage from class realities and functions, and from class guilt; that 'objective traitor,' as Sartre characterized him, who, disengaging from whatever class of origin (not to speak of race, gender or ethnicity), is never fully welcomed into the group ideologi-cally adopted; whose disinterested intellectual and epistemological commitment finally (as has been suggested above) always risks being unmasked as this or that practical subservience to social forces of a scarcely altruistic nature.

So it is that the social detective – whether generically still a police-man or private investigator, or an investigator of a different sociologi-cal type, which can range from the reporter or the correspondent to the archeologist scholar peering into ancient mysteries – will either be an intellectual in the formal sense from the outset, or will gradually find himself/herself occupying the intellectual's structural position by virtue of the premium placed on knowledge or the cognitive by the form itself (perhaps the last contemporary narrative type in which the lone intellectual can still win heroic dimensions). In any case, it will be the more general positioning of the intellectual in the social structure which endows the individual protagonist with collective resonance, which transforms policeman or journalist, photographer or even media figure, into a vehicle for judgments on society and revelations of its hidden nature, just as it refocuses the various individual or empirical events and actors into a representative pattern symptomatic of the social order as a whole.

But this representativity of the event or crime is by no means so easy to secure, and flexes or rehearses the old tension between the universal and the particular, which, exacerbated in bourgeois society, cannot be solved or resolved, but which equally – on Adorno's view – constitutes the productive contradiction of its greatest art. Indeed, not all such narratives still look like the detective story, particularly when the individual event-mystery of that form is replaced by some more general social one, or better still, by the sense that it is society as a whole that is the mystery to be solved. This is most dramatically the case when the conspiracy turns out to be war – both the guerrilla war of national liberation and at one and the same time the counter-revolutionary war, the war of intervention and repression. Yet the apparent realism and the seemingly overt political content of such films, which range from *Under Fire* (Spottiswoode, 1983) and *Salvador* (Stone, 1986) to *Missing* (Costa-Gavras, 1982) and even *The Year of Living Dangerously* (Weir, 1983) or (marginally) *Who'll Stop the Rain?* (Reisz, 1978), should not be allowed to distract us from the deeper problems of representation and representability they all confront.

If the realism-effect is traditional and old-fashioned, then certainly such films mark a formal regression over the collective and conspiratorial intrigues of our first moment. In particular, we witness here the return in force of the old narrative category of 'point of view,' along with the ideological category of the 'main character' or protagonist-hero. It is as though an empirical singularity, which in our first moment gripped the category of the *event*, as in the crime or murder, releasing its character system to the possibility of more collective dynamics, here absolves from that singularity the events themselves (which become a state of things, rather than a punctual occurrence), and now returns upon the category of the *character* to recontain it by compensation, and enforce again a certain singularity and individuality.

The conventional or generic war film (from the World War II artifacts to *Platoon*) remains a narrative about us, a narrative whose elements do not involve any radical cultural difference. Such films deploy the male collective in exotic settings called into being by their hardships and unfamiliarity, but where the content of the setting is relatively indifferent: on some deeper formal level, the rawness of penitentiary space will do just as well as the jungles of South-East Asia. The *Bildungsroman* or 'point of view' hero is not indispensable here, although frequently enough present, but what is 'learned' generally has more to do with the eternal human than with the radical difference of other cultures and communities (what remains of this last, in American films, is mostly a weak after-image of social class which dares not speak its name).

It is therefore clear that the new 'guerrilla-war correspondent film' is structurally very different from this older war-film genre (of recent attempts, only *Latino* [Wexler, 1985] attempts to combine features of the two forms, without great success). The journalist-witness, whatever his professional camaraderie, is alone; the collective exists on the other side, as his object, in the twin forms of the insurgents and the forces of order. Such films are therefore structured in advance as films-for-us, for the North American public, and seem to raise the issue of difference only at the price of consenting in advance to a structure that will ensure their failure to overcome it.

But we would be wrong to conclude that this structure always necessarily locks us back inside our own heads and involves what used to be called psychological projection (if not even irony). For one thing, filmic 'point of view' is a misnomer to the degree to which it suggests anything like the incorrigible situatedness of narrative language, in which the most 'objective' sentence is always sooner or later fatally drawn back into an attributional process causing us to rewrite such sentences as though they were somebody's thought (the author's, at least, if not the character's). Images, while not objective in the sense in which people used to use the term 'photographic,' are nonetheless material and open to inspection in ways the much weaker identification dynamics of film can never completely master (this proposition, which can be said to argue for a kind of general *dissemination* of meaning in the filmic image, is also the central tenet of Bazinian 'ontological realism').

It is certain, however, that a dual narrative perspective is established in the guerrilla-war correspondent film which leaves us relatively free to read the text as the story of the subject or as the story of the object alternatively: either the protagonist's drama as an outsider and a witness, or the convulsive realities of Central America itself. Yet the alternative is only apparently symmetrical: *Under Fire* – with all its very real aesthetic and political merits[12] – surely ends up reprocessing its materials into a vehicle for the conventional pathos of the old-fashioned individual protagonist. Meanwhile, the ideology of the individual character here even distorts the historical nature of the social situation to which the Nick Nolte character is witness. For if the memory of the martyred leader played a significant role in the ideology of the Sandinista revolution (from Sandino himself to Carlos Fonseca), the ingenious episode of the death of this particularly fic-

Under Fire

tional leader utterly misrepresents the revolutionary process in Nicaragua by attributing to it the structural need for a charismatic figure which it was precisely the originality of the Nicaraguan revolution, with its collective dynamics and leadership, to have been able to do without. This reproach is only apparently based on some philistine commitment to the 'facts' and to empirical accuracy over against imaginative or 'fictive' freedoms; rather, it confirms Adorno's insight that palpable anachronism or historical falsification in the work of art are privileged symptoms of the latter's deeper representational dilemmas and contradictions. It is not because the facts have some prior claim over fiction that such 'flaws' are significant; it is rather because this violence to the logic of the facts betrays a deeper weakness within the very fiction itself, and a structural incapacity, for whatever reason, to construct a narrative that can map totality. The causes, here, in this otherwise meritorious piece of film-making, only too sadly and evidently seem to lie in some generalized ideological incapacity of North Americans to imagine collective processes in the first place, and their tendency, in consequence, to fall back on the emotional securities of individualizing narrative paradigms wherever possible.

Yet the formal alternative to paradigms of this kind is not really the documentary as such, the seeming effacement in advance of the subjectivity of the outsider-witness.[13] *Salvador* offers an interesting formal contrast to *Under Fire* in this respect, even in those features which it seems to share with it. For if *Salvador* seems less laundered and sanitized than *Under Fire*, more raw, and more a matter of what the Cubans used to call 'imperfect cinema' than Spottiswoode's technically polished Hollywood product, this is an impression which has little enough to do either with the technique or with the content, that grisly record of corpses and assassinations that it reads into the record (but which a second viewing of *Under Fire* shows to be matched body for body). Such an impression strikes me rather as testifying to the power of recontainment inherent in subjectivized 'point of view' and in its narrative forms. The interposition of a 'subjectivity' between our reading minds and the 'thing itself' – which Henry James was once able to celebrate as the surest path to the most vivid apprehension of the object – now comes before many of us, in a new and different historical situation (that of postmodernism rather than modernism), as a debilitating instrument in the service of relativism and irony.

It will be paradoxical to position *Salvador* (again starring the ubiquitous James Woods) as a triumphant example of some strong formal alternative to this subjectivizing narrative, since in this film the 'drama' of the protagonist-witness is if anything even more insistent than in *Under Fire*. The appeal to pathos has, to be sure, here been replaced by an implacable anatomy of self-pity. But this is by no means the crucial feature in the differentiation to be established between the two narrative paradigms, a differentiation which lies rather in the historical *content* of the two personal dramas. What must be stressed is not merely a quantitative increase in attention to the details of the James Woods character's marital and financial problems (or even a quantitative increase in the problems themselves), but rather a qualitative shift from Nick Nolte's still relatively moral dilemmas (objective treason to his cuckolded friend, art versus life) to features of a life situation of which money and jobs are only the external signs and which no longer seems to raise ethical or moral choices at all in the first place, in the sense in which 'changing one's life' is not the same kind of choice as that posed by competing loyalties.

In fact, one is tempted to grasp these rather different anxieties ('allegorically') within the informing context of some larger virtual nightmare, which can be identified as that of the 60s gone toxic, the drug and schizophrenic counter-cultural 'bad trip,' psychic fragmentation raised to a qualitatively new power, the structural distraction of the decentered subject now promoted to the very existential logic of late capitalism. 'I have to talk to you about my whole life,' the James Woods character says, 'it's such a mess ... disgusting.' This is not the way one would have found the classical modernist heroes formulating their metaphysical problems – not Hans Castorp, or Marcel, not Ulrich or Joseph K., or even Roquentin. Nor is the chaos and bewilderment of the honest schizophrenic life really the 'problem' of modernist film-makers either, having little enough to do with the obsessions of the hero of *Vertigo* (Hitchcock, 1958), or the neuroses and psychoses of Bergman or Antonioni characters, although in this last arguably we come close, and in *La Dolce Vita* (Fellini, 1960) we're already on our way. The metaphysics of existential disorder; the 'mess' of schizophrenic filled time without any spaces for withdrawal or for distance; the abolition of boredom (and along with it, of any sure-fire distinction between pleasure and pain); the perpetual present of the postmodern, its caricatural fulfillment of the old idea of human life as sheer unrelenting activity: all this is what it would be better not to call a new theme, but rather a new content for literary or cultural representation.

It is of course scarcely exempt from sentimentalism or pathos in its own right, as is the case with most direct representations of this dimension of the 60s as 'official' subject-matter. In *Salvador*, however, the co-existence of the second narrative, the Central American reality, ensures the freshness of this new content by perpetuating that structural ambiguity or Gestalt reading alternation mentioned above where your eye is always on the wrong nutshell. What happens therefore is that as long as you read the movie as a film about Central America, the dilemmas of the protagonist (now positioned in secondary perspective) have representational authenticity. But the inverse is also true: and one is tempted to conclude that – owing to the radical otherness and difference of the Salvadorian class war from North American experience – we read its nightmarish objectivity by way of the subjective nightmare of the protagonist's messy existence, which we know much better and which 'computes' within our experience. More than a metaphor, therefore, the subjective narrative has the function of an *analogon* with respect to the objective or social narrative – a quasi-material object of perception off which we read, as from a material *interpretant*, the narrative language of another set of events: using a nightmare we understand to conjure up a nightmare we cannot even imagine.

Nor does this seem a solution merely local to the film in question, for something similar can be detected in a whole range of significant literary approaches to this same content of postmodern or interventionist warfare. Much of the extraordinary linguistic and representational power of Michael Herr's *Dispatches* (1978), for example, spring from a creative fusion of drug, schizophrenic and rock cultural materials (and sub-languages): the resultant new language experiment does not *express* the nightmare of the Vietnam War, but substitutes a textual equivalent for it. Meanwhile, in retrospect (particularly since his 1985 Hollywood novel, *Children of Light*), the work of Robert Stone – whose *Flag for Sunrise* (1981) we took to be the extreme verge of both Vietnam and Central American war literature – can be perceived (not without a certain disillusionment) to have constituted 'in reality' one long passionate sermon against the 'messiness' of drugs and alcohol, and to have borrowed its 'objective' representational power from a similarly 'subjective' content.[14]

43

Here, then, the problems of motivation mentioned above run structurally very deep indeed; and it was predictable that under certain conditions an elegant autoreferential solution would be found for them, which, by taking motivation itself as the central feature of the 'mystery,' turns the form inside out.

The form-problem that has been tracked thus far, with as much a view towards registering its fitful moments of appearance as its 'solutions' – which can never be anything more than provisional – can also be posed in terms of the empirical and the conceptual content (or meanings) one would like it to vehiculate. In principle, indeed, the here-and-now ought to suffice unto itself, and need no further meaning; but that would only be the case in Utopia, in a landscape of sheer immanence, in which social life coincided fully with itself, so that the most insignificant situations of its everyday life were already in and of themselves fully philosophical. This was presumably what Hegel's slogan about the real being the rational and the rational being the real was supposed to designate; while in aesthetics the canonical New Critical vision of an absolute fusion of form and content is ideological to the degree to which it attributes to the actually existing work of art what it is the latter's impossible vocation to strain for without ever achieving (or so runs the more plausible variant of this aesthetic of immanence, in Lukács' *Theory of the Novel*).

In the absence of Utopia, however, things, remaining as they do contingent and 'unequal' to their own concepts, have to be pumped back up and patched together with allegory. The characterological traits of the protagonists required by the plot have to be remotivated, and made to mean something of a 'supplementary' and symbolic nature. Even the plots themselves must be made to mean something a little extra: a war like Vietnam or El Salvador means the larger imperialist conspiracy, true enough; but as an empirical event, a unique occurrence in that particular latitude and longitude, on that particular date in the calendar, it must also be *made* to mean its meaning: it must in short be *allegorized*, however discreetly, in order to pass for some more general logical class of which it is itself a member. The problem would scarcely be solved by suppressing the mediation: the narrative cannot but remain allegorical, since the object it attempts to represent – namely, the social totality itself – is not an empirical entity and cannot be made to materialize as such in front of the individual viewer. In effect, the new figure we are here asked to supply continues to suggest something other than itself, in the occurrence a conspiracy that is in reality a (class) war.

But we have not yet exhausted the formal possibilities and permutations: leaving aside the victim for the moment, we began from the basic scenario of the classical detective story, in which both the murderer and the detective were individual agents. A first modification and amplification then suggested itself, in which the murderer becomes identified as a collective instance, even while the point of view of the detective remains an individual one. In this modification, certain kinds of social or political investigations (such as the Abdrashitov film) are rarer than the more schematic surface manifestation in terms of civil war: this being, however, from a North American viewing standpoint, as science-fictional as *Videodrome* since it evidently has no equivalent within our own 'current situation.' Its actantial problems are thereby compounded, since the individual social detective still in question here will in the guerrilla/civil-war film also carry the narrative onus of being a foreigner and a foreign speaker.

But there remain two narrative permutations which have not yet been examined. Suppose, for instance, that the murderer (or indeed the victim) remains an individual, while the detective has somehow already been transformed into a collective instance? And even if this peculiar formal possibility can be conceived (let alone empirically realized somewhere), how would it be possible to imagine moving forward to the ultimate and most satisfying transformation of the form, in which both crime and detective, murderer and investigator (not to speak of the victim), have finally, like chrysalids, been transmogrified into that final manifestation of which they were supposed to be allegories in the first place, namely, the collective – the group or class – as agent, actor, or communal agency. That would presumably be a civil war, but somehow within the US, and with a domestic rather than a foreign-language cast.[15]

But at least the first of these structural possibilities can readily be identified, if looked for in the right place, since it is one of the most frequently rehearsed motifs or fantasy-narratives, not to say obsessions, of the current political unconscious, namely, *assassination*, which, owing to the mediation of the public sphere and its technologies, is one of the few individual crimes upon which a whole collectivity broods like a many-headed private investigator, noting the insufficiencies of the official police procedures all the while it revels in ingenious speculations of its own devising. Meanwhile, few plot structures so dramatically illustrate the constructional dilemmas of allegory, and the problems that obtain when events of an individual, empirical nature are worked over by force with a view towards endowing them with this or that more general meaning.

From the very outset, indeed, the assassination plot poses two

46

preliminary questions that are virtually unanswerable: not merely why the death of this particular political figure should hold any more general interest – particularly within an aesthetic frame which is commonly supposed to suspend in advance our interests in and commitments to the real political world outside it; but even more fundamentally (and in a question that clearly violates that frame in advance), what relationship this particular fictional assassination plot is supposed to entertain with the one real-life assassination that has, in our time, had general philosophical significance (above and beyond its more immediate practical consequences). I want to argue that these two questions or problems largely transcend the more familiar aesthetic question about the value of *'romans à clef'* or even of topical allusions within the traditional work of art. Or if you prefer, those traditional problems anticipate these, which now – in the context of the new representational issues of the world system – raise questions in their very form about the public and the private spheres which were not yet problems under an older dispensation, problems which can, for example, be glimpsed by asking ourselves whether there still exist sub-genres and narrative classifications such as the 'political novel' or 'political film.'

In another place,[16] I have made the suggestion that the paradigmatic political assassination in (Western) modern times – that of John F. Kennedy – cannot be said to owe its resonance to Kennedy's political meaning, nor even (save for an emergent youth culture) to the deeper social symbolism and fantasy investment associated with him as a figure (in that respect, Malcolm X, or Martin Luther King, or Bobby Kennedy probably generated more intense experiences of mourning). Rather, what ensured the well-nigh permanent association of assassination in general with this particular historical one was the experience of the media, which for the first time and uniquely in its history bound together an enormous collectivity over several days and vouchsafed a glimpse into a Utopian public sphere of the future which remained unrealized.

However that may be, it means that henceforth any structural deployment of the assassination narrative necessarily faces two supplementary problems. First, it must specify its distance from this specific historical referent, that is to say, it must give us the means to determine whether it is meant to offer a commentary on the Kennedy event itself, or whether it is designed to bracket that topical reference point and direct our attention towards other themes. Then too, it must somehow handle the new and historically original problem of the media which the Kennedy event brought into being for the first time (and this is the deeper sense in which Kennedy's assassination was paradigmatic): henceforth assassination and the question of the media are representationally related and mutually implicit (in ways in which they were not in popular or collective representations of Sarajevo, for example, or of Lincoln's death).

These are, as it were, the new features, the new problems, associated with the assassination narrative. They do not, however, annul the inherited problems associated with political themes as a *genre*. What has to be explained here, in other words, is why we no longer grasp *The Parallax View*, or even *All the President's Men*, as narrative artifacts that can be classed under the rubrics appropriate for, say, *Advise and Consent* (Preminger, 1962) or *Fail-Safe* (Lumet, 1964) or even, perhaps, *The Dead Zone* (Cronenberg, 1983). These last evidently presupposed a specialization of political thematics as a local subject-matter associated with Washington, DC, or with electoral politics, something no longer terribly relevant or meaningful after the 60s (and a more widely disseminated Marxian view of historical dynamics) enlarged our perception of what is political well beyond this narrowly governmental material. But it would be wrong to grasp this more traditional category of the genre of the political novel (or film) as one uniquely correlated with parliamentary or representative democracy, since specialized notions of the court and its intrigues, in the baroque political drama (or *Haupt-und-Staatsaktion*), for example, played an analogous role in the period of the absolute monarchy (and perhaps in other imperial cultures).

Such a pre-bourgeois genealogy, however, reminds us to take note of a rather different (though in another sense equally 'traditional') way of cutting across the generic signals of a specifically 'political' literature: Lukács' discussion of the historical novel as such (and the historical drama), which subsumes the narrowly and sociologically 'political' back under the more philosophical and universal concept of the 'historical'. But the newer assassination and conspiratorial narratives under investigation here seem also to have coincided with a significant waning and obsolescence of just such 'historical' genres – in film and the novel, fully as much as in drama: only Gore Vidal's remarkable American chronicles have seemed to constitute the straw in the wind of a momentous revival (if not of a whole new type of historical representation). What Lukács' line of reflection reminds us to inscribe is, however, the classical opposition of public and private, which constituted the foundation and the fundamental structural presupposition of the notion of a distinct, specialized 'political' literature about public life. The waning and disappearance of this literature may therefore now offer valuable clues as to the specificity of the conspiratorial narrative, whose emergence may indeed equally well stand as a symptom of the tendential end of 'civil society' in late capitalism.

What is certain is that both of these categories – the nature of the 'political' as a literary, representational or narrative constraint or feature, and the structural opposition of private and public spheres – are decisively modified, if not transformed beyond all recognition, by the enlargement of the social totality or operative context out into the uniquely distended proportions of the new world system of late capitalism. If already, in Brecht's time, the social forces and realities invested in the Krupp works were, as he once put it, no longer susceptible to representation of a photographic sort, how much more is this the case for a kind of production that can scarcely be spatially identified as an individual factory in the first place? Better still, the very problem or theme of its possible photographic reproduction would under post-contemporary circumstances now have to be factored into the attempt itself; while any intent to map a network of just such productive nodes or provisional centers would have to include within the description an account of their mode of communicational relationship and command transmission. Multinational capitalism, in other words, is a concept that has to include within itself reproduction as well as production.

In more political terms, the Nixon tapes may offer some (conspiratorial) equivalent to the 'photographic realism' discredited by Brecht, suggesting, as they do, not merely a unity of place and action, but also a strongly representational aesthetic (powered, no doubt, by a Freudian scoptic drive) in which, as in so much historiography and historical fiction, what the reader/spectator really longs for is to be present at the scene: to see, to hear, to find out the secret truth. The limits of such categories of personal or anthropomorphic power are not only evident intellectually – in the incompatibility between a complex bureaucratic system and the arbitrary caprice of individual psychology – but representationally as well: where the dramatization of the most powerful conceivable 'world-historical' figure, whether Hitler, Stalin or whatever occupant of the Oval Office, pushed to its extreme, still fails to yield anything more suggestive than the inside of a room – 'power' at best manifesting itself in banks of telephones or the arrival and departure of written messages or heralds whose actantial form is shrouded in antiquity. But this is the narrative stock in trade of Oriental Despotism and not of late capitalism: the hold over our imagination of such antiquated narrative categories ought to tell us something about the dilemmas of cognitive mapping in the world system today.

So it is, for example, that one's first thought of an adequate representation of the Cuban Missile Crisis of 1962, inevitably projects a conference in the War Room onto the screen of the mind, with Kennedy and his advisors hunched over enlargements of strategic maps and high altitude surveillance photographs. What we are here really looking at, however, are the formal stereotypes and kitsch narrative paradigms and archetypes inside our own minds: not even the most concrete visuality in detail and reconstruction, nor the historical accuracy and 'truth' of the re-enactment, can rescue such images from the realm of simulacra and the imaginary. 'Even if it was a fact it

49

wouldn't be true' (Adorno); and the historians have known, at least since the Higher Criticism of the Bible, that familiar paradigms must by definition be wrong, just as Cornford demonstrated the suspicious operation, within the stoic and glacial factuality of Thucydides, of patterns of Athenian tragic drama that are not likely to have shown up, by accident, in nature or in 'real life'.[17] But are fresh paradigms possible any longer, or even the raucous mockery of the parodic satyr play (*Dr Strangelove*, for example [Kubrick, 1964]), in which high convention is mimetically remastered by the gross human productivity of farce?

In fact, we do possess a rather different 'rendering' of the October Crisis from the point of view, as it were, of the Other. This is Tomas Gutierrez Alea's now classical *Memories of Underdevelopment* (Cuba, 1968, from the novel by Edmundo Desnois), in which 'Kennedy' exists, not as an old-fashioned fictional character in the round (played by the appropriate look-alike movie star), but rather as a well-nigh disembodied television image, inserted, intermittently flickering but full of menace, into the daily life of Cubans in Havana, in an urban routine unchanged in everything but the imminence of the nuclear flash. This is the ominous silence of the new kind of nuclear 'phony war' that at best, in First World representations, shows up in pathology or obsession, like that Bergman character muttering darkly and compulsively about the peril of millions of Chinese. The media image or photographic reproduction thus offers a provisional me-

Memories of Underdevelopment

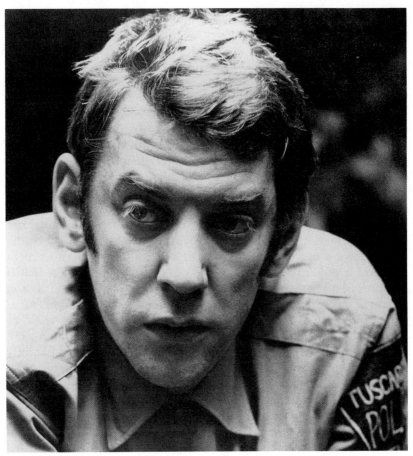

Klute

diation between the category of the old-fashioned narrative character or agent and the information transmissions of the new global communication systems, binding these incommensurable levels punctually together in an unstable kind of ion-exchange: from Kennedy to 'Kennedy,' not to say from the referent or signified to the simulacrum.

Nixon also remained just such a television image and a constitutive absence in Pakula's *All the President's Men*, which, framed in video close-ups of the protagonist of the convention and the reinauguration, faithfully transmits the more successful dramatic touches of this theatrical president (not the notorious operetta uniforms of the White House guard, but rather the splendidly timed helicopter touchdown at the joint session of Congress staged as the climax of his world journey). Oddly enough, however, this residual Nixoniana does not reintroduce the shadow of a fictional White House redramatization 'behind the scenes,' as in our imaginary Kennedy scenarios, but rather succeeds triumphantly in here splitting reference from narrativity. Indeed, virtually the most interesting formal feature of Pakula's achievement here lies in its evasion of the traditional category of the costume drama or narrowly 'political' film or sub-generic Washington 'exposé'. 'Nixon' here remains an absence: a technical stroke of no little interest that at one blow produces and solves a qualitatively new form-problem, and which, by cutting across the traditional opposition between public and private, has virtually, in Pakula's most successful films, become his trademark.

It is therefore worth looking for the antecedents of this effect in the earlier panels of his so-called paranoia trilogy, in *Klute* of 1971 and *The Parallax View* of 1974, in which the public-private opposition is already rehearsed in unusual and untraditional ways. Indeed, it is precisely this opposition that makes up the originality of *Klute*, not officially a 'political' film at all. A neutral plot summary might wildly misrepresent it as the touching story of a love affair between a prostitute and a policeman, omitting the essentials, namely, that it is a question of a big-city prostitute and a small-town policeman. For in this film, exceptionally, the tension between public and private is played out upon the opposition between what is still the city itself, or the urban, and what is no longer the country in any traditional sense but not the suburb either: rather, a kind of bedroom community outside, in the former countryside, where new and presumably high-tech industries have established themselves, their upper-level employees adopting the rural style of the former farming culture just as urban yuppies reinhabit brownstones and appropriate a classical nineteenth-century American city culture for technocracy.

What this means is that, in the powerful reversal of this axis staged in *Klute*, the countryside becomes the public realm and the city the private one. Such is indeed the burden of the mystery's exposition: the respected family man at Thanksgiving dinner with his friends, in the bright sunlight of the small-town community, where this seemingly domestic persona is in reality the public image – Manhattan becoming the place of the hidden perversion and the secret life. The disappearance and possible murder only conceals this spatial axis which was there all along, hidden away within the fragility of a domestic prosperity which is also a corporate one. Nor does it matter much later on when we find that the two lives never did co-exist within the same individual after all. As for the protagonists of this film, a similar (but narratively unrelated) reversal gives their relationship its bite and freshness. For it is the official or professional figure, the policeman John Klute (Donald Sutherland), who is the bearer of private feelings, of love and affection as well as of therapeutic consolation; while the prostitute (Jane Fonda), who might be supposed to be associated with the double life and the sexual underworld, in reality represents professionalism and business life with a well-nigh Brechtian irony (she

The Parallax View

has her answering service and her own 'private life,' her hobbies, her therapist, and her career prospects – acting lessons and a possible career in fashion modeling). Such is the hypocrisy of North American culture, however, that, unlike *The Threepenny Opera*, the effect in late capitalism is not to turn the public formalities of business and big-city bureaucratic life to ridicule, but rather to stand as a social statement, with political and even activist consequences, by portraying the hooker as belonging to a genuine sub-group in her own right and thereby deserving of public attention (demonstrations, unions, legal rights, and so on). *Klute* seems to have accomplished this despite the (equally American) therapeutic overtones (prostitutes are frigid, they want attention and power over others, above all – shades of neo-Freudianism and the soaps! – they are unable to face 'serious' relations with others). But I would argue that these social messages, which seemed at the time to mark out the boldness of *Klute*'s subject-matter, are little more than the (necessary) pre-text for the unsettling of our conventional notions of private life and the public sphere. Simmel, indeed, liked to point out that what is scandalous for the middle classes about prostitution is not the degradation of the body, sexuality and love that it seems to imply, but rather, the other way round, the way money finds itself degraded by this association with the sexual functions.

At any rate, in Pakula's trilogy, such Brechtian changing of the valences of private and public does not so much have the effect of defamiliarizing either of these poles (for some specifically satiric purpose) as much as it does of holding them apart and freezing their incompatibility in such a way as to 'produce' their incommensurable antagonism as an object of aesthetic contemplation, if I may use this Althusserian way of speaking. What transpires, particularly in the public figures, is an absolute dissociation between their public and private realities, in ways consistent with an image culture but which then block that older kind of 'political' genre literature in which the character or personality of the politician remained a substantive issue.

In *The Parallax View*, it is the disparity between the two senatorial victims of assassination that is designed to disjoin and to problematize the mystery of the private-public allegory. (They are of course by no means the only victims, in this greatest of all assassination films, which takes as its premise that famous rumor about the deaths in mysterious circumstances of a high and statistically improbable number of eye-witnesses in the years immediately following the Kennedy assassination. Here it is the public on the Needle that begins to disappear improbably after the equivalent shooting: a fact that determines the newspaperman protagonist to infiltrate the organized conspiracy he thinks he has begun to glimpse. Only too successful in doing so and in passing himself off as a potential assassin, he finds himself trapped in the wings and causeways of the sports arena in which the second senator has just been shot, becoming an only too plausible, indeed a fatal, suspect in the crime.)

Here, then, the representational dilemma is inscribed in the text and thereby acknowledged, rather than repressed or resolved: the gap between the private individual and the public function or meaning is

The Parallax View

held open and exacerbated; resolution is not even presupposed in advance; and the very problem of representability now becomes in some sense its own solution – the thing being done, as it were, by showing it cannot be done in the first place. Meanwhile, a third term silently associates itself with the other two, and that is assassination or conspiracy itself, which sets private life and public reputation side by side, before sweeping both away into meaningless contingency and externality, thus rendering old-fashioned political questions irrelevant. A new kind of political narrative thereby emerges, which is more consistent with the dynamics of the world system than an older anthropomorphic or 'humanist' kind (in which personal agency still had to be attributed to individual politicians by virtue of their narrative significance as characters). Its operation above the level of representative democracy in *The Parallax View* does not, however, lead into the abstractions of the spy thriller, nor even into the science-fictional loops of *Videodrome*, but rather paves the way for the return to what looks like the most classic political intrigue and Washingtoniana in the 'victimless' conspiracies of *All the President's Men*.

Meanwhile, its social detective must now also be remotivated, but in a way that somehow transcends sheer reportorial curiosity (the purely epistemological) in order to take root in the ontological, in a world in which conspiracy is the fundamental law. The problem to be solved here is then that characterological one we have already observed in *Salvador*, where the existential messiness of the protagonist's psyche somehow corresponded to the messiness of revolution and civil war itself. But in *Salvador*, the James Woods character's mission was personal redemption, and redemption of a sort – finally nailing a story, putting his personal life back together, saving his career – which does not particularly connect back up with the objective situation; it could not do so, indeed, for that situation speaks Spanish and comes from out of another world (the Third), while the Woods-style neurosis is necessarily a North American product. *The Parallax View*, however, confronts this formal problem head on, by trying to give figuration to the equivalent of a civil war within an 'advanced' capitalist society whose contradictions no longer express themselves in that fashion.

Nonetheless, the Warren Beatty character is inscribed in a tradition of North American revolutionary and political literature by way of the characterology that allows his story to be read as the last in that series, if not the beginning of something else. It is not enough to describe him as a rebel, unless we take the trouble of noting the historical disappearance of this kind of figure from a bureaucratic and corporate universe, and also of interrogating the paradoxical sources of such violence, which can also be described as 'anti-social' as it brushes the psychotic and the pathological. At the beginning of the century, indeed, in his path-breaking study of the emergence of modern drama, Lukács underscored pathology as a fundamental aspect of the wresting of dramatic action from the complacencies of the new bourgeois social life and culture. The stylization demanded by a contemporary drama, he observed,

> can no longer simply be the pathos of an abstract or self-conscious heroism as such. It can only be found in the stylization of a specific character trait, on a gigantic scale beyond anything found in life, and to a degree that dominates the entire human being and his destiny. Or, to put it in the language of everyday life: pathology. For what else can this most extreme form of intensification prove to be but morbidity and the pathological excess of one particular feature over everything else in human life? And this is clearly exaggerated by the motivational compulsion that derives from the style of the drama itself: if the excessiveness is to be confirmed on psychic grounds, these cannot be drawn from the limits of normal psychology, and even less to the very degree that the situation of the character is itself dramatic. ... If there is no mythology ... everything must be based on and derived from character itself. But a motivation thrown back exclusively on character, and the exclusive interiority of that character's destiny, now always drive character to the very borders of pathology.[18]

The dramatic, in other words what shakes the status quo and produces crisis as such, is difficult to derive or produce from out of the status quo of a non-transcendent universe, and must therefore be housed, as a disturbing and unsettling force, within the individual herself. But in the various European national traditions, which are more intensely socialized, the representation of such a force must take into account the class context, and the rebel will either be a sympathizer with another class or else someone viewed as sick or aberrant from the perspective of this one. In the frontier dissolution of the older North American classes, however, the rebel can incarnate sheer unmotivated violence, an energy that blasts open social convention and needs no other ideological justification than the hatred of masters and of the social order: something which shows up in sheer aggressivity as such.

Yet all American political ideologies have sought in one way or another to remotivate that aggressivity and to draw its energies back within their own programs: most recently the great political images of the 30s and of American socialist realism, in which characterological violence is necessary in order to oppose the whole weight and force of the system itself. But the paradoxes of such violence (dramatized in a film like *Bound for Glory* [Ashby, 1976], based on the life of Woody Guthrie) do not seem to have been registered until the 60s and the contemporary feminist movement: namely, how anti-social violence can with impunity be tapped for social reconstruction; how a temperament suited for the demolition of the old order can participate in the formation of a new one; how the purifying negative act can be Utopian; how the destructive personality can be productively used. Not only the deeper constitutive tensions between anarchism and communism are resonated here, but also a whole set of Freudian presuppositions about the childhood sources of violence and aggressivity and their possible redirection, as well as the classical ideological arguments about the goodness or irrecuperability of human nature itself.

But in *The Parallax View* a positive contribution on the part of the protagonist is unnecessary, save in whatever resistance is required to overcome the concealment of the conspiracy. The Warren Beatty character's unruly belligerence and temperamental uncooperativeness already stand in the service of the epistemological, and in a bureaucratic world in which cognitive mapping is the supreme remaining form of praxis, aggressivity in following up the truth becomes Utopian, at least for a time. But it also becomes ironic, an irony which may have its deeper origins in the disabused refusal of this political film, as in so many others in recent times, to project even the shadow of some older 'positive' hero. The postmodern period generally has been described as the era of universal cynicism, not least because of the triumphant process whereby it has demystified all value and reduced everything to instrumentality: the remnants of value then come before us as so much propaganda or sentimentalism. But the rhetoric of cynical demystification demands a certain modesty. No one should profit from the universal corruption of the system (it is the old paradox of the satirist: if everyone has become tainted, who is left to say so but the misanthrope?), so that only the absence of heroes authenticates the document and proves the point. So also in that muted new version of *The Parallax View* which is Pakula's Watergate film (*All the President's Men*), where the conspiratorial reporter's well-nigh physical pugnaciousness (in the earlier film misleadingly attributed to alcoholism) has instructively been diminished to the characterologically unpleasant traits of the two reporters: everything awkward and inarticulate about Hoffman as a character actor is here mobilized in the service of manipulation, while the Redford figure is so vacuous and shabby as to cast a more fundamental doubt on the very category of the 'good guy' in the first place. Meanwhile, their combination in what has elsewhere been termed the pseudo-couple deprives them of all possible dignity (while formally allowing anything resembling subjective experience to be externalized as dialogue and exposition). In any case, the detective story classically required a pair in order to sift through the findings; only here priority status shifts back and forth in order to pre-empt a definitive by-line.

The Parallax View

In *The Parallax View*, however, the protagonist's pathological character is functional and is systematically looped back into the narrative: only psychotic candidates are able to pass the screen test (psychologically calibrated reactions to a carefully chosen and suggestive series of images involving family, state, race, violence, and social and psychological inferiority and *ressentiment*) and thus to qualify for the Parallax Corporation's openings as professional assassins. Yet it is the very rebelliousness inherent in his pursuit of the conspiracy that allows him to pass for potentially psychopathic in the first place. But here is the supplementary turn of the screw: everything that qualified him to be a professional killer also confirms his identity as lone assassin, without any ties to an 'organized conspiracy'; everything that equips him to penetrate the organization also makes him vulnerable to the latter's manipulation.

What must be stressed is that the institutional construction of the conspirator figures is not to be confused with the essentially satiric portrayal of 'organization men' and the new corporate personality which culturally precedes it and of which it is no doubt, in another sense, a kind of structural variant. The allegorical indices that enable the rewriting of individual actors in the register of the collective no longer have anything to do with satire in that older sense in which the structural 'opposite' of the faceless corporation man remained the true individual, most often a rebel and a non-conformist in just that great American tradition of individual protest and resistance already evoked.

For, as I have implied above, all forms of opposition are today also collective and organized into political protest groups and movements of various kinds: at which point the corporate fact and the corporate style is somehow no longer merely an aberrant business subculture, but some deeper, quasi-ontological law of the social world itself. In this sense, indeed, the Beatty character in *The Parallax View* can be taken as a comment on, and a definitive dismissal of, the older narrative paradigm of the rebel; for he still looks like that, and the violence and anti-social nature of his personality is here insistently set in place. It is not, to be sure, the tragic fate of this protagonist that differentiates his story from the rebel plot, since those stories draw their heroic qualities from the very sense of the inevitability of doom and failure. The Beatty character, however, ceases to be the rebel figure for which he still takes himself because the oppositional impulses within himself and in his character and unconscious have become the very instruments of the conspiracy proper, which uses and welcomes them specifically for its own purposes. In a kind of Hegelian ruse of reason, it is precisely the will to revolt and to destroy the conspiracy which allows this last to write him into their scenario and to destroy him in the process, something for which the popular term 'co-optation' is probably not a very adequate characterization.

The detective is thus murderer and victim all at once: two mirror-image conspiracies begin to confront each other, except that one has more people and is better organized. But this means that finally bureaucracy wins out over the rebel, whose last glimpse in life (as his killers move in on his hiding-place) cancels the definitive closing door of the nineteenth-century carceral imagination, substituting instead the more intense nightmare of an open door that gives onto a world conspiratorially organized and controlled as far as the eye can see. The rebel's paradigmatic narrative is thereby retired along with him. The final silhouette of the enemy on the causeway is if anything grimmer than the blank video-screen of *Videodrome* insofar as it is followed by the Warren Commission-style judicial announcement ('Beatty' acted alone) that translates all this back into new and current events, into that segment of daily life to which we now confine 'history' and the public sphere and which, in its rapid obsolescence, becomes associated with the historical referents from which the film had so triumphantly kept its distance; only at this point it is an association as dusty as the closed file or the wastepaper-basket.

Here, then, the motivation of the social detective reaches back into, and is overdetermined by, the 'crime' it is his mission and his destiny to detect. In some immense postmodern Hegelianism the same structures contaminate the fields of the subject and of the object alike, making them infinitely substitutable and susceptible to endless trans-

The Parallax View

formation into each other – something which is not without its consequences for filmic language as well. For the detective, Benjamin's
Grübler, the saturnine melancholic brooding among things and reading their fragmentary, allegorical messages – the message of the frag-
ment, in late capitalism, always being the totality itself and the world
system – the visual knows a primacy which is congenial indeed to the
development of film as medium (as the pivotal constructions of Hitchcock demonstrate).

That both detectives and assassins need to be at least in that respect
analogous to documentary film-makers is clear enough. But *The Parallax View* trumps this general thesis about the intimate relations of
suspicion and perception with a whole reading test – the Corporation's photographic 'fascist reaction scale' – that seems to drop us
back into the crudest kind of associationism or experimental psychology (this last, to be sure, remaining a fertile breeding ground for
paranoia as well as superstition, as its institutional links with the CIA
and various forms of counter-insurgency training testify). Yet the
testing sequence in *The Parallax View*, like its predecessor in the
programming sequences of *A Clockwork Orange* (Kubrick, 1971),
comments on image society and advertising fully as much as it hints at
darker sources of manipulation and control; the deck is here shuffled
differently than in *Videodrome*, where commodities (television programs and/or pornography) stood in for political conspiracy. Here
the fact of consumption is underscored by discontinuity; narrativity is
deliberately interrupted by the insertion of still photographic images

61

The Parallax View

which are then renarrativized on a second level by the suggestive music that forges them into an allegory of good and evil, family and country versus the enemy, the heroic comic-book persona of the avenging hero, and the pathos of rich and poor, ins and outs, in a oscillation finally becoming so fast as to endow the positive presidential images with the quotient of loathing associated with 'evil' Nazi and communist leaders.

The sequence recalls both narrative interpolations – such as the wondrous silent-film flash-back tale of Alma's humiliation in *The Naked Night* (Bergman, 1953) – and the inserted competition with a rival medium: the television monitor itself, or an interruption by photography proper, as in the pack of snapshots that invades *Last Year at Marienbad* (Resnais, 1962). The rivalry with another medium – it has been suggested that it is always staged, in film, to demonstrate the primacy of this one[19] – will return again and again in the following pages. Here it is enough to pause on the way in which film here is used against itself and to suggest something beyond itself. As in the euthanasia sequence of *Soylent Green* (Fleischer, 1973), where Edward G. Robinson's last moments are fulfilled with a lush travelogue of the great natural images that no longer exist on the film's near-future polluted earth, the insertion is also distinguished from its narrative context by style as such, that is to say, by a garish bad taste meant (at least in the American context) to signify the popular or mass unconscious in which such images function. In *Parallax*, this unconscious is home-grown American comic-book fascism, as native as apple pie; in *Soylent Green*, it is the deeper longing for *National Geographic* pictures as the most authentic domestic contact with nature itself. To use style as an instrument for Barthesian connotation in this way, as a vehicle for a specific ideological message, is perhaps always to ensure its qualification as bad, meretricious, kitsch, or

The Parallax View

degraded: only in the various modernisms are there ways distinct from camp of turning the connotative use of such vulgarity back into 'art'. In *Parallax*, however, the quoted style authenticates the filmic narratives all around it as a reliable kind of realism; while the very excursus through impersonal collective and cultural stereotypes ends on a chilling note indeed, reducing the Beatty character to a sociological type and driving a new kind of wedge between the private and the public by its disclosure of a non-individual unconsciousness made up of thoughts and myths belonging to nobody in particular.

These supplementary images may indeed comment more generally on the filmic language of *The Parallax View*, which is more brassily orchestrated than the other films in the so-called paranoia trilogy. In *Klute* color was used against the nocturnal interiors and closed urban scenery, and it is indeed as if a bright palette there were designed to demystify that floral and pastoral, sunlit suburban village space with which, as I have already observed, the film had to begin. *All the President's Men*, for reasons I will return to, must retain a certain drabness as a sign that, like Washington itself, it is beyond the opposition between city and country. But *The Parallax View* enfolds a variety of landscapes within itself by way of documenting its model of the social totality as conspiracy. As with *Videodrome* (and also, in a different way, *North by Northwest*), the multiplicity of landscapes becomes something like an *analogon* for aesthetic as well as epistemological closure: so here we have all the elements – the high seas and a boat in flames, the needle of the Seattle Tower high up in the stratosphere, a raging river in the mountains, a faceless glass modernist office-building in a corporate no man's land, rented rooms in the tenderloin, the classical airport, the classical shopping mall, the classical morgue and also the traditional newspaper office – all of them sewn together, if not by typically US parades and marching bands,

The Parallax View

then by the miniature train in the zoo where the protagonist learns how to go about changing his identity.

Still, none of this yet tells us the essential: namely, how the villains are to be allegorized in this particular film, how – after the appropriate operations on the victim and the detective – the third position of criminal agent is to be de-individualized, if not collectivized. Here too a totality-effect must be achieved; the conspiracy must not simply be a collection of individual characters, but project something like a corporate structure: in *The Parallax View*, this is achieved by the division of labor between two notable villains, who constitute something like the president of the company and the chairman of the board, respectively. But even that structural collectivity must now be hollowed out and made capable of bearing the weight of allegorical generalization. It is an a priori formal dilemma about which virtually the only thing that can be said in advance is that the recourse to the stock languages of older melodrama is an immediately identifiable sign of failure or of the admission of defeat. What strikes the viewer of *The Parallax View*, however, as well as of the other related films by Pakula already mentioned, is an unexpected solution by displacement, a local innovation in a different zone of the text, where one would not at first have sought the elements of some new kind of compositional allegory. These films are all indeed characterized by a nagging stylistic peculiarity, which can at first distract the viewer: namely, something like an arbitrary decision to work up very close to the actors and to substitute the obsessive close-ups of their faces for the long or medium shots of conventional filmic story-telling. What is imperceptibly unnerving about all this has been astutely registered by James Monaco, who, invoking Dreyer, observes that 'a film shot mainly in close-ups ... deprives us of setting and is therefore disorienting, claustrophobic.'[20]

The Parallax View

It is a stylistic mannerism that seems at first to operate indiscriminately, lingering on innocent or guilty alike, and dwelling on the whole range of curious or indifferent, interested or suspicious people in any way involved in the events in question (the camera thereby itself replicating the attention of the conspiracy, since an improbable number of bystanders to the assassination end up dying accidental deaths). The close-up style here therefore signals some outer problematic limit of visual interrogation: the camera seems to look more closely at these people, to examine their features and to surprise their secrets – only the face itself marks the boundary and the limits of what it can explore. Meanwhile, shorn of its bodily and gestural context, facial expression is in the process depersonalized and dehumanized. The variety of human emotions (or more properly, of our concepts of emotion) – that distinct collection of names for the muscle contractions and grimaces of which the human mask is physically capable – now finds itself somehow sharply reduced, everything coming to stand as the changing sign of some deeper underlying mood tone, that can variously be characterized as anxiety, concern, *Sorge*, harassed bewilderment, apprehension, confusion, or disquiet. At the same time, this peculiar standardization by depersonalized fear is accompanied by something rather different – an unpleasant sense of intimacy, as is normal enough (in the Anglo-Saxon world) when faces come too close.

This is the context in which the distinctive treatment of the agents of conspiracy must now be specified: for alone among these troubled faces, the villains, the members of the conspiracy, are calm and unruffled, with a complacency it may not be too hasty to connote as that of corporations and corporate officials. The faces of this second species are male, well-fed, utterly lacking in personal idiosyncrasies, and above all deeply tanned (the connotator, in our society, of privilege).

Yet they are also *sweating* faces: a film of oiliness is always present which marks these faces as haunted by preoccupation, but by a pre-occupation of a very different type than the fear that grips their victims. For the agents of conspiracy, *Sorge* is a matter of smiling confidence, and the preoccupation is not personal but corporate, concern for the vitality of the network or the institution, a disembo-died distraction or inattentiveness engaging the absent space of the collective organization itself without the clumsy conjectures that sap the energies of the victims. These people *know*, and are therefore able to invest their presence as individual characters in an intense yet complacent attention whose center of gravity is elsewhere: a rapt intentness which is at one and the same time disinterest. Yet this very different type of concern, equally depersonalized, carries its own specific anxiety with it, as it were unconsciously and corporately, without any personal consequences for the individual villains. Sweat does double duty, as the badge of that collective responsibility, and as the tangible locus of everything that is unpleasant in the intimacy of the close-up; an index sometimes projected onto other sensory levels, as in the telephone exchanges of *All the President's Men*, or above all in the murderer's whispering voice in *Klute*, near and hoarse enough to be obscene. What we have here called 'intimacy' is the discovery that we are caught in a collective network without knowing it, that people are already up much closer than we realized, even in moments of solitude, their alien body warmth testifying without melodrama to our own vulnerability. From Sartre to Foucault, and beyond them in contemporary feminism, the look has been the privileged ontological space in which our disempowerment as manipulatable objects is dra-matized and deployed. Yet the dynamics of the visual and of the gaze always project a space of 'power' – the absent Other, the watch-tower of the panopticon – which is somehow itself immune to sight and escapes its own logic by taking refuge behind the recording appar-atus. Pakula's world here seems to me to move into a new and more generalized sensory space in which there are no longer any ontologi-cal hiding-places of that kind: the conspiracy wins, if it does (as in *The Parallax View*), not because it has some special form of 'power' that the victims lack, but simply because it is collective and the victims, taken one by one in their isolation, are not.

In the preceding sections we have been able to observe one of the most peculiar indirections characteristic of allegory in general: the laterality with which the levels, like the hollow nutshells of the shell game, must be conveyed. If you want to say something about economics, for example, you do so with political material (such is indeed the general interpretive premise of this chapter, that the economic organization of multinational capitalism is in the conspiracy form conveyed by the shifting shapes of power). On the other hand, if you want to say something about politics (as in *Videodrome*), it is by way of economic raw material – in that film, the great corporation, and its relation to small business achieves figuration. Now, in *All the President's Men*, we approach the squaring of the circle of this allegorical law: a political film that deceptively looks like a political film, a representation that seeks to convey some conception of political relations by way of overtly political material.

But this first impression may be misleading – a good deal of the overtly political content has, indeed, been trimmed off this Washington movie, from which all elected officials have been removed. The state is thereby not merely transformed into one immense appointed bureaucracy; this last is then – practical politics removed, the basis for Nixonian power presupposed without discussion, the backdrop of the war tacitly effaced – easily reorganized into the figure of a conspiracy. But the originality of *All the President's Men* is to have staged its chain of events virtually from the outset as the struggle between two conspiracies, two collectivities, two suprapersonal organizations: the plumbers versus the newspaper; the White House versus the *Washington Post*; the voices on the telephone versus the in principle equally disembodied voice of 'Deep Throat'; the amoral arrogance of the Nixon officials versus the equally brutal and ruthless determination and ambition of the young reporters. The viewer's sympathy is in fact denied to either side and granted in passing only to Segretti or to the secretaries, as will be seen below. For the place of the victim is essentially taken by these last, in a situation in which the 'crime' has

All the President's Men

become a victimless one.

Meanwhile, since one of the peculiarities of Watergate (something it shared with the paradigmatic spy narrative) was that it turned from the outset on information and representation rather than anything substantive – how to smear the Democrats in the public view, an operation that can be metamorphosed without any great difficulties into the symmetrical one of concealing from public view the Republicans' shame – the characteristic two-tiered structure of the traditional detective story is conflated into a complementary and unimpeded circulation, content now becoming form. The detective story presupposed an absolute distinction between the story of the crime and the story of its resolution: here the distance between the two has been reduced to an absolute minimum by the positing of a 'crime' as informational and media-centered as its own solution.

What results is a remarkable diminution of effect, which dialectically transforms such limits into a whole new positive rather than privative type of representation. Tact here becomes a new genre, conspiracy turns into providentiality, and *All the President's Men* thereby offers the spectacle of a kind of chamber music in the realm of melodrama, a remarkable *Kammerspiel* from which a whole range of brassy instruments is excluded and none of the effects is allowed to exceed a certain very delicate and muffled *forte,* like the famous chord in Haydn's *Surprise Symphony,* sounded with such tact and tentative-

All the President's Men

ness that you imagine the timid agent on the point of running away at the moment of striking so cushioned a blow. Such is for example the very satisfying moment in which, after Deep Throat's final warning, Woodward breathlessly turns to confront his pursuers, only to find the lights of the empty streets of a sleeping Washington staring him in the face. This purely formal climax – sheer syntax, from which all the grossness of content has been sublimated – constitutes the ideal empty Mallarmean category of an encounter with the absolute Other, and replaces any number of villains, torture sequences, struggles, agons, kung fu or wrestling collisions, thrown up by garden variety melodrama (*The Parallax View's* fight in the bar in the Northwest Coast woods, itself imitated from the horrific sequence in Dalton Trumbo's *Lonely Are the Brave* [1962], is, however, a more than average embodiment of the alternate strategy). At any rate, the later disclosure (to Bernstein) of the actual physical danger only apparently continues to manipulate the basic tokens and raw materials of melodrama. In fact its typing sequence (they can't speak for fear of hidden microphones) blossoms into a full-throated triumphant outburst of baroque music whose transcendental joy annuls the literal content and seals the victory of the reporters over their adversaries. In any case, villainy is peculiarly problematic in *All the President's Men*, and it is its essential absence which is most disturbing (but in a different way than the conspiracy of *The Parallax View*, whose sinister certainties at least afford some epistemological reassurance). Even 'Nixon' does not name this absence, about which it is indeed never really even clear whether there is anything there at all ('the fact is,' as Deep Throat puts it, 'that these are not really very bright guys').

Pakula himself (in an interview) registers two basic formal constraints which may have something to do with the special mode of being we have attributed to this particular film. The first has to do with the complexity of the facts and of the problem of exposition: a comparison with the reporters' own book (as well as the larger constellation of events) reveals much to applaud in the way of an admirable and expert set of strategic choices and omissions. Most of the materials – leads and topics alike – come from the first few weeks of the investigation; John Dean and Ehrlichmann have been completely excised; the cover-up itself, the White House, the tapes, are gone; the climactic movement is built around the emergence of Haldeman, and so on. This has led to a second peculiarity, namely a top-heavy predominance of dialogue: 'I don't think there's a more verbal film that's ever been made,' Pakula says,[21] 'not even *Claire's Knee*.' The Rohmer comparison is apt and significant, suggesting a form that remains profoundly cinematographic, that does not return to the filmed theater of the early talkies, but in which the centrality of language and the scenario is endowed with a specifically filmic mode of being by the way in which the new form promotes dialogue into a kind of action or event in its own right. What in Godard is spectacularly reified in the

All the President's Men

form of the interview, here becomes an extraordinary kind of one-on-one playing, in which minimal facial expressions are, as in the earliest close-ups, blown up into crucial spaces for narrative meaning. Not in order to produce the mask, as in silent film, but rather in order to emphasize a kind of tennis match in which you sit on your hands as it were, and mobilize the glance, the lifted eyebrow, the most minute tics and reflexes, on a level with the value of the verbal intervention, the retort, the question thrown down. The new form is displayed at its outer limits with technical virtuosity and no little daring during the telephone conversations, of which there can never have been so many in any preceding film, and which – like Godard's interviewees pinned like firing-squad victims against a blank wall, but reversing the basic relational hierarchy – allow us to watch the reporters at work as character actors restricted to the minimum, producing and simultaneously consuming fresh information before our eyes.

In the sequence of episodes, then, what this means is a remarkable anthology of character acting and of miniature encounters; and who is to say that our most essential knowledge of other people is not calibrated on this middle distance of the strong but occasional contact, rather than the far glimpse of a well-nigh represented figure, or the Other up so close we can scarcely distinguish the features? But if the distant stereotype yields something called realism, and the interpenetration of some absolute Other the space of the modernist language experiment, what can we call this series of representations

All the President's Men

All the President's Men

(which assuredly has nothing postmodernist about it)? It is also important to raise the issue of gender in these encounters, where the proximate other – secretary or intermediary for those absent others who hold supreme power – is almost always a woman, who must in some way or other be victimized or tormented in order to release her secret, or – in the stunning Miami sequence – to remove her from the crucial door. In effect, there are no real contacts with men – the significantly nicknamed Deep Throat being the only emissary from that shadowy realm and the only voice from across that chasm. Even these male contacts are feminized at the moment of revelation, betrayal, disclosure, or exposure: something most interesting in the ultimate instance, that of Segretti, in which a whole symbolic seduc-

tion begins with the visible relief of the informant at having finally been tracked down. So maybe there is something pornographic in the very form of this inquiry (in the sense in which it has been said of the detective story that it replicates the search for the primal scene); or perhaps at this level of formal abstraction the agon and sexuality fold back into one another. What does seem absolutely certain is that the sociological conditions of possibility of this particular narrative lie in the older gender-hierarchical office style and business management characteristic of the Nixon ethos if not of this period altogether. That means that this is an archaic story, a narrative of yesteryear (which presumably could not be resuscitated for the Irangate period); and I'll come back shortly to another way in which this film marks itself as belonging to a now vanished past, rather than to our own present.

Finally, it must also be observed that the one-on-one format has decisive effects on space; or better still, has decisive spatial consequences which release and enable new kinds of spatial effects: a kind of claustrophobia is built into the form which endows open space – the open-air lunch, for example, in which all of Washington in summer is spread out on the large screen – with an extraordinary but only provisional power. I put it that way because the interview situation will then slowly draw the open air back inside of its own formal constraints, enfolding the little neo-colonial free-standing houses back into itself as the sequence broadens out and Washington itself

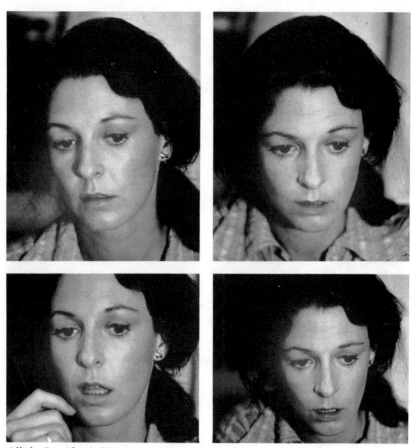

All the President's Men

becomes a list or set of names and addresses to be explored.

But space is scarcely an incidental player in this particular work of art, where the relative withdrawal of the narrative actants or characters in some sense determines the enlargement and investment of hitherto incidental spatial features into protagonists in their own right. If anything, indeed, it would be this unusual and unexpected spatialization of the narrative that could be characterized as postmodern, or at least as proto-postmodern. How an essentially spatial medium like film could in any meaningful way be supplementarily described as being more or less spatial, as somehow significantly becoming spatialized (after having presumably once been less so) is a matter of great tact, but not at all, I think, meaningless nonsense. For one thing, a good deal of the film theory we classically associate with *Screen* magazine could be rewritten as the proposition that in the process of naturalizing narrative or the realistic story, Hollywood was very systematically obliged to organize, that is to say, to repress

74

and to neutralize space as such, since space is what interrupts the naturality of the story-line. Most often, however, the thesis of some spatialization of a spatial medium like film amounts to little more than a pretentious way of drawing attention to the expanded place of architecture as such within the medium in question.

Here, in *All the President's Men*, architecture is of course supreme, and ranges from the cavernous parking garages in which Woodward meets Deep Throat – the Watergate is itself first approached through one of these garages – all the way to the newsroom of the *Washington Post*, the quintessential bureaucratic office space of the post-contemporary period, whose importance Pakula stresses: 'I shudder to think what it would have been like if the *Post* hadn't moved into its new quarters ... their old offices, I gather, were like most old newspaper offices.'[22] But he thinks the *Post's* openness and harsh fluorescent lighting is the sign of Truth itself and everything uncomfortable about it: actually, its light is fully as unnatural as the darkness, and is also in some sense a replay and an unfolding of the primal offices at the Watergate with which we began. Yet the office can be the space of extraordinarily expressive camera movement, later on in the camera's dizzying pursuit of this or that reporter on his way to desk or door, but first of all with the Bradlee figure, of whom Pakula says:

> The major 'star entrance' in the film is Robards'. Up until he comes on, there's almost no camera movement; very little. When he comes out of his office, arbitrarily out of nowhere, we move with him down half the set: we give him a star entrance out of Belasco, all the stops out. And you say, here comes the king.[23]

Both kinds of space thus derive from this primal built space, about which we must now stress its initial presentation as a model that can be manipulated and examined perspectively from a variety of different points of view. The Watergate building here offers the *jouissance* of the miniature, which is to say essentially a pleasure in implicit symbolic praxis: we see it from across the street, selected floors illuminated; we see it from the underground parking garage; from the point of view of insiders walking its narrative trajectory; and as the quintessential decorated shed, whose façade peculiarly bespeaks that combination of anonymity and power, of the imposing-fearful and the empty-trivial, to which I have already referred and which was somehow the essential mystery of the Nixon years. The point, however, is that when space itself is thus foregrounded, it is itself thereby deprived of any natural background, as which a kind of inert and conventionalized space normally serves. Reality and matter are released from their ground, and become peculiarly free-floating, something that can be even more strikingly detected in the other great axis of this film, alongside the light-dark axis just mentioned.

That other axis – of scale – is laid in place in the memorable first

All the President's Men

image, in which the eye comes to distinguish the paper on the platen and the typewriter key. This is clearly only one item in a list of writing materials that includes 'xerox machines, library slips, special copy-paper sets,'[24] along with notes scribbled on pieces of toilet paper, entries in diaries, lists of names, cancelled bank checks and reproduced credit records, and all the other objects which the hermeneutic of detection at once transforms into traces and signs. I hope these things do not signify, as Pakula tells us, the old adage that the pen is mightier than the sword (if only because – following Miriam Hansen's dictum, to which we have referred above,[25] that film includes other media to dramatize its superiority over them – we might thereby be led to wonder what was mightier than the pen). Still less is this a complacent proliferation of *écriture*, by which, as in an Escher drawing, the camera-style doodles all over itself. Surely, as the demise of the ticker-tape only a year or so ago reminds us, the operative feature in such detail is the periodizing one: these are all older forms of reproductive technology, already outmoded when the film is shot and released (Pakula is significantly careful to note, in his comments, that 'the use of the television set is something apart[26]). Such incomplete modernization is in striking contrast – if not, indeed, significant contradiction – with the bureaucratic modern sanitation of the new offices. And it seems to be crucial that the Library of Congress' slips are still on paper; that the checks and Segretti's credit card receipts are not yet stored away in the computer; that the typewriter – whose two-fingered virtuoso rehearsal is supremely characteristic of the classic newspaperman (not yet a 'print journalist'!) – should thereby be allowed to celebrate an anachronistic if not indeed a posthumous triumph. As I suggested earlier, such archaic technology impacts on the possibilities of representation to the very degree that the newer communicational machinery – the data bank, for instance – evades conventional representation altogether. It was thus altogether characteristic for Pynchon to regress to the 50s in *Vineland*, and to stage his most contemporary evocation of the computer network within a henceforth old-fashioned supermarket. It will not, indeed, be until the era of cyberpunk that literary narrative attempts to evolve new forms commensurate with the networks of late or global capital.

Still, some deeper logic may well also be at work here. Aragon was the first, in *Le Paysan de Paris* (1927), to observe that we can most adequately represent the contemporary by way of what is already just slightly out of style, or in the process of historical obsolescence. Walter Benjamin followed him in this: indeed the plan of the latter's Arcades project was structured on this very principle. Clearly, a dialectical view of history (and of the ways in which its very laws and internal dynamics are modified from period to period) would be reluctant to presuppose some ahistorical persistence of just such a 'principle of anachronistic representation' from the Second Empire to the 1920s, and thence to the eve of our own era, in the waning of the 1960s. Yet if what we call postmodernism is characterized by a far more complete and thoroughgoing modernization than anything that obtained in the historically uneven period of so-called modernism proper – which is to say, marked by a far more systematic effacement of all the anachronistic traces even of a recent historical past – then it seems possible that historical representation in the postmodern age is doomed to cling with something more urgent than mere nostalgia to just such traces. At any rate, it seems clear that, in *All the President's Men*, the representability of this narrative material is somehow deeply related to what is already archaic about it, to what is already secretly no longer actual, what is outmoded and already old-fashioned, whether or not the participants or indeed the first viewers are aware of it. It is as though somehow the film bore on itself in a kind of calibration the rate of the trajectory of its own contents into the distant past, the heroic legendary moment of a vanished medium, the newspaper, a news sensation that was always somehow in its generic nature a fairy tale.

But it was essentially for spatial reasons that I raised the issue of the use of typeface in the credits (although the sound values are also significant). For this initial episode – which should be expected to program our habits of perception more energetically than anything that follows – now reorients us towards an axis of scale that runs from the microcosm to the macrocosm. This is to my mind more significant, if only because less obvious, but above all because it is less 'symbolic' and symbolically freighted with ready-made meanings of a portentous type than the axis of light and dark of which mention has

All the President's Men

already been made. Here, the very small – in the sense of Benjamin's well-known pages on the 'surgical' vocation of cinema to probe into dimensions of space (and time) that are inaccessible to beings of our particular size and metabolism[27] – prepares that manipulation of the Watergate building-model of which I just spoke. It gives us a new distance from objects and their spaces, which is not quite the Brechtian-scientific distance of experimentation and the forging of alternatives (pre-empted by the postmodern), but distantly comparable to it.

But this axis is not complete, nor is it perceptually functional, until we reach its other, well-nigh cosmological term – in which, as in the pre-Socratics, a virtually spherical vision of the nature of the universe comes into view. This is of course the famous and seemingly gratuitous shot of the Library of Congress, which literally rises from the very small (the reading-room call slips) to the social totality itself.

Pakula's own observations, indeed, begin by trivializing this wondrous effect:

Starting with those little library slips as clues, filling the screen at first, enormous in their size, and then pulling back to the top of the Library of Congress, where the reporters are so small, gave me a chance to dramatize the endless time it takes to do these things, without being boring about it. It also gave me a sense of how lost they are in this thing, how tiny these figures are in terms of the enormity of the task, and the heroic job they're trying to achieve.

But then, virtually as an afterthought, he modifies the register in which the initial remarks were made:

> There's also something about the Library of Congress that moved me, particularly in that shot of the hallway, something I didn't expect audiences to share, a personal thing. That pseudo-Renaissance hallway they walk through to the reading room, and indeed the reading room itself, have a romantic conception of power behind them, also a romantic ideal of the human being: the antithesis of what's going on in this film.[28]

This does not seem quite right either, since the traditional, religious or metaphysical, architecture of the Reading Room and its dome are not here in some ironic counterpoint with the positivist and bureaucratic reality of these characters, but very precisely now begin to coincide with their research. Yet Pakula's words now begin to suggest the emergence of the allegorical level for the first time, from behind the sweaty close-up social reality of the empirical plot.

For it is the impossible vision of totality – here recovered in the moment in which the possibility of conspiracy confirms the possibility of the very unity of the social order itself – that is celebrated in this well-nigh paradisal moment. This is then the link between the phenomenal and the noumenal, or the ideological and the Utopian. This mounting image, underscored by the audible emergence, for the first time in the film, of the solemn music that so remarkably confirms the investigation's and the film's *telos*, in which the map of conspiracy itself, with its streets now radiating out through Washington from this ultimate center, unexpectedly suggests the possibility of cognitive mapping as a whole and stands as its substitute and yet its allegory all at once. The mounting camera shot, which diminishes the fevered researches of the two investigators as it rises to disclose the frozen cosmology of the reading room's circular balconies, confirms the momentary coincidence between knowledge as such and the architectural order of the astronomical totality itself, and yields a brief glimpse of the providential, as what organizes history but is unrepresentable within it.

To Pakula's account, then, may be preferred this description, by

Toute la mémoire du monde

Jacques Rivette, of the analogous shot in Resnais' *Toute la mémoire du monde* (to which indeed the Library of Congress shot may be seen as an allusion):

> the most crucial thing that's happening to our civilization is that it is in the process of becoming a civilization of specialists. Each one of us is more and more locked into his own little domain, and incapable of leaving it. There is no one nowadays who has the capacity to decipher both an ancient inscription and a modern scientific formula. Culture and the common treasure of mankind have become the prey of the specialists. I think that was what Resnais had in mind when he made *Toute la mémoire du monde*. He wanted to show that the only task necessary for mankind in the search for that unity of culture was, through the work of every individual, to try to reassemble the scattered fragments of the universal culture that is being lost. And I think that is why *Toute la mémoire du monde* ended with those higher and higher shots of the central hall, where you can see each reader, each researcher in his place, bent over his manuscript, yet all of them side by side, all in the process of trying to assemble the scattered pieces of the mosaic, to find the lost secret of humanity; a secret that is perhaps called happiness.[29]

All the President's Men

Yet even the 'secret of happiness' – like the sentimental defense of the US constitution with which Pakula's film overtly ends – may not be the best way of specifying the way in which, here, the solemnity of a working out of destiny is conjoined intermittently with a well-nigh ecstatic glimpse of the paradisal. One thinks of the perverse arguments of the so-called Capital-logicians: that what Hegel, in the process of making his exhaustive inventory of it, called Absolute Spirit, is now from our perspective rather to be identified as Capital itself, whose study is now our true ontology. It is indeed the new world system, the third stage of capitalism, which is for us the absent totality, Spinoza's God or Nature, the ultimate (indeed, perhaps the only) referent, the true ground of Being of our own time. Only by way of its fitful contemplation can its future, and our own, be somehow disclosed:

> We can see that philosophy too may have its *chiliastic* expectations; but they are of such a kind that their fulfilment can be hastened, if only indirectly, by a knowledge of the idea they are based on, so that they are anything but over-fanciful. The real test is whether experience can discover anything to indicate a purposeful natural process of this kind. In my opinion, it can discover *a little*; for this cycle of events seems to take so long a time to complete, that the small part of it traversed by mankind up till now does not allow us to determine with certainty the shape of the whole cycle, and the relation of its parts to the whole. It is no easier than it is to determine, from all hitherto available astronomical observations, the path which our sun with its whole swarm of satellites is following within the vast system of the fixed stars; although from the general premise that the universe is constituted as a system and from the little which has been learnt by observation, we can conclude with sufficient certainty that a movement of this kind does exist in reality. Nevertheless, human nature is such that it cannot be indifferent even to the most remote epoch which may eventually affect our species, so long as this epoch can be expected with certainty.[30]

Notes

1. David Ehrenstein, 'Raoul Ruiz at the Holiday Inn', *Film Quarterly* XL, 1, Fall 1986, pp. 2–7.
2. See my 'Spatial Structures in *North by Northwest*', in S. Žižek (ed.), *Everything You Always Wanted to Know about Lacan (But Were Afraid to Ask Hitchcock)* (London: Verso, forthcoming).
3. Karl Marx, *Capital, Vol. 1* (London: Penguin-Verso, 1976), pp. 279–80.
4. Thomas Pynchon, *The Crying of Lot 49* (New York: Bantam, 1967), p. 13. The equivalent cinematic breakthrough in the representation of conspiracy via the media has often been attributed to Sidney Lumet's 1972 *Anderson*

Tapes (to which, in that case, the later authorial achievement of Peckinpah's *Osterman Weekend* (1983) ought to be added).

5. Thomas Pynchon, *Vineland* (Boston: Little, Brown, 1990), pp. 90–1.

6. See for example the work of Marie-Claire Ropars-Wuillemer (*L'Ecran de la mémoire*, [Paris: Seuil, 1970]); Rick Altman (ed.), *Cinema/Sound, Yale French Studies* 60 (1980); Michael Chion, *La Voix au cinéma* (Paris: Editions de l'Etoile, 1982); and Kaja Silverman, *The Acoustic Mirror* (Bloomington: Indiana, 1988).

7. *Signatures of the Visible* (New York: Routledge, 1990), pp. 191–7.

8. *Signatures*, pp. 218ff.

9. *Postmodernism, Or, The Cultural Logic of Late Capitalism* (Durham, NC: Duke University Press, 1990), chapter 8, and pp. 416–18.

10. I take it that Proust's great theme is not memory but rather our incapacity to experience things 'for the first time'; the possibility of genuine experience *(Erfahrung)* only the second time round (by writing rather than memory). This means that if we stare at our immediate experience *(Erlebnis)* head-on, with a will towards assimilating it at once, without mediation, we lose it; but the real thing comes in, as it were, at the corner of the eye, and while we are consciously intent on something else.

11. See Introduction, note 1, p. 10.

12. *Screen* magazine conducted an important polemic several years ago on the effectivity of Costa-Gavras' *Missing*, which the participants judged to be less truly political, owing to the conventionality of its realism and to its failure to problematize the central issue of representation itself, than any number of formally experimental and anti-representational filmic texts. I would have said myself that it was a liberal, rather than a truly radical, document (and this is in effect what I am saying about *Under Fire*); but that for that very reason its political effect in the movie-houses of the great North American hinterland could only be enhanced. Aesthetically, both films seem to me excellent work – or workmanship – in a conventional form; their value therefore probably lies more in the contextual history of the period and its political issues and struggles (the resurgent right, intervention) than in the history of the form.

13. In any case, the most interesting contemporary documentaries are those in which the film-making process is recognized as intervening between the viewer and the documentaries' raw materials (*Signatures*, pp. 187–90).

14. See for more on Robert Stone my 'Americans Abroad: Exogamy and Letters in Late Capitalism', in Steven M. Bell, Albert H. LeMay, Leonard Orr, (eds.), *Critical Theory, Cultural Politics and Latin American Narrative* (Indiana: Notre Dame University Press, 1991).

15. I have here omitted gang war films, which, at least during a certain period, might well have been read as visions of internal civil war: see, for example, *Escape from New York* (Carpenter, 1981), *The Warriors* (Hill, 1979), *Fort Apache, The Bronx* (Petrie, 1981). On my view these films shade over into what is called, in Science-Fiction terminology, 'near-future' representations and this is a distinctive genre in its own right, its form and structure sharply distinguished by the viewer from 'realistic' verisimilitude or immanence.

16. *Postmodernism*, pp. 355–6.

17. See F. M. Cornford, *Thucydides Mythhistoricus* (London: Cambridge University Press, 1907).

18. Georg Lukács, *Entwicklungsgeschichte des modernen Dramas* (Neuwied: Luchterhand, 1981 [1911]), pp. 117–18.

19. Speaking of the power of visual hieroglyph over print and script in Griffith's *Intolerance*, Miriam Hansen notes: 'The self-conscious mixing of heterogeneous materials throws into relief a dialectical tension between written

characters and images. ... In terms of the film's metafictional economy, the hieroglyphic discourse exceeds and unmakes the confines of the book, literalized in the Book of Intolerance (title-card), whose defeat is dramatized in the happy ending of the Modern narrative' (*Babel and Babylon* [Harvard University Press, 1991], pp. 190–4). Meanwhile, speaking of the competition of television in *The China Syndrome* (James Bridges, 1979), Bordwell and Staiger observe: 'Classical narration aims to create the impression that it proceeds directly from the story action (owing to multiple motivation and other factors). Television is the perfect foil for this process. ... Television mediates reality; it disjoins and fragments. Film, on the other hand, is immediate' (David Bordwell, Janet Staiger and Kristin Thompson, *The Classical Hollywood Cinema* [Columbia Univesity Press, 1985]), p. 371. It does not seem abusive to generalize these insights into the general hypothesis that whenever other media appear within film, their deeper function is to set off and demonstrate the latter's ontological primacy.

20. James Monaco, *How to Read a Film* (Oxford: Oxford University Press, 1977), p. 167.
21. Interview in *Film Comment* 5, September–October 1976, p. 13; and see also the excellent accompanying article by Richard T. Jameson.
22. Ibid., p. 18.
23. Ibid., p. 15.
24. Ibid., p. 16.
25. See note 19, above.
26. *Film Comment*, p. 16.
27. Walter Benjamin, 'The Work of Art in the Age of Its Mechanical Reproduceability', in *Illuminations*, translated by H. Zohn (New York: Schocken, 1968), pp. 233, 236.
28. *Film Comment*, p. 16.
29. Jim Hillier (ed.), *Cahiers du cinéma, Vol. I (the 1950s)*, (Harvard University Press, 1985), p. 60.
30. Immanuel Kant, 'Idea for a Universal History', in Hans Reiss (ed.), *Kant's Political Writings* (Cambridge University Press, 1970), p. 50.

Part Two

Circumnavigations

Chapter 1

On Soviet Magic Realism

Soviet Science-Fiction was always instructively different from its Western counterpart; meanwhile, what now in retrospect looks like a Soviet cinematographic 'new wave' – emerging underground or 'shelved' between the early 70s and the new Western-style commercialization heralded by *perestroika* films and the influence of the market – is also formally distinctive and seemingly without parallels in the various Western art or independent films. These both now momentarily intersect in Alexander Sokurov's *Days of Eclipse* (1988). It is what I would rather call a translation than an adaptation, in order to mark the lexical work of constructing equivalents which the film presupposes and which we must now retrace. The original novel, by the most famous Soviet SF writers, the Strugatsky Brothers, who also collaborated on the screenplay, was entitled *A Billion Years to the End of the World*.[1] What the original title meant was something like the threat of an incremental disaster resulting from minute changes in the present that alter the course of history. These novelties, then, are not likely to have immediate results, but insofar as they interfere with the homeostatic controls built into the very heart of the universe, will in a billion years result in its destruction:

> Don't ask me, Vecherovsky said, why you and Glukhov became the first swallows of the coming cataclysm. Don't ask me about the physical nature of the signals that disturbed the homeostasis in that corner of the universe where you and Glukhov undertook your research. In fact don't ask me about any of the mechanisms of the Homeostatic Universe – I know nothing about them, the way people know nothing about the functioning of the law of the conservation of energy. All processes occur in such a way that in a billion years from now the work by you and Glukhov, when combined with the work of millions upon millions of other people, does not lead to the end of the world. Of course, it was not a question of the end of the world in general but of the end of the world as we observe it today, the world as it has existed for a

billion years, the world that you and Glukhov, without even suspecting it, are threatening with your microscopic attempts to overcome entropy. (103–4)

The meaning of this motif remains the same, I think, in the film version, but the differences in its manner of staging are interesting and need to be examined first.

In the novel, mysterious things begin to happen to four scientists working on unrelated problems in different fields, at the moment in which all of them are on the point of this or that scientific break-through. Something wants to prevent these breakthroughs, and it tries to do so using both the carrot and the stick, delivering mysterious packages of vodka and caviar to one of the researchers, and causing another to commit suicide. The movement of the plot will then be a dual one, in a first moment registering the attempt of all four to co-ordinate their experiences and to come to the conclusion that something similar is happening to all of them together; in a second, generating hypotheses about the mysterious agency itself and its intentions – is it a supercivilization jealous of its higher technology, which is not to be shared with earthlings, or is it, on the other hand, a mystical religious conspiracy of a suspiciously Slavophile type? Are not what look like a series of events rather to be understood as a spasmodic, instinctive gesture, of the kind with which we swat an insect? Is all this finally to be grasped not at all anthropomorphically, but rather as the automatic reflex mechanism of natural law itself, 'the first reaction of the Homeostatic Universe to the threat of humanity becoming a super-civilization' (103)? Clearly enough, the novel cannot 'decide' between these options. What I have called its meaning does not lie in one or the other of them, but rather in the problem of the indeterminacy itself and that of assessing the nature of an external force that does some-thing to you, but which, by virtue of the fact that its power transcends your own and cannot be matched, by definition also transcends your capacity to understand it or to conceptualize – better still, to repre-sent – it. The novel, and the film as well, are fables about this epis-temological problem, this ultimate challenge to cognitive mapping. The meaning of the fable then lies not in making a stab at interpret-ation anyway, in a situation in which it has been shown to be impos-sible; but rather, as we shall see, in locating and hypothesizing that feature of the national culture and the national experience to which this peculiar interpretive dilemma can be said to be relevant.

What must be said first is the obvious: namely, that the film system-atically discards or lightens a good deal of the science-fictional bag-gage and trappings; a few of the mysterious events remain, but they are no longer discussed and interrogated in a science-fictional mode. All that survives of the alien presence in the film, for example, is the passage, at night, of an enormous spotlight over this sleeping hamlet,

Days of Eclipse

and, in the day, the ominous shadow of a terminator slowly blotting out the sun for a moment and testifying that something very large is looking at you (the 'eclipse' of the title, reduced to the merest passing figure).

Indeed, I'm tempted to say that virtually the only overt extra-terrestrial motif retained here is one that was not in the book in the first place: that is, the great travelling shot at the beginning in which the point of view of what can only be supposed to be a spaceship comes to rest on a peculiarly arid stretch of landscape. But in my opinion this is comparable, less to the crash of David Bowie's starship in *The Man Who Fell to Earth* (Roeg, 1976), than rather to the great balloon voyage that opens *Andrei Rublev* (Tarkovsky, 1966), even though its sense is diametrically opposed to that of Tarkovsky's sequence. In the latter, what was wanted was to flee the horror and the butchery of earth, the monstrous cruelty of human nature; in *Days of Eclipse*, the longing is somehow to draw closer to human misery and be at one with it, filthy with the same yellow dust, sweating with the same heat, breathing in the same dry air. But the heroes of *Days of Eclipse* are intellectuals, who can never 'share the destiny of the popular masses' no matter how much good will they bring to the effort.

There can therefore be found in *Days of Eclipse* something of the same muting of generic signals we observed (for a very different genre indeed) in *All the President's Men*: a diminution of genre-distinctive conventions which is not quite the same as that relatively more frequent secularization of SF narratives into bestsellers (as, for example, in catastrophe film) or that equally familiar promotion of sub-generic discourse (such as the mystery thriller) into high art. *Days of Eclipse* is rather something like *sublated* Science-Fiction, in the Hegelian sense in which the latter is both cancelled and preserved all at once, lifted into something rather different (which I have abusively called magic

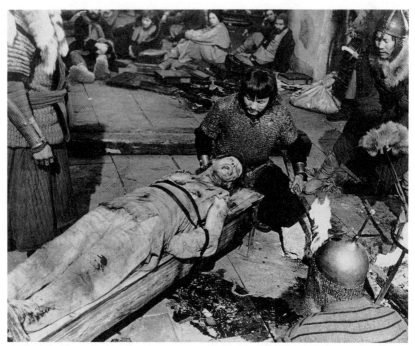

Andrei Rublev

realism for lack of a better characterization) without losing its deep structural affinities for the sub-generic form, with the result that it can be read either way. Indeed, anxieties about the appropriate public seem to play no little part here, since what makes for a durable sub-generic structure that can be repeated indefinitely is also what systematically repels whole other segments of the public (who do not go to thrillers, romances, occult films, or science-fiction films, respectively).

But 'high art' or 'art film' used to be a sub-genre as clearly differentiated from the unmarked Hollywood product as the specific genres enumerated above, something that no longer seems to be the case in the postmodern period (but which could just as easily be attributed to the gradual waning of high art fully as much to its assimilation by mass culture). Modernist traditions, however, are still very much alive in the Soviet Union today, and this is why it is worth stressing the refusal of *Days of Eclipse* to take this particular generic path, and to cross that thin line that separates Lem or Dick from Kafka. I consider it illegitimate to cross that line very precisely because of the implied intent to endow a paraliterary or subcultural genre with the legitimacies of high literature and high art proper, legitimacies that in any case many of us no longer recognize. Indeed, we have a closely related example of what happens when this particular generic boundary is transgressed, in another Soviet movie adaptation of a Stru-

Stalker

gatsky novel: Andrei Tarkovsky's *Stalker* (1979), based on a book called *Roadside Picnic*,[2] an incomparable novel, whose superiority to *A Billion Years* may well account for the chagrin one feels at seeing Tarkovsky's treatment of it.

Roadside Picnic gave figuration to the third hypothesis enumerated above, the possibility that 'mysterious events' of an analogous kind were to be considered little more than accidents, the involuntary reflexes of a higher power. In it, a motif unique to the Strugatskys is elaborated: the brooding presence of an enormous 'zone', a kind of magical Gulag in real physical space, cutting across the older city boundaries, its line running imperceptibly through houses and vacant lots, with the most peculiar and dangerous psycho-physical phenomena at play on the other side of the border. Only intrepid smugglers and criminals with a very specialized set of capacities cross over periodically, to bring back samples of the high technology of the future or of outer space, samples of the greatest interest to the military-industrial complex, which may, however, turn out to be an unknown plague, and which in any case generally end up costing the smuggler health or happiness, if not life itself. The premise of this extraordinary novel is that the zone very precisely constitutes the leavings and the garbage of a roadside picnic, stray beer-cans and foodwrappers tossed nonchalantly on earth by aliens of an unimagi-

Stalker

nably higher technology and civilization on their way somewhere else. This novel Tarkovsky made over into the most lugubrious religious fable, his camera and his actors moving if anything more slowly than real time itself, with a solemnity quite intolerable to any but the truest believers (in Tarkovsky, I mean, and I speak as one who has a great deal of tolerance for the longueurs of this auteur). Only the scene with the little girl, and the ominously rattling glass of water, sticks in the mind with all the vividness of the greatest moments of Tarkovsky's work; while one would like to forget the allegories themselves, and the drearily suffering Christ-like solemnity of a protagonist who, in the novel, was still an attractive trickster and social deviant.[3] The objection is not so much to the religious content (although see note 4 below) as it is to the artistic pretentiousness. The operation consists in trying to block our resistance in a two-fold way: to forestall aesthetic qualms with religious gravity, while afterthoughts about the religious content are to be chastened by the reminder that this is, after all, high art.

But that 'high art' is also what we would now identify as modernism, so that what is objectionable about it is not the art as such, but rather the rehearsal of now tiresome and old-fashioned auteurist paradigms. To Sokurov's credit, then, *Days of Eclipse* does not attempt to convert its science-fictional premises into a symbolic modernist – that is to say, existentialist or absurdist – parable of that kind. It leaves the

SF scaffolding intact, while attenuating its presence so that the un-forewarned spectator need not raise the kinds of questions that occur to a spectator who has also read the Strugatskys' novels. If a generic modification has taken place at all here, then, it is an inflection towards the fairy tale rather than towards what in the language of SF analysis is technically called fantasy or sword-and-sorcery.

For the novel took place in Moscow, in the worst big-city summer heat; its protagonists were grown, middle-aged men with wives and lovers, careers, ambitions, corrupt impulses, the guilt of capitulations, the lust for success and achievement; and the social element of the action was essentially that of male bonding and mateship (or collegia-lity). All this is now gone without a trace from the film which is transported, if I may say so, to a kind of pre-adolescent realm without sex or desire, before the forbidden fruit or the fall, but very much including the adolescent's passionate relationship to knowledge and learning, along with adolescent idealism and social commitment.

Meanwhile, we are transported far from Moscow to Turkestan, and to what looks in effect like another planet (not the least science-fictional element of the film). We are in a yellow dusty world, the very camera's light is a faded, jaundiced orange, so that its subjects look as sick and feeble as the survivors of Auschwitz, grinning toothless at the apparatus, sitting against the mud walls in emaciated inanition, a population of in-bred genetic freaks and mutants, going about their incomprehensible business in the unpaved streets and alleys of what looks like a refugee camp but turns out to be a national minority village, about which you hesitate to decide whether it exemplifies the worst traces of that 'development of underdevelopment' whereby once flourishing Third World trading settlements have been reduced to some genuinely urban big-city misery and poverty in the midst of open natural space and ecological drought, or whether it is not in fact a kind of ultimate sink-hole or end of the line in which all the detritus of manufacture – broken machinery and manual typewriters, the torn pages of outdated engineering manuals, unmatched wooden chairs with legs renailed, old gramophones, broken dishes – have somehow collected at random, as in some ultimate First World junk pile of obsolescent merchandise and unwanted inventory. The dust that transpires through the pores of all that broken matter as through the skin of organic substances and living beings – what Philip K. Dick, evoking the end of the world through entropy as some enormous scrap heap, called *kipple* – rejoins the saffron filter of the lens to transform the visible universe itself, whose physical reality film pro-mised to redeem, into unpainted woodwork palpably dissolving in time before your eyes.

Into this pathology of the visual, this incurable illness of the mani-fest volume of the seen, of the perceptible landscape stricken by a sickness unto death of airless heat and premature old age, is now

Days of Eclipse

inserted, so suddenly and unexpectedly that the generic shock is only registered subliminally, a cartoon character of an utterly different style: the ineffectual Malianov of the novel transmuted into what the Russians call a 'golden child', a ruddy blond youth as imagined by small children, a kind of Scandinavian or ur-Russian Prince Valiant, dwelling incognito among the rachitic population of the alien town from whom he sticks out like a sore thumb, their misery reduplicated within his own four walls by the cobbled together furniture, the piles of yellowing paper, the ancient machine on which he tirelessly picks away, making clacking sounds that float oddly across the chickens in his neighbors' backyards. He is writing a study of the local diseases: actually, of the relationship between susceptibility to illness and religious fundamentalism;[4] and it is worth noting, at this stage, the way in which the natural sciences of the novel have here been transformed into life sciences. In the novel, Malianov was an astronomer; here, his training as a medical doctor makes the relationship between his scientific research (and even his putative 'great discoveries') and tangible human need and suffering a good deal more visible and dramatic. It gives him, as it were, a vocation (he tries to care for a small boy, visibly undernourished and neglected), thereby justifying his otherwise inexplicable appearance in this place so far from home. (The other characters' specializations are also moved closer to the locale and the natural habitat of this society: Vecherovsky is a geologist in the film; Snegovoi a military engineer.)

But much uncertainty about his presence still remains: is this an exile or an assignment, a sentence or a mission? Is it a life term far from loved ones or from the center of things, or on the other hand the need to get away from the city for a while to do one's work in relative calm and isolation? Or is it finally the self-sacrifice of an idealistic youth (who has little enough to give up anyway) intent on placing his skills at the service of the under-privileged? Is this the Peace Corps or that extra-terrestrial assignment the Strugatskys' ensigns are often given to planetary cultures at a lower level of development? Much speaks, indeed, for the hypothesis that Malianov is a Fulbright to an underdeveloped culture, an exchange student to a plague-ridden city, going to the post office to look for his check, waiting in line like everybody else for his weekly ration, and idly taking in the occasional street fairs or folk music. In that case, he is the alien, and not the people among whom he dwells; and the most objectionable feature of this racism of fairy tales, this orientalism of a kind of magic-realist cartoon, is not so much its physical caricature of the Other (physical features constituting the principal language of children) as rather its denial of their daily life. For if, forewarned or on a second viewing, you peer more intently through the yellow filter, you will see that the misery of the natives is greatly exaggerated. Glimpses testify to the fact that this is a daily life like any other, people saying hello in the

Days of Eclipse

morning, shaking hands in passing, setting out their wares, and going out for haircuts. It is the filter that converts all that into the most sinister of documentary footage, reminiscent of Buñuel's *Las Hurdes*, in which the surrealist camera, primed for the libidinal image, records the stark desolation of a culture of malnutrition and premature mortality, among mountains in which there is nothing to eat.[5]

The novel's other characters have been reduced in number, but also dwell here as foreigners and outsiders, in a palpable exile that waxes and wanes generationally. The older man, Snegovoi, in the novel a physicist, in the film still apparently a suicide, seems redolent of political exile. The episode of the engineer Gubar, a womanizer saddled in the novel with an unwanted and frighteningly precocious child, has been transformed into something ostentatiously Kafkaesque and melodramatic, a crazed rebel whose final act of armed resistance is repressed by the authorities in a virtual army mobilization. However, if we are permitted to extrapolate from the spirit of the novel, it seems clear that this defiance is based on a misunderstanding, since the mysterious enemies it addresses are not located in the inefficient bureaucratic state but rather in outer space. Still, the sense of exile is again reinforced by the family background of the school chum Vecherovsky, in connection with which the fates of both the Volga Germans (his own ancestry) and the Crimean Tatars (that of his foster parents) are evoked, shipped en masse by Stalin beyond the Arctic Circle during the war. Another older exile, finally, the quisling Glukhov, has found his profession equally humanized or socialized. From the orientalist of the novel he has been turned into a local historian, equipped with mesmerizing images of the city's past, as well as with the wisdom of capitulation: don't make waves, give up your research, enjoy life as it is, don't be a troublemaker. As for daily

96

life, however, the motif of exile retroacts upon it, inasmuch as daily life is in any case always the daily life of other people. There thus re-emerge some of its pleasures in the weekly routine of the expatriate in familiar foreign streets, domesticating the culturally exotic, like a neighbor's pet snake that periodically gets away and has to be returned to his masters.

About the filters, however, something more needs to be said, for this seems to be a Soviet innovation and a significant formal response to the image culture of postmodernism itself, in a situation in which the return to black-and-white photography is the impossible Utopia of the lost object of desire. The calibration of black-and-white, indeed – with its precisely determinable range of intermediary hues that the trained eye can learn to read like a bas-relief on a stone pilaster or as the ear registers the barely perceptible variation in the intonation and inflection of a trained voice – this system, indeed, to which the phantasm and the unrealizable ideal of a Bazinian realism cling like an after-image, offers a possibility of the exact and multiple operations of translation that is at once lost when the colors of the real world are simply replicated with other colors. So it is that the perceptual precision of high modernist black-and-white film is at one stroke annulled by the blossoming of color stock in the postmodern, with its mesmerization of the visual organ by expensive technicolor stimuli.

What must now be reckoned into the equation is the specific place and role of Tarkovsky in the Soviet version of this story: for his grandiose mysticism depended very much on a kind of naturalization of the color image. Indeed, the mystique of nature in his films was specifically validated by the splendor of the shots themselves, whose essential *naturality* was then itself subscribed, documented and vouched for by their contents, namely, the varieties of primal matter.

Tarkovsky's screen is notoriously the space in which we once again

Days of Eclipse

Ivan's Childhood

apprehend or intuit the natural world, or better still its 'elements', as though we could sense its emergent constitution out of fire, earth, water and air, which show through in the crucial moments. This, no doubt, rather than Nature or some concrete fascination with the object-world as such, is Tarkovsky's religion, whose camera tracks the moments in which the elements speak – from the persistent rain of *Ivan's Childhood* (1962) to the glorious fire which ends *The Sacrifice* (1986). That fire was in reality dual, and we should not receive it without somehow including the more gruesome pyre of the human sacrifice in *Nostalghia* (1983) – which was, if you like, a way of securing the body's participation in the image, of warding off the disembodied contemplative vision of a spectator who might admire the house in flames without paying the price, without existential sweat, seeing it as sheer apocalyptic aesthetics that omit the ultimate active grimness and despair of immolation. The image remains beautiful and false unless that Kantian disinterested viewer's body can be somehow tricked back inside of it, to lend it truth: an uncertain matter, which the 'ban on graven images' was meant to solve, too simply and peremptorily, by removing the problem. If, however, film is given in advance and here to stay, then what arises for a Tarkovsky is the rather different, but no less delicate, problem of the relationship between asceticism and visual pleasure, between a life-denying fascination with sacrifice and the wide-screen libido of a created world that gorges the eyes rather than putting them out (or, like a Bresson, starving them).

Rain was of course with film since its very invention, something of its fascination surely lying in the depth with which it necessarily

The Sacrifice

endows the screen at the same moment that it fills it up and abolishes it. Only in rain is the 'magic cube' of filmic space utterly saturated, 'as full as an egg,' both transparent to sight and yet everywhere visible as a thing or object whose inside is also its outside: rain and the mystery of space are somehow cognate:

> Today he remarked how a shower of rain
> Had stopped so cleanly across Golightly's lane
> It might have been a wall of glass
> That had toppled over.[6]

Rain becomes the camera's sacrament, therefore, which it cannot perform too often or degrade, but which recovers its force at certain moments of film's utmost solemnity.

Tarkovsky has meanwhile invented a substitute mystery, rarer and thus more immediately fascinating: it is the sponginess of wet soil into which the soaking shoe presses, and from which it is then withdrawn, with the faintest of sucking noises. It is the truth of mosses, Being itself as swamp, in which the faint human traces still persist for a time, the water seeping into their contours – no longer Robinson's clue, nor the mystery of the Other, but instead the late and catastrophic anticipation of the tendential extinction of the human species from a technologically exhausted planet. Yet that particular 'disappearance of Man' would draw its occurrence from the exhaustion of a Nature which in Tarkovsky on the contrary seems to *revive*, thriving on human sacrifices and drawing its blood from the extinction of the human, as though it had rid itself of planetary vermin and were now restored, at least on the screen and in the image, to some rich and archaic ur-natural flourishing. The deepest contradiction in Tarkovsky is then that offered by a valorization of nature without human technology achieved by the highest technology of the photographic apparatus itself. No reflexivity acknowledges this second hidden presence, thus threatening to transform Tarkovskian nature-mysticism into the sheerest ideology.

One's impression, as an outsider and a layman, is, however, that contemporary Soviet cinema does not spring exclusively and fully armed from Tarkovsky's brow, but knows another, cognate progenitor: the Georgian film-maker Sergei Paradjanov, whose 1965 *Shadows of Our Forgotten Ancestors* (in Russian, *The Little Horses of Fire*) inflects the color image in another, more properly magical-realist direction, substituting nationalism and folklore for Greater Russian religious mysticism and inflecting the guilt and sacrifice that obsess Tarkovsky in the direction of a more vulnerable and more human shame and humiliation, the smarting of a well-nigh sexual inferiority feeling.[7] In any case, both of these massive achievements confront contemporary Soviet auteurship with a very special problem of heritage-liquidation which is quite unlike the current Western one (that could be defined as an inner Third-World struggle against a hegemonic commercial postmodernism): how to efface such vibrant imagery and to find some new minor key or language to set in the place of an achieved and positive one.[8]

This is what the filter accomplishes, in films like this one by Sokurov or the equally extraordinary *My Friend Ivan Lapshin* (1984) of Alexei Gherman. The filter desaturates images in such a way as to mute the autonomy of multiple colors in *Days of Eclipse* or destabilize the stark polarity of black and white in *Lapshin*, thus opening a spectrum of tones that recover the complexity of the Chinese aesthetic or of the twelve-tone system at its most complex, in which a note realized in one timbre on one kind of instrument is considered distinct and given a different value from the same note plucked from a different kind of material. Here tonalities like the gauze-softened, the misted, the rounded and swelling, are each as different from the hard-edged as the system of tastes in the *combinatoire* of classical gastronomy. (Indeed, such effects can also be seen as a return to the procedures of 'tinting and toning' in silent film, in another involution characteristic of the postmodern period.) This now makes for a pulse in the transmission of the shots, and a rhythmic variation of visual opposites and alternatives as complex as anything theorized by late Eisenstein in his conceptual models of the co-ordination of sound or color itself. It peculiarly affects and destabilizes narrative, and discredits the traditional categories of identification and point of view, by submitting even the already familiar actants and narrative elements, such as the face and body of our protagonist, to well-nigh physical variations, as though he had been rolled in dust, crumpled like a rug, or carefully posed in bright moonlight. In *Days of Eclipse*, however, the yellow persists within the image as a sense of faded photographs and of an antiquated documentary whose subjects are all long-since dead: a kind of suspended historicity that scarcely seizes on the principal players, while for the enchanted village itself (which, to be sure, at one point shrinks to the dimensions of a field of dolls' houses, and at another vanishes altogether against the empty meadowland), it is held in check by the peculiar timelessness of the fairy tale that may be Science Fiction in disguise.

Meanwhile, a genuine range of color emerges in Sokurov's outdoor shots, as though sharpened by the filter and as it were miniaturized by it. The yellow remains, but a wondrously delicate combination of hues becomes visible through it like a garden or carpet; a true invention of saffron pastels, as though saturation of an extremely low level heightened the intensity and revitalized the visual organs, making the viewer capable of feats of minute perception quite impossible in the grander official full-color achievements of high Hollywood or Tarkovsky, for example.

This gap between the hero's fairy-tale adventure and the yellowing documentary of its inhabitants opens up a space in which the most remarkable visual experiences are available:[9] most notably the aimless, endless investigation of the suicide, which the camera observes tirelessly and without boredom, scarcely moving at all from a position from which it sees across a long room into a smaller one, virtually without perspective, with the body covered with a sheet as the least important part of the matter, stored away at the rear of the deep shot, and occasionally viewed idly by a policeman with nothing better to do. We had seen these lodgings the night before, during the hero's visit, when they looked somehow smaller, cramped, full of books. Now, angling oddly above the floorboards, our view seems enormous, filled with milling police officials and bureaucrats, in uniform and in civilian clothes, who don't know how to proceed but intermittently and without conviction rummage here and there at random in order to seem to be active. None of these people face each other directly, nor are they spread around a center – as in the later, complementary scene, theatrically staged between two mountains and virtually bearing the monumental title, The Hunting Down and Killing of the Guerrilla Zakhar Gubar. Here on the contrary I am reminded of Erving Goffman's description of the insane, so characterized most fundamentally because of their loss of any sense of the existence of other people: their bodies at angles to each other, the plane of the faces failing to be held over against each other like reflecting mirrors, the inner unity of the features themselves (no longer understanding what it is to make another's face a unity by looking at it) drifting apart into separate, twitching organs. Bureauc-

Days of Eclipse

102

racy would then offer the collective or social equivalent of this inner disorder, as its members aimlessly pursue their isolated many-headed tasks, the anamorphic focus turning over the outside of the inexplicable volume they form without finding a reassuring, perspectival position for the viewer. They are, indeed, within this anamorphic space a little like the lobster in aspic in an earlier scene, carefully unwrapped by the protagonist as though, 'exotic monster', it were an extinct relic of the past that might stir into life on extraction.

This scene then, held at extraordinary length, is something like a *mise en abysme* of the film itself, encapsulating as it were the very concept of the Investigation as such, under mysterious circumstances, in which the investigators cannot yet even grasp what a clue might consist in, let alone the nature of the events to be clarified.[10] One thinks of Benjamin's characterization of Atget's classic turn-of-the-century photographs of empty Paris streets, of which it has been said that 'he photographed them like the scene of the crime,'[11] except that, since this is in some sense already the scene of a crime, we would have to outtrump this first-level allegory and suggest that the crime itself was the cipher for pure scene, the locus of an unknown, unimaginable event as such, an annunciation we grasp and which these milling bureaucrats – professionals of the report and the dossier – are least of all capable of handling.

Meanwhile, the death itself is registered less by the body it leaves behind than by the incredible disorder of the former dwelling place, the floorboards of which are strewn with papers of all kinds, reminding one irresistibly of Claude Simon's account of the passage of war, as the sight of festoons of toilet paper along the roadways, as though an eviscerated suitcase released 'an unbelievable quantity of cloth, most often black and white (but there was a faded pink rag flung or caught on the flowering hedge, as though it had been hung out to dry).'[12] The sadness of Simon's figure, however, lies in its revelation of the seemingly irrepressible tendency of human life to bear with it so many useless quantities of objects of all kinds, auxiliary items and articles without any drama or symbolic value, like the junk emptied out of a shaving kit. Here, in Sokurov, the quantities of paper rather betoken something else, like the scribblings and obsessions of a maniac or a hermit, devising urgent messages not to be shown to anyone. Endlessly, with rapt fascination, we watch this room of the enigma that has been thrown open to us without ever disclosing its consequences; and the scene is appropriately closed by the formal departure of endless fleets of official cars from the square outside, as enormous as some textbook example of Renaissance perspective blown up in size over an entire city.

Nonetheless, we will later on finally hear the message of the corpse, at night, in the empty silence of the morgue, where the protagonist, roused by mysterious voices, comes to watch a dead jaw move and

Days of Eclipse

emit a message from outer space. The use of the dead human body as an intergalactic wireless or transmitter hearkens back to other Strugatsky novels, in which genetic eggs from alien species are planted in human time-bombs that look just like you or me. But the point here is that the message is a lie and a deception, designed to trick the protagonist into inaction and to stop his dangerous research: don't leave your own circle, warns the corpse in a spirit of submission and humble good behavior.

The film equally retains, but mutes, the more minor irritants introduced by the novel's aliens – the repeated phone calls that interrupt the hero, the mysterious telegram that quite unnecessarily summons his sister to his side – it being well known how even the most desirable guests can interfere with your schedule. But I think that when he actually burns his manuscript, it is more on account of the sick child than because of this spurious warning (echoed in any case by the local historian, who has himself set a good example of giving in).

So Malianov drowns his book, but in fire, from which the great

Days of Eclipse

Days of Eclipse

Tarkovskian ethos again briefly flares: the sheets of stray paper carbonized in an intolerable flame in the heat of the sand and dust outside the city walls give us a momentary shot at real fire itself, if you are willing to detest it as passionately as only those are capable of doing who, drenched in sweat, still have to light the match. But the most wondrous effect of this magical conflagration is a kind of action at a distance in which, if I'm not mistaken, the charring of the flames unexpectedly translates into a kind of supernatural incineration of Malianov's young colleague's living room walls, which are now strangely hairy, as though the plaster to which this strange disaster is affixed were alive and exuded pus.[13] I cannot help but connect this great feathery black spot with another peculiar marking, namely, the strangely blackened and silvery side of Snegovoi's face, which he wears like a mask or the scar from some unearthly encounter. It is a multiple transfer enigmatic enough to suggest methodological as well as libidinal after-images. Pascal Bonitzer's concept of the spot or *tâche*, for example, that sharpens Barthes' photographic punctum

Days of Eclipse

Days of Eclipse

into a crucial category of Hitchcock's camera work – the key in the hands, the luminous glass of milk, the telltale detail that leaps out of the screen at the viewer – does not seem irrelevant here, where this supernatural *spot* or stain becomes something like the technique's meta-image and its way of designating itself autoreferentially.[14]

As a symptom, however, the spot does not so much demand interpretation of the traditional type as rather draw attention to its own conditions of possibility, and ask us to 'interpret' the implications of the interpretive options offered here or, better still, of the range of interpretive possibilities to which we have here been restricted.

But we cannot do so without noting the Utopian stirrings of the final scene, the journey by boat across a water whose very presence and existence in this dusty yellow world is problematical, since it is itself the Utopian dimension that fails to spill in relief on the screen, although prompted by Offenbach's *Barcarolle*, with its intimations of the canals and lagoons of Venice. Utopia in that respect would be the staff striking the dry rock, the transformation of this arid, thankless, doomed countryside into some unimaginable Venice.

But this is surely a way, albeit an intolerably figurative and flowery one, of talking about the protagonists' project in the first place, the intention of this multiple research that a higher force has it in mind to check. The novel remained epistemological, after the fashion of Science Fiction generally, which need not show its credentials or document its reason for being. There, all we need to grasp is the essential premise: that great work, breakthroughs, the scientific discoveries of the next century, are on the point of being made – the value of science, socially unspoken, being presupposed, along with some vague generic curiosity as to what the future of such science might look like. The content, however – the novelistic Malianov's spirals and planetary nebulae – has to be fudged. Nothing can tell us why, besides a commitment as readers to SF, we should be interested in this 'problem', which it is of course an advantage to have Malianov him-

Days of Eclipse

self systematically forget (owing to the machinations of the Enemy).

But the film now removes the layers of abstraction from this narrative shape as a sculptor disengages the ultimate statue from a mass of plaster. The positioning of the plot within the co-ordinates of medicine and social misery neutralize the unspoken question: this activity no longer needs justification. The interpretive mind can now turn away from that to contemplate its systemic blockage: not the intent to make great scientific discoveries, but the great project of social amelioration and the relief of human suffering that is dashed again, that has once again, with the best will in the world, come to naught! The SF structure has thereby been revealed as a fable, with all the fable's determinant characteristics, above all the substitutability of the explanation's content. Like a proverb, it can be applied to any number of concrete situations; any number of inexplicable defeats offer themselves as what the film might have been devised to express in the first place. And with the fairy tales, its indefinitely renewable narrative meaning is unfortunately dependent on the re-emergence of just such unhappy situations over and over again throughout history: why can't we succeed in doing what we are so well equipped and motivated to do? Its immediate historical fascination would then lie in the deeper places in which that failure has been locally, painfully, gained, experienced in the form of this or that unique concrete project to which we were committed above all others, and next to which all the others are worthless. The reader abstracts and generalizes, the sufferer rememorates the collapse of this particular life that sticks in his craw, there is no other.

The content of the interpretation of such a fable may thus be substitutable, but it has to correspond to the limits narratively prepared, which is in the novel still essentially a matter of the contact and interference between two cultures, two civilizations, two societies (or indeed, since we are in SF, between two species). Lem's obsession (and I mention him only because he is often 'compared' with the

Strugatskys, on the rather flimsy strength of being another Eastern European, and also of having been filmed by Tarkovsky) is with non-contact. His works[15] can thus not really be fables, since they engage a very specific point in which you are supposed to be interested in and for itself, namely, how we could ever communicate with an alien intelligence if we found one (the answer is: we couldn't!). The Strugatskys, on the other hand, are better grasped as near-contemporaries and socialist versions of the American series *Star Trek*. Both superpowers came to be interested, in their diverse ways, in the course of the 1950s and 60s, in the question of the impact of their technologies and social achievements on the undeveloped, the underdeveloped, the developing, and the not yet overdeveloped. The fundamental shared theme is then something like the ethics and the responsibilities of imperialism (the Prime Directive). As can be expected, the two traditions are as similar and as different as the wars in Vietnam and Afghanistan: destroying counter-insurgency and making an example of the repression of a revolutionary movement is comparable to the attempt to bring enlightenment, education and medicine to a feudal and medieval country locked into clans and vendettas only in the number of dead bodies produced by both efforts. Equally predictably, the focus of the US narratives is individual and ethical even where the interaction of populations is concerned, while over the Soviet ones the concept of a mode of production, with all its historical irony, now presides. So it is that any number of *Star Trek* episodes show how difficult it is – and how personally agonizing for the leadership – to decide when to intervene in a barbarous situation for the good of the natives themselves: it is, to borrow the title of the relevant Strugatsky novel, 'hard to be a god.'[16] But the difficulty in *Hard to be a God* is compounded by the laws of development of the modes of production themselves: you cannot export advanced bourgeois or socialist forms of behavior back into precapitalist or feudal situations, unless you undertake to change those situations structurally and to accelerate the transition out of feudalism itself. But, as in the later novel that concerns us here, you may well change the very course of that evolution by your own intervention (so that, in the 'billion years' of the original title, what will emerge is not a better society but the end of the world).

These narrative situations are then elaborated by the Strugatskys into their version of the American 'galactic council,' a kind of interstellar KGB whose agents dwell incognito within lower modes of production and make the appropriate reports on progress and regress, radical movements and the other kind. Indeed, the shock of *Hard to Be a God*, in particular, involves the unexpected emergence, within a feudal mode, of a fundamentally more modern fascism, or at the least one as 'modern' as that, say, of interwar Romania. The plot then turns in part on the problem of causality, and whether it was not the intervention of the higher 'socialist' forces that triggered this anticipatory anachronism and its grisly results. But as in the paradigm of all modern Science Fiction, Wells' foundational *War of the Worlds*, the situation can also be explored in its inversions. Wells, contemplating the genocide of the Tasmanians at the hands of his own contemporaries, set out to see how we would feel if a 'higher power' tampered with us; the Strugatskys' *Second Martian Invasion* then rewrites Wells in a delicious neo-colonial way, with human collaborators and a sophisticated use of the modern media. *A Billion Years*, finally, restages an equally contemporary version of the ultimate problem: 'they' don't really want to use force (although they will 'suicide' opponents if they have to) – they would rather send you lobster (in the novel, it's vodka and caviar) to take your mind off your troublesome ambitions.

In the film, of course, the 'they' is less precise, and the failure more poignant. But it will be clear on my reading that the failure must be a collective one, and that the fable specifies, at the least, some connection with the problem of the mode of production itself, however it inflects that parabolical lesson. In both novel and film, then – at least for contemporary readers, leaving posterity's uses out of it – what is blocked and thwarted is the construction of socialism itself, of a society in control of its own destiny, that sets its own, human agenda for itself. The fable then sharpens the incomprehensible question, in its novelistic form drawing on the high scientific and technological capacities of the Soviet Union, to wonder why, in spite of all those achievements, something nevertheless gets in the way. But in the years in which the novel was published, the Brezhnev years, the era of stagnation, the answer solicited by the fable seemed clear enough: it lay in bureaucracy and in the incestuous burgeoning of the *nomenklatura* system, the corruption and nepotism of what used then to be described as a 'new class'.

What is historically interesting about the filmic version of 1988 – aside from the extraordinary aesthetic and formal merits we have attributed to it – is that rare thing, a convulsive shift of reference, a radical change in the historical dilemma the fable now seems to address and project. For now Stalinism and Brezhnevism are both gone, bureaucracy is in the process of being replaced by the market, and so on. The question thereby wins a redoubled poignancy – why in spite of all these changes, when we no longer have the old pretexts to blame, is it still not possible to achieve social transformation? For in a period in which the Soviet Union, while hoping for promotion from Second to First World status, is more likely to find itself degraded to the condition of a Third World country, the SF enemy turns around, and what blocks socialism is no longer 'socialism' itself, or Stalinism, or Communism or the Communist Party – it is the capitalist world system into which the Soviet Union has decided to integrate itself.

Days of Eclipse

This is now the mysterious 'alien' power that enigmatically impedes development and thwarts the projects of social transformation at every path, by way of the carrot of consumers' goods and the stick of intimidation by the IMF and the threat of the shutting off of Western loans.[17]

But of course one cannot propose so vulgar or unmediated an allegoresis without specifying the more indirect mediations whereby these – to be sure catastrophic – current events find their way into an autonomous artistic fantasy whose more plausible and immediate determinants would seem instead formal (the dynamics of fairy tales and SF) and technical (the recent traditions of Soviet and world film). Could the film-maker be imagined in any way consciously to have sponsored this kind of topical allusion; could his public in any way be argued to have thought these thoughts and interpretations in the process of watching it?

A long polemic, over several generations, has probably complicated the matter of artistic intention beyond such simple uses; while precisely for an esoteric film like this – which would be classified, I imagine, as a 'festival film,' had it been made in a First or Third World country – the matter of the public also becomes problematic, above all owing to the emergence of new international artistic relations. Indeed, I think that it is the fact of the new global system, and the modification of intellectuals' roles within it, that can serve as the justification for what is actually an interpretation of *Days of Eclipse* in terms of an international, or geopolitical, allegory. For it is the national artists and intellectuals who first sense the modifications imposed by the global market on the relative standing of the national artistic production within which they work. Artists (outside the center or the superstate itself, certainly) sense the dilemmas of national subalternity and dependency much earlier than most other social groups, excepting the actual producers themselves.[18] In particular they find themselves keenly aware of the external damage to that paradigm of national allegory within which they used to work[19] and are well placed to readapt it to allegorical structures of a global and world-systemic type. Economic dependency and political subal-

110

ternity here also signify the emergence of a new kind of desire for the Other – a longing for First World acknowledgment and international recognition – alongside that dialectic of internal publics that used to be the fundamental terrain of the aesthetic gamble and the formal act, and which now finds itself reduced and forcibly devalued into the regional and the nativist. I cannot therefore myself – regrettably! – feel that there is anything far-fetched or improbable about the reading I have proposed for this remarkable film. Power does not go away when you ignore it, the West is near, late capitalism weighs on the globe like a doom, and now, in the transformation of this little fable by History, it becomes the mysterious, unknowable outside power (from some higher plane of civilization and technology) that incomprehensibly sets limits to the praxis of those neo-colonial subjects the Soviets are in danger of becoming.

Notes

1. A title idiotically rendered in English as *Definitely Maybe*, translated by Antonina W. Bouis (New York: Macmillan, 1978); all page references in the text are to this edition (Russian original, 1976). And see Stephen W. Potts, *The Second Marxian Invasion: The Fiction of the Strugatsky Brothers* (San Bernadino: Borgo, 1991) for a useful discussion and an extensive English bibliography; and also D. Suvin, *Russian Science Fiction 1956–1974: A Bibliography* (Elizabethtown, NY: Dragon Press, 1976).

2. Arkady and Boris Strugatsky, *Roadside Picnic*, translated by Antonina W. Bouis (New York: Macmillan, 1977 [Russian original, 1972]).

3. It may not be altogether fair to say so: the authors tell us, in an interview with *Locus* magazine, that a first filming of the novel was faithful; but that, the film stock being unprocessable in the USSR, a second filming had to be undertaken on a shoestring, necessitating the allegorical rewrite here complained of. May we deduce from this that, among its other determinations, the postmodern preponderance of the allegorical over the symbolic has fiscal and budgetary grounds?

4. He discovers it to be five times lower! Besides a lengthy emission from the Vatican, in Italian, about the beatification of a new saint, this is Sokurov's only concession to current Soviet religious trendiness in this particular film. Still, may one in passing express exasperation with the various religious revivals in the East? The Roman Catholic wedding in *Man of Steel* (complete with Lech Walensa!) was already disgraceful; we have now seen the consequences. As for the rates of infection, even if it were so that believers catch fewer diseases, this would not necessarily redound to their greater moral or psychological credit. Surely an anti-foundational era is able to satisfy its aesthetic, philosophical and political needs without the trappings of superstition, and is at last in a position to jettison the baggage of the great monotheisms (the animisms and polytheisms might still be acceptable on other grounds; while Buddhism is in our sense atheistic). Perhaps we might minimally agree that stories about priests are in whatever form intolerable, whatever religion they purport to serve; in that sense Paradjanov's *Color of Pomegranates* is as detestable as Bernanos, despite the naïf folk-art splendor of its images. Sokurov need not be omitted from this diatribe: the gratuitous introduction of a priest into the Platonov materials that make up *A Lonely Human Voice* is particularly unforgivable.

5. Sokurov has indeed made a number of remarkable documentaries (which I have so far been unable to see), something that leads me to assume that *Days of Eclipse* incorporates (or cannibalizes) an unfinished documentary on life and production in Turkestan, from which both the initial views of city life and the extended digression later on in the film about production and construction derive. *Eclipse* thereby not merely unites two distinct generic aspects of his extraordinary talent – the narrative-fictional and the observational – but also dialectically allows each one to batten off the other: the fairy tale drawing unexpected new strength from this *ciné vérité* and vice versa.

6. Paul Muldoon, 'The Boundary Commission', in *Why Brownlee Left* (Wake Forest, N.C.: Wake Forest University Press, 1980), p. 15.

7. See, for a cognate phenomenon, Platonov's conception of the 'eunuch of the soul,' in *Chevengur*, discussed in Valery Podoroga's important essay on the writer in *South Atlantic Quarterly* Vol. 90 No. 2, Spring 1991.

8. Paradjanov's own retreat into the puppet play and the oriental miniature (in the film mentioned in note 4 and others) is surely to be understood not only as the expression of Georgian and Armenian cultural nationalism and separatism, but also as a critique of the representational as such.

9. Among other bravura features of this film (and besides the striking vertical shots, mostly from above) must be mentioned the soundtrack. Above all in the scene in which the sick child's father reappears to thwart Malianov's plans for his future and his cure – behind a shot of the child's face, a very long sequence of muffled grunts from the off-camera doorway, which we can only take to be a wordless struggle between the two men. The music (by Y. Chanin) is absolutely remarkable and seems to mingle ethnic Asian musical traditions from various sources: see D. Popov's excellent 'Alexander Sokurov's Film "Tage der Finsternis"' (*Kunst und Literatur* vol. 38 no. 3, May–June 1990, pp. 303–8). Popov stresses the symbolic value of the setting as a protest against the centralized and Russian-national state; see also Yampolsky's useful accompanying article (in the same issue) on Sokurov's next film, *Save and Protect*, a version of *Madame Bovary*.

10. Indeed, his 1990 film, *The Second Circle*, is something like an exfoliation and an extended commentary on this short sequence: an implacable account of the burial of the protagonist's father, complete with analogous spatial problems in getting the corpse out of the apartment. Already in *Skorbnoe Beschuvstvie* (in English, *Anesthesia Dolorosa*) his remarkable film version of *Heartbreak House* (complete with film clips of World War I and the aged Shaw himself nodding away in an upstairs room and having fitful visions of apocalypse, as in the zeppelin raid on London), Boss Mangin's peculiar fainting spell has been replaced with a simulation of death so absolute that the autopsy is on the point of being performed before our very eyes.

11. See his comparison of the camera with the surgeon's scalpel in 'The Work of Art in the Age of Its Mechanical Reproduceability', *Illuminations*, translated by Harry Zohn (New York: Schocken, 1969), p. 223.

12. Claude Simon, *La route des Flandres* (Paris: Minuit, 1960), p. 29.

13. My student Chris Andre suggests, I think plausibly, that the immediate 'explanation' of this local disaster is to be found in the putative explosion of the stray dog which, like Mephistopheles, unaccountably turns up one day to visit Vecherovsky (a present, presumably, from the mysterious powers, and a kind of non-Andalusian pendant to the visiting serpent). Another school of thought, rigorously mindful of Freud's most rudimentary lessons, takes a somewhat more impure view of the matter: I suppose I have to confess that my own first free association with this image (the armpit hair in *Un chien andalou*) suggests some agreement with them on the part of my unconscious.

The conscious mind, however, continues stoutly to defend its earlier pre-Freudian position ('a pre-adolescent realm without sex or desire').

14. Pascal Bonitzer, *Le Champ aveugle* (Paris: Gallimard, 1982), pp. 53ff.: 'Hitchcock's cinema is organized as follows: everything proceeds normally, within the average of a general mediocrity and insensibility, until someone notices that one element of the ensemble, behaving inexplicably, stands out like a spot or stain [*fait tâche*].'

15. Any number of Stanislaw Lem's most important novels could be adduced: *Solaris, The Invincible, His Master's Voice, Fiasco.*

16. *Hard to Be a God* (New York: Seabury, 1973 [Russian original, 1964]), now a Franco-Soviet co-production directed by Peter Fleischman.

17. This hypothesis of an unconscious geopolitical allegory is reinforced by the suggestive analysis (by Konrad and Szelenyi) of the substitution of the West for a hostile and threatening nature in the Eastern bureaucratic or party states: 'Rational-redistributive [that is, communist] societies treat economic growth as an external challenge, a politically defined goal dictated by the desire to catch up with the developed Western economies. In this externality of the goal of growth rational distribution resembles the more traditional variety [that is, the so-called Asiatic mode of production], for whom the challenge of nature appears as an external menace'. George Konrad and Ivan Szelenyi, *The Intellectuals on the Road to Class Power* (NY: Harcourt Brace Jovanovich, 1979), p. 49.

18. See, in particular, for a remarkable mapping of the impact of the new world system on national labor movements, Caroline M. Vogler, *The Nation-State: The Neglected Dimension of Class* (Gower Publishing Co., 1985). I am indebted to Susan Buck-Morss for this reference.

19. See Introduction, note 1.

Chapter 2

Remapping Taipei

The social totality can be sensed, as it were, from the outside, like a skin at which the Other somehow looks, but which we ourselves will never see. Or it can be tracked, like a crime, whose clues we accumulate, not knowing that we are ourselves parts and organs of this obscenely moving and stirring zoological monstrosity. But most often, in the modern itself, its vague and nascent concept begins to awaken with the knowledge function, very much like a book whose characters do not yet know that they are being read. So it is that the spectator alone knows that the lovers have only missed each other by five minutes, or that Iago has lied to the hero's uncle, giving him a view of the partners' motives that will never be corrected in this life, with appropriately disastrous consequences. These known misunderstandings bring into being a new kind of purely aesthetic emotion, which is not exactly pity and fear, but for which 'Irony' is an exhausted word whose original acceptation can only lend to conjecture. That it is purely aesthetic, however, means that this effect is conceivable only in conjunction with the work of art, cannot take place in real life, and has something to do with the omniscient author. These occurrences remain disjoined, unknown to each other, their interrelationship, causal or other, being a non-existent fact, event, or phenomenon, save when the gaze of the Author, rising over miniature roof-tops, puts them back together and declares them to be the material of story-telling, or Literature.

But the author must discover such ironies and not invent them — omniscience is like providence and not like creation. Nor does the chance seem to come often, or in every kind of social formation: the urban seems propitious to it, infinitely assembling the empty spaces of such meetings or missed encounters; while the modern (or the romantic) seems to supply the other vital ingredient, namely, the sense of authorial function or of the omniscient social witness. Perhaps it also serves to seal in the monads in some more airtight way, thus heightening the astonishing fact of their synchronicity. *Tom Jones* and indeed the Byzantine novel itself all made their living off the fact of sheer

114

coincidence (which generally involved the mysteries of birth and genealogy). But only the age of the modern is notoriously the moment in which the individual life is driven so deeply into its isolated 'point of view' that it is no longer capable of peeping out above the barrier. Modern relativistic plot, and its fundamental category, the unity of 'point of view', only come into being at the moment of late Victorian individualism, in which the monadic closure of the individual self becomes a desperate case, projecting just such an abstract representational form – a kind of relativistic synchronicity, in which a multiplicity of monads is imagined separately, and as it were from above, in but the most fitful relationship with one another – as its expression and its compensation alike.

The supreme plot-formation of this period then undertakes impossibly and paradoxically to reunite all these isolated monads, taking the older providential form mentioned above as its distant pattern. But we may be forgiven for thinking that its spirit is the inverse of that earlier one. There, unification of the multiple destinies and strands had the effect of reassuring its subjects of the ultimate unity of the social totality, and of God's design. Here, everything that is stunning about the accidents and peripeties that draw these isolated subjects together (crossing their paths, often, on the mode of showing their own individual ignorance of that momentary co-presence to space) would seem, by its very ephemerality, to have the effect of driving us all individually and privately back ever more deeply into our isolation, and of assuring us that the Providence-effect is little more than an aesthetic one: the bravura gesture of a Romantic or a modern, which corresponds to nothing in lived experience.

I think, for example, of a wonderful book by Ann Banfield on another narrative and representational peculiarity, so-called *style indirect libre*. Her very title, *Unspeakable Sentences*,[1] conveys the argument that such sentence structure can only be found in written and printed narrative and not in any speaker's mouth. So also with the Irony of synchronous monadic simultaneity: no human subject has ever known it as an existential experience (save in reading a book), nor has ever witnessed it as an observing eye. To attribute it to God is as grotesque as to imagine God following our innermost thoughts and muttering them out in His own distinctive form of *style indirect libre*. On the other hand, a return to our present context draws us up sharply and reminds us that the movie camera is also just such a non-human apparatus apt to produce effects and simulated 'experiences' that no one can possibly have had in real individual or existential human life. In fact, a filmic 'point of view' is less realistic than the other, written kind, since it shows us the viewer along with the viewed and has to include the viewing subject's body in the contents of the allegedly subjective experience, as if to mark the latter as seen by someone.

115

Such artificial constructs then pose the philosophical problem thereby implied: how to evaluate seemingly artificial or secondary 'experiences' generated prosthetically. They are evidently real, but at the same time inauthentic or untruthful insofar as they include the suggestion that the new experience-construct is somehow natural or 'the same' as ordinary or everyday viewing or experiencing. But this philosophical problem of film (which impossibly offers us, as Cavell has argued, the world viewed without ourselves present) is no doubt already implicit in the problematic of McLuhanism, and in the evaluation of a then equally new experience (writing, reading, printing) which is not natural either and which offers just such peculiar non-existential experience-constructs as the one Ann Banfield describes.

The phenomenon of the providential plot, therefore, and of the narrative of synchronous monadic simultaneity (henceforth known as SMS), is thus compounded by the intersection with film and its philosophical problems. And it is time to say that those compounds are in turn multiply compounded by the matter of modernism and postmodernism, which respecifies the SMS plot as a peculiarly modernist phenomenon and also, in the era of video, raises some questions as to the positioning of film itself as a medium. Historical and periodizing questions of that kind, however, require attention to the ambiguity of the term postmodernism itself, which must designate a whole historical period and its 'structure of feeling' in the preceding sentence, but which risks slipping inappreciably in this one into the rather different sense of an aesthetic style or set of formal properties. The slippage is significant, since it has been argued that much of the content of what has been called, in art, architecture or thought alike, postmodern is in reality modernist – indeed, that a pure postmodernism may well a priori be impossible as such, always involving the treatment of essentially modernist residues. The return, therefore, of what looks like a Western modernist narrative paradigm (the SMS) in the work of a Third-World film-maker (in the thick of postmodernity as a global tendency, if not a global cultural and social reality) can be expected to raise new questions, which do not include the relatively idle one, debated by critics and journalists at the film's first showing in its native Taiwan, as to whether the director had not sold out to essentially Westernizing methods or style.[2]

Indeed, I am tempted to say that this particular question disqualifies itself today, by standing revealed as a specifically modernist one. In the great debates in colonial countries over nativism and Westernization, modernization versus traditional ideals and values, fighting the imperialist with his own weapons and his own science or reviving an authentic national (and cultural-national) spirit, the West connotes the modern as such in a way that it can no longer do when the modernization process is tendentially far more complete and no longer particularly marked as Western (no one seems to have asked the Ayatollah whether the use of audio-cassettes marked a corrupt surrender to Western technology and values).

I suspect, in any case, that the opposite of Westernization in such contemporary arguments in Taiwan cannot be China itself (even assuming that each individual speaker or participant had some relatively clear conception of Chinese aesthetic values and social realities), but that its empty place must rather be filled by the question about some putative Taiwanese identity that is itself as much a problem as it is a solution. In that sense, perhaps what is objected to in Edward Yang's film is not so much its failure to be Chinese or Taiwanese so much as the relative absence from it of any ostensible worry about the nature of Taiwanese identity, of any rehearsal of its very possibility. Indeed, it does seem to be the case that *Terrorizer* (a peculiar and pointed translation of *kong bu fen zi*, 1986) assimilates modernization, and the toll it takes on psychic subjects, more generally to urbanization than to Westernization as such. This lends its 'diagnosis' a kind of globality, if not a universality, which is evidently what has made Yang's critics uncomfortable – yet it cannot be said that Taipei is a modern and Western-style city, in the same way that one could affirm this of Shanghai, for example. Rather it is an example of some generally late-capitalist urbanization (which one hesitates, except to make the point, to call postmodern), of a now classic proliferation of the urban fabric that one finds everywhere in the First and Third Worlds alike. But if, as I am arguing here, it no longer makes much sense to talk about such cities in terms of an opposition between the Western and the traditional, then it would seem to follow that the opposite term is equally problematized, and that notions of national or ethnic identity (of the modernist type) are equally threatened by postmodernity. (What the television brings us in the way of civil war and nationality struggle – most notably from the former Soviet Union and Yugoslavia – is something quite different from the above, something which we have every interest in identifying properly as the media phenomenon of neo-ethnicity, a simulacrum in which it is no longer a question of *belief*, in any religious sense, but very much a question of *practices*. Ethnicity is something you are condemned to; neo-ethnicity is something you decide to reaffirm about yourself.[3])

In any case, nothing is more distant from the stylistic features and formal problematic of the so-called Taiwanese *new wave* than the People's Republic of China (PRC) 'fifth generation' film-making that is contemporaneous with it. This last indeed seems marked by properly epic ambitions, in particular reaffirming its landscapes in an utterly different fashion from the ways in which Hong Kong or Taiwanese space is given, constructed, and experienced. A specific stylistic mannerism marks this particular ambition (about which this is not the moment to 'decide' whether it is authentic or manipulatory, or to attempt to separate out from within it what belongs to propaganda and the staging of power, and what can be traced back to new and original modes of being-in-the-world). This mannerism is what may be termed a kind of aspiration to the bas-relief, the privileging of an epic mid-shot that associates film and frieze and scans a middle realm of landscape below the mountain peaks and eschewing the foreground plain, sweeping humans and horses along with it in an endless procession of moving figures without feet or heads, like a cinematographic scroll. This new technique of a mid-panoramic perspective becomes not merely a stylistic signature for the newer PRC cinema: it affirms its epic narrativity, by directing attention to a panning across the frieze, as in traditional painterly story-telling, at the same time as it defamiliarizes the conventional relationship of human bodies and their landscape contexts, allowing them to be grasped not independently (in old-fashioned ways), but rather in some new symbiotic relationship of volume to each other which remains to be determined. This epic shot is thus a symbolic act which promises some new Utopian combination of what used to be subject and object. Politically it claims to constitute some new way of appropriating tradition which is neither iconoclastic nor given over to Western individualism – with what truth one cannot say (save to register the claim as a rival form in competition with *nostalgia film* as the current dominant Western or postmodern form of telling history).

Epic of this kind must necessarily include the countryside (even when the shots are limited to city space). Its perceptual allegory, indeed, implies a reduction of the city to human praxis and politics, and reaffirms the immense agricultural hinterland of the peasant masses as its incontrovertible mid-perspective and wall in depth. Urban PRC film, however, seems to take a very different stylistic turn, as though its relations were not those that led into the Chinese land mass, but rather the discontinuous vertical openings onto the media and the Pacific Rim, that is to say, onto whatever is fantasized as the West. What one notes here, in a film like the 1987 *Desperation*, for example, directed by Zhou Xiaowen in the Xian studios, a thriller whose sheer physical violence takes second place to no equivalent Western product, is a peculiar process whereby the signs and identifying marks of all specific named cities have been systematically removed, in order thereby to foreground the generically urban. It would be too simple and functional to impute this particular stylistic motivation (whose implementation must, as one can imagine, be very complex indeed) to marketing strategies alone and an attention to a potentially international public; or rather, it would be crucial to affirm such base, external motivation, such determination by the extra-aesthetic, as realities in the object-world that ultimately, at some wider level of analysis, always rejoin the subject (and the formal and aesthetic) in unexpected internal ways. In this case, surely, the problems of the market in situations of dependency always somehow rejoin the logic of the collective imaginary and the positioning of that Other to whom cultural and aesthetic production is then also implicitly addressed.

Here what seems initially clear is that the marks of the socio-economic system must be removed: the consumer of entertainment in the overseas communities must not be distracted by politics, that is to say, by the reminders of a socialist economy in the PRC. The high-tech espresso bars and bullet trains of *Desperation* thus dutifully construct a world of contemporary industrial production and consumption beyond all ideological struggle. Meanwhile, by the same token, the identifying marks of the mainland cities must also be excised, since few viewers of this product will be likely to imagine that Xian, say, or Tientsin are located somewhere in the 'free world'; they must therefore not be allowed to ask themselves such questions, or to begin to identify the city in question in the first place.

It is interesting to compare such neutralization and de-identification procedures – a kind of representational laundering of ideologically marked contents – with those I have elsewhere[4] described at work in Western (or, perhaps even more specifically, in US) post-modern films in which, however, it is not the locale but rather the time period which is generalized. In *The Grifters*, for example, a Stephen Frears movie version of Jim Thompson's novel about the 1950s, pains have been taken to remove the markers of 1991–contemporaneity from the Los Angeles–San Diego–Phoenix axis in which the story is played out. Leaving aside all the other problems involved in transferring Thompson's plot to the Reagan-Bush era, the impulse can surely also be identified as the (not altogether successful) attempt to create a time-free indeterminate nostalgia zone for the thriller narrative in which unpleasant reminders of contemporary social – and thereby political – issues and contradictions have been removed.[5] Thus, a postmodern aesthetic – which at its most vibrant aims at the ideal or Platonic reconstruction of some eternal 30s or 40s art-deco Miami in a film noir beyond historical time itself (as in my earlier example of Kazden's *Body Heat*) – can be socially retraced to its class and ideological roots in a form of collective cultural repression (in the literal sense of an exclusion from consciousness of painful or disturbing material); and it can in this sense be juxtaposed with a specifically Second-World form of aesthetic repression (removing the marks of socialism as a system).

Both are in any case relatively distinct from the packaging of specifically Third-World international or festival films in national, cultural and one is tempted to say, tourist-friendly ways, in which it is the fact of a brand-new locale and unprecedented national provenance that is stressed and marketed. As Peter Wollen has observed, what are henceforth termed 'new waves' are fresh entries of this kind into the international market. I won't belabor at any great length the interesting theoretical issue of whether Taiwan is to be counted as a Third-World country: if you think the label means Southern-Tier poverty, then it is clearly inappropriate, if not worse; but if it merely affirms something as structural and descriptive as the non-adherence to what is left of the socialist bloc, coupled with the constitutive distance from one of the three great capital centers of the 'new world order' (Japan, Europe, the USA), then it may be less misleading.

In any case, the Taiwanese 'new wave' has tended to mark its images as specific to the island, in ways quite distinct from the PRC evocation of landscape. The city is also focused differently here (and *Terrorizer* will be an index of its richness and possibilities), for the obvious reasons that Taipei does not possess the profile or the historical resonance and associations of the great traditional mainland cities, nor is it that all-encompassing closed urban space of a virtual city-state like Hong Kong. Still its dominance has effectively transformed the natural countryside into a kind of extended suburban space, one in which the survival of more traditional agricultural villages is nonetheless sublated and somehow modified by their linked association on an intricate web and map of electric trains that lead into the capital. The image of these small suburban trains indeed has in the camerawork of Hou Hsaio-hsien's films become a virtual new wave logo, particularly in his beautiful *Dust in the Wind* (1986), in which the very shot of the empty station and the sound of the train in the distance end up articulating the narrative and standing as signs or shorthand for mutations in the Event. The commuter train here includes the landscape and is open to it, in that utterly unlike the high-speed projectiles that propel the narrative forward in *Desperation* (or in such precursors as Kurosawa's 1962 *High and Low*). The palpable interweavings of the social (no longer, in the late capitalist world system, characterizable as provincial), which are both expressed and signified by this system of recurrent imagery and then peculiarly overdetermined by such intertextuality as the casting of Hou Hsaio-hsien himself as the protagonist in Edward Yang's *Taipei Story* (1985); along with the material itself, which with the political opening of liberalization begins to evolve towards such ambitious historical chronicles as Hou's *City of Sadness* (1989) and Edward Yang's *A Brighter Summer Day* (1991) – all this makes of Taiwanese new wave films a kind of linked cycle more satisfying for the viewer than any national cinema I know (save perhaps the French productions of the 20s and 30s).

From this cycle, *Terrorizer* stands out starkly as uncharacteristic. Sharing none of the potential sentimentalism of the nativist films, its visual elegance has frequently been characterized as cold, as one would characterize a glassy surface that repels identification. Yet *Taipei Story* combined fashion-plate visuality with pathos, and its hero – played, as I have said, by Hou Hsaio-hsien – was a non-intellectual, fumbling his way, in the manner of American populism, through a series of odd jobs and reversals of fortune. What marks off *Terrorizer* is not even the class status of its characters, who are now, as we shall see, professionals and lumpens, but rather the now archaic modernity of its theme: art versus life, the novel and reality, mimesis and irony. The co-protagonist indeed is a writer with a writer's block (Chou Yufen), who is freed up by an anonymous phone call denouncing her husband's adulterous affairs, at which point she sits down to write a prize-winning novella about this situation (which has no basis in fact), leaving him in the process. Under other circumstances, the situation whereby the possibility of attributing guilt to the husband suddenly grants independence to the wife would offer interesting material for interpretation. But Chou Yufen's story is only one of the film's four distinct plot strands, the alternation of which, I would argue, leaves no distance for reflection of this kind, for interpretive rumination, particularly of this motivational-psychoanalytic type. What does stand out, rather, is the old-fashioned reflexivity of the theme, the residual modernism of the now familiar mystery of the imitation of art by life and the correspondence of the novel to the aleatory realities of the real world outside. The embodiment of the theme around the writing of literature and the pathos of the precarious role of the literary 'creator' strikes a regressive note within a film of this decidedly contemporary stamp (none of the chronological laundering and neutralization of nostalgia film here), produced in the age of the simulacrum and of the dominance of technological media (in Taiwan, as elsewhere, the aesthetically ambitious now want to become great film-makers rather than great novelists). This anachronism of Literature and its once interesting reflexive paradoxes – foregrounded and as it were quoted here, in the midst of the other plot lines we shall be examining in a moment – is what makes *Terrorizer* relatively conspicuous within contemporary Third-World production, where there are plenty of intellectuals and even writers, but perhaps somewhat less 'modernism' in this Western sense.

André Gide's *Counterfeiters* (1925) is the very prototype of this older classic modernist text, whose protagonist, Edouard, keeps a journal within the novel about the novel – called 'The Counterfeiters' – which he is writing but will perhaps never finish (unlike Gide, who was then able to publish, under separate cover, the journal he himself also kept while writing and actually finishing his own novel of the same name). Edward Yang does not seem to have made a separate film about the making of *Terrorizer* (although Godard did so, after completing his film *Passion*, as we shall see in a subsequent chapter). At any rate, the archetypal scene in Gide's intricate novel (or *roman*, a term he reserved for a form that marked the confluence of a number of stories, plot lines, or *récits*, and used only once in his own work, for this book) is the moment in which, during a discussion of the novelist's theories about the ways in which contemporary intellectuals counterfeit social and spiritual values, another character flings a 'real' counterfeit coin upon the table, suggesting that the referent itself might interest him as well. But theories about counterfeiting are more interesting to this protagonist than the reality (which belongs in fact to another of the novel's multiple plot strands), and Edouard is thus himself ironically dispatched along with the other hapless characters about whom he has himself ironized. More significantly, in a move that has traditionally seemed canonical for high modernism generally, the very theme of counterfeit value is thereby itself ironized and left to float in mid-air and mid-reference, passing slowly in all its optionality from the status of a social comment or critique into that of sheer aesthetic decoration and back again.

One's sense is that modernist constructs of this kind cannot be filmed. It is a proposition that could be tested against three very different candidates. Jean Renoir's *La Règle du jeu* (1939), for example, has its author inside it as well (the director playing the meddling and matchmaking – 'authorial' – character of Octave), along with multiple plot lines and artificial mechanisms 'en abysme'. The social content on which Renoir's bravura formal operation is performed is certainly very different from Gide's, turning as it does on an aristocracy of blood, culture and merit, and posing questions about heroism and about authentic love. But if this reflexive form constitutively includes a rift between form and content, the shift in period and social class, or in ideological preoccupation, should not make any fundamental difference. More relevant, perhaps, is the glacial distance of *La Règle du jeu* from even those characters about which it seems to be sentimentalizing – a gulf seemingly too broad to be spanned by Gidean (or indeed Jamesean) irony, at least in a situation in which the terms are of two distinct modes of being (since the familiar sentimental complacent relationship of viewer to character is staged by way of the visual image; whereas the judgment takes place somewhere else, in a non-visual, non-filmic mind). Quite distinct from this is the interpenetration of empathy and otherness enabled and indeed encouraged by narrative language in the point-of-view ironies of high literary modernism.

Meanwhile, Nabokov's coy and mannered version of these games does not work on film either: Fassbinder's version of *Despair* (1979), whatever its other considerable merits, is absurdly – perhaps even pointedly – unfaithful to the novel in this respect, since in the reading we are persuaded of a virtual physical identity between the narrator and his double which is instantly dispelled by the latter's first appearance on screen. The very different reflexivity of Dziga Vertov's *Man with a Movie Camera* (1929), however, in which the place of the novelist and language is taken by the apparatus itself, yields a stream

La Règle du jeu

of visual images the equivalent of which would surely not be the introspective complacencies of a Gide, but rather the *Sachlichkeit* of a Dos Passos or a Döblin (experimental objectivities whose fit with the medium of language time has itself rendered questionable).

We must conclude, then, that the media sharply diverge in their capacity for what, to use a properly Gidean term, we may call complicity with the fictional characters themselves; and that, whatever fascination and self-identification, unconscious mimesis, mirror-stage jubilation by proxy, we are capable of developing in the presence of the images of movie actors, it can have little enough to do with the games high modernist writers played with the expanding and contracting distance available within the reading of the fictional sentence.

It is something that can be said the other way round, in terms of judgment rather than of empathy, and shown by means of a famous chapter in *The Counterfeiters* (Part II, chapter vii), in which an ostentatiously omniscient narrator now, after the fashion of the eighteenth-century novel, pretends to pass his fictional characters in review and to acknowledge their weaknesses and defects: 'Edouard annoyed me more than once, and even made me indignant. ... Lady Griffith quite impressed me in the beginning, but I quickly realized the mistake I was making. ... Vincent interested me more ...' and so on. One never quite believed it for a moment; yet it may seem in retrospect that Gide succeeded in fooling us with this ruse, and in encouraging a habit of

Terrorizer

judgment in the reader by virtue of annoying us with his own. Such judgment tends to ratify a certain moral or personal commitment to these characters on the reader's part. 'Liking' them is certainly not the word for it (although Gide takes pains to make sure we dislike some of them); but some minimal willingness to compare the temperatures within this or that point of view, this or that subjectivity, is involved.

Nothing of the sort in *Terrorizer*, whose characters are all signally lacking in any of the secret merits that might encourage our complicity. Nor are they, however, antipathetic, something that might be easier to achieve but which Yang does not really manage even for the Eurasian girl (who on some accounts seems to have been for him the eponymous villain of the piece). At least in my opinion, they are neither likeable nor dramatically evil, but rather mildly, and secretly, repulsive. The self-pity of the protagonist, Li Li-chung,, the doctor (and husband of the writer already mentioned) is not enhanced by his betrayal of a colleague (let alone his massive obtuseness about his wife's unhappiness). Chou Yufen herself, meanwhile, is so narcissistically unhappy (and so complacent in her subsequent moment of happiness and triumph) as to make it very easy to separate out any

Terrorizer

feelings one may have about her victimization as a woman from one's judgment of her own personality as such. Nor do the protagonists of the other plot strands fare much better. The young photographer with whom the film opens (paparazzo-like, he is trying to get some action shots of a shoot-out between drug dealers and the police) is surely as self-centered an idle rich youth as one would like, not quite as repulsive as the hero of *Blow-Up*, but only because he doesn't have to make a living out of it in the first place. Meanwhile his immediate target (the fleeing Eurasian girl, nicknamed the White Chick, and initially mixed up with the criminal elements in question) offers yet another version of self-centered ego-indulgence and narcissistic indifference to the outside world, even leaving aside her criminal nastiness and the well-nigh impersonal ferocity with which she fights for her existence in a world of rich and stupid, corrupt johns and gulls. Her mother, floating alcoholically in her memories of the 1950s night life among American servicemen, is not much better in her own way; and the bureaucrats are appropriately repellent and the underworld flora and fauna unromantic and bestially uninteresting. To say that the policeman (the doctor's childhood friend) comes off best is only to register the fact that we learn least about him, and that, of all the things people do in this movie, being tired out, lying in a hot tub, doing some drinking, and listening to a 'younger brother's' complaints or boasts, are the least calculated to arouse antipathy.

To be sure, at the end of the chapter mentioned above, Gide also tosses all his characters in the trash-can:

> 'If ever I find myself inventing another story, I will only allow into it tempered characters, whom life makes sharper, rather than blunting their edge. Laura, Douviers, La Pérouse, Azais ... what am I doing with people like this?'

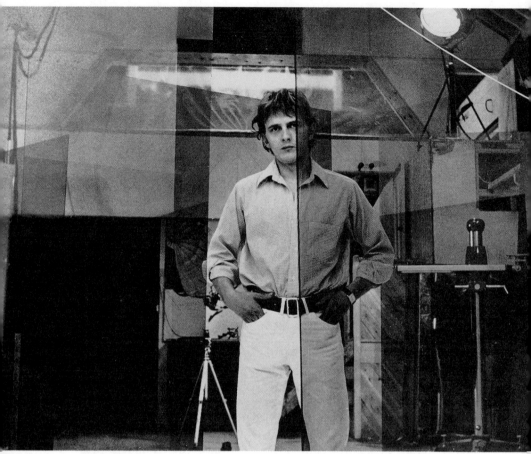

Blow-Up

Yet it is the very standard of judgment that allows Gide to say so which is lacking in Edward Yang's film, for reasons historical and social, rather than cultural or personal, reasons ultimately rooted in the differences between the modern period and our own.

In that separation of form and content I have already evoked, Gide's 'novel' also formally exploits and organizes a social and personal content given in advance and somehow contingent, dependent on the vicissitudes of the writer's own life and background. Clearly enough, all the varied forms of a high modernist abstraction must in one way or another confront this particular contingent seam, which is necessary for some minimal content in the first place (the last sparse image residue of the Mallarmean vase or curtains blowing). It is an open question whether authenticity consists in acknowledging such contingency and allowing it to persist within the work as such, like a foreign body, or in attempting a symbolic recuperation whereby at some higher level it again becomes 'motivated' (in all the Russian Formalist senses) and thus meaningful or post-contingent. In the event Gide does both, attempting to endow his homosexuality with symbolic meaning, while the fact of his social background in French Protestantism is mainly taken as a given and a contingent starting-point. In *The Counterfeiters*, for example, with its multivocal and collective formal vocation, Gide is obliged to draw on the French Protestant background far more extensively than in the individual *récits*, in which the problem of the individual destiny and the individual choice fairly well ensures a 'motivation' of the initial situation in terms of this or that meaning (whether 'hedonistic', as in *L'Immoraliste*, or 'ascetic', as in *La Porte étroite*). In retrospect, the Gide of *The Counterfeiters* may instructively be reread as an ethnic novelist, for whom 'French Protestantism', uniquely in French society, has something of the enclave and subcultural dynamics we associate with ethnicity in the United States. The residues of a relatively prim and pietistic moralizing in the judgments of the omniscient narrator are then overdetermined by this particular social content: in some deeper ideological sense, Gide remains a Christian novelist, whose attention is above all focused on matters of character (in the moral sense of what can manifest rectitude and steadfastness, or on the other hand weakness and irresolution). From Weber all the way down to David Riesman's 'inner-direction', then, these matters of characterology are social in their causes as well as in their effects. If they reinforce the emergent ethos of capitalism or later on the spirit of the entrepreneurial moment, such moralizing categories also remain intimately bound up with a particular stage of social development, from which their judgments cannot be separated.

This is clearest for categories of evil or of moral weakness and corruption. Gide can still produce a diagnosis of the social condition

Terrorizer

and identify forces for social evil: in the irresponsible and corrupt Cocteau-figure of Edouard's rival novelist Passavant, and even more starkly in those genuine nihilists for whom Passavant is a kind of façade and who operate by way of genuine crime ('real' counterfeiting) and an atmosphere not unlike the kind of anarchism and terrorism indicated by Conrad in works like *The Secret Agent*. But this Manichaean and apocalyptic view of social disintegration is much less convincing in the radical Gide than in conservative and right-wing authors. Moral weakness, susceptibility to evil influences, corruptibility, the failure of nerve or the sapping of moral fibre – these judgments are here more plausible, but seem applicable to almost everyone, from the corrupt grande bourgeoisie on the side of social order all the way to the various prototypes of youth. Edouard's second nephew Olivier is thus momentarily seduced by Passavant, while the latter's older brother Vincent is irredeemably corrupted by the fashionable novelist and his partner Lady Griffith, whom Vincent murders in a tropical drama of madness and self-destruction which we only glimpse fitfully between the lines.

It is enough to juxtapose these figures with the characters of *Terrorizer* to see that in postmodern times, in the international urban society of late capitalism, such moral judgments are irrelevant or at least inoperative (to use a once fashionable corporate word). Gidean moralism, and the monitory portraits of evil and corruption it enables, can have little to do with the maimed figures of the Taiwanese film, if only because it presupposes what the various poststructuralisms most often call the 'centered subject', the old inner-directed ego of the modern period. In a postmodern universe, after the so-called 'death of the subject', or at least after the end of the 'ideology of the subject' as such, it follows that nobody is evil exactly any longer or at least that evil is no longer the word for it. In this film, the Eurasian girl and her pimp are dangerous and violent (we witness, for example, the – not unjustified – murder of one of her clients), but given the context of urban capitalism, they are surely not much worse than anybody else. Indeed, I would argue that within the prodigious expansion of the concept of rationality in our contemporary post-natural society (taking rationality in the Habermasian sense of what you can understand or argue for), the traditional opposite numbers of this concept – the irrational, madness, and even evil itself – have become increasingly implausible or unfunctional. The occult revival, the taste for demonology, strike one as a desperate or nostalgic attempt to pump life back into these moral conceptions, which remain as quaint and inappropriate in the post-contemporary period as Victorian bustles at a disco.

But already in *The Counterfeiters* crime and violence had begun to secure a somewhat different narrative function from that of moralizing judgments. In a system of parallel narrative strands, indeed,

Terrorizer

violence and crime tend to mark an 'ultimately determining instance' in which the various plots come together in an explosive climax. But this is narrative rather than ontological logic, so to speak, and bears less on the ultimate meaning and interpretation of the events in question than on their visibility and their eruption as symptoms to be read. So the police investigation of counterfeiting and vice ('crimes roses') continues throughout the surface unfolding of the final sections of the novel, but the conspiracy finds its surface inscription in the related schoolboy prank in which the student Boris shoots himself in front of his class and under his grandfather's eyes. In *Terrorizer*, meanwhile, the criminal incident – the shoot-out – stands at the starting-point of the intrigue, as what accidentally links a group of destinies together – in particular, it is the occasion that lets the young photographer glimpse the Eurasian girl (whom he photographs). In film, however, crosscutting can just as plausibly connect these plot strands with others, merely contiguous, with which they have not yet concretely intersected. Thus the doctor drives to work through traffic which contains both the police vans going the other way and the ambulance that carries the wounded girl to treatment: it is a connection the camera makes for us long before the effects show up in the doctor's own life. Here at any rate violence has come to be associated with narrative rather than with ethical categories, and is a matter of closure or of the interrelationship of strands and episodes rather than of judgment and evaluation.

We have not yet, however, identified the positive term in Gide's moralism, a term which knows an equally instructive evolution and displacement in the postmodern period. This positive term surely has to do with youth, equally an emphasis in *Terrorizer*, although its omnipresence as a theme in media culture means that it need no longer be a marked term. The accompanying ethical conceptions of character and characterological weakness (as well as Gide's own characteristic staging of pederasty as a pedagogical matter) make it clear that it is the residual Goethean value of *Bildung* or 'formation' which is here foregrounded, in a novel whose polyphony excludes the older *Bildungsroman* form as such. It is in the light of the residual concerns of *Bildung* alone that the Gidean attention to weakness and corrupting influences can be properly understood. The juxtaposition with *Terrorizer*, however, makes it clear that, despite the omnipresence of the category of the generation here as everywhere else in postmodern global urban culture, categories of *Bildung* or pedagogy, ideals of character formation, are now peculiarly inappropriate. Education manuals of the type of the *Cortegiano* or the *Mirror for Princes* might well be imagined for the world system of late capitalism, but they would surely bear little resemblance to the traditional models. Meanwhile, the very notion of reinventing a form of Goethean *Bildung* consistent with the age of Andy Warhol or MTV is problematical, to say the least. Our *Wilhelm Meister* is called *Falsche Bewegung*; and current debates about pedagogy and the humanities in the superstate give some idea, by way of their very aimlessness and the utter vacuousness of any intellectual content, of the difficulties involved in papering over 'the reification of consciousness in late capitalism', and indeed in reconciling the ravages left by the triumph of 'cynical reason' and commercial media or corporate culture with any of the canonical or traditional moral and educational paradigms.

What has come to replace this kind of characterological focus is instead, as *Terrorizer* shows, a displacement from the ethical and the pedagogical-formative towards the psychological as allegory or symptom of the mutilation of individual subjects by the system itself. It is an allegory that finds its most intense embodiment in the situations in this film of women, whose centrality can be measured against their relatively secondary position in Gide's *Counterfeiters*. There, Laura and Lady Griffith clearly mark the extremes of passive victimization and manipulative domination, respectively; and in retrospect Gide's sense of the crippling effects of bourgeois marriage is as vivid and as critical as any of his more dramatic protests in the name of youth (which were in any case also accompanied by a denunciation of the bourgeois family). But, as we shall see in more detail below, in *Terrorizer* it is the women's destinies – the situations of emprisonment of Chou Yufen and the Eurasian girl – which are paradigmatic, and that of the hapless Li Li-chung which is merely reactive. It is a historical difference or modification which can perhaps best be characterized by a shift in the object of the sociocultural critique. In both periods, that of the first classical feminism around World War I, of social democracy and the suffragette movement, of Shaw and Virginia Woolf, as well as that of the 'second wave' of feminism from the late 60s onwards, attention to specific forms of injustice or oppression is articulated with a larger project of social change. But in the first period, which was still Gide's, it is in terms of a specifically bourgeois culture of the family and of middle-class Victorian hypocrisy and puritanism that both feminism and socialism are staged. In our own postmodern world there is no longer a bourgeois or class-specific culture to be indicted, but rather a system-specific phenomenon: the various forms which reification and commodification and the corporate standardizations of media society imprint on human subjectivity and existential experience. This is the sense in which *Terrorizer*'s characters – and most particularly the film's women characters – dramatize the maiming of the subject in late capitalism, or, in terms of the language of the centered subject referred to earlier, indict something like the failure of the subject under the new system to constitute itself in the first place.

Yet all this merely characterizes the variable content organized by a form about which one wants principally to know how it will then itself be historically modified by modifications in the social raw material which is its enabling pretext. For the Gidean project – the novel as a multiplicity of plot strands – presumably survives and persists in *Terrorizer*, with this further difference (of degree, rather than of kind): namely, that the urban framework is here intensified and becomes something like the primary message of the narrative form itself. Yet in its earliest forms (as in the Byzantine novel), the providential plot, based on the coincidental interweaving of multiple destinies, was not particularly urban in its spatial requirements. The following authorial complaint by Manzoni is indeed a standard trope of the form well up to the end of the nineteenth century:

> More than once I have seen a nice, bright little boy – somewhat too bright, to tell the truth, but showing every sign of intending to turn out a good citizen – doing his best, as evening falls, to round up his little herd of guinea-pigs, which have been running free all day in the garden. He would like to get them all trotting into the pen together; but that's hopeless. One breaks away to the right, and while the small swineherd runs after him to chase him back with the others, another one – or two, or three – dash off to the left – or all over the place. After a little impatience he adapts himself to their methods, and begins by pushing inside those who happen to be nearest to the pen, and then goes to fetch the others, singly, or two or three at a time, as best he can. We have to play much the same game with our characters. We managed to get Lucia under cover, and ran off after Don Rodrigo; and now we must drop him and catch up with Renzo, who is right out of sight.[6]

If the urban comes to predominate, it is because the inns and high roads in which the protagonists of the older novel met by accident and rectified their mistaken identities necessarily required such characters to be travellers with destinies of a specific type – exiles, runaways, pursued or pursuer – so that the plot itself is thereby always moulded according to a distinct sub-genre or narrative type. The city frees up all this: its chance meetings and coincidence allow for a far greater variety of character-destinies, and thereby a web of relationships that can be spread out and unfolded in a dazzling array of distinct ideological effects. Gide's novel – surely one of the great bravura performances of all narrative literature, the first 150 pages of which can only be compared, for the breathless momentum with which it catches and drops its characters along the way and sets its stage, with the analogous opening gambits of *Heart of Midlothian* or *Lord Jim* – must properly be assigned to a specific historical trans-European generic context I am tempted to identify (anachronistically) as the Edwardian SMS or novel of synchronous monadic simultaneity. (It is instructive, besides its strong form in books like Forster's *Howards End*, to add in Virginia Woolf on the one hand and *Ulysses* on the other, both of which look different when they are read as work in a pre-existing formal project, namely, that of uniting the classical closed plot with the spatial multiplicity of the new industrial city.)

Gide's novel outtrumps these in its manipulation of representational levels. The *mises en abysme* of the related novels enumerated above necessarily had to pass through the needle's eye of gossip or the orally transmitted anecdote, the eavesdropping omniscience of third parties and the pathos of missed encounters that might have changed everything. Gide's narrative now includes the journal as an inner-worldly object which, opened up and read by our initial hero, Bernard (something of a false start, this young man, who solves his problems and ceases to interest the narrator), now allows the past to enter like a fourth dimension within an absolute unity of time, from which the ineptitude of the psychological flashback is rigorously excluded for formal and aesthetic reasons. I would be willing to argue that we do not like to shift textual levels, and are most reluctant to shift reading gears in order to scan interpolated texts and lengthy quotations inserted like a foreign body into unrelated discourse. How Gide's interpolation, which spans three chapters and some fifty pages, negotiates this particular reef is then a crucial issue, although the remarkable timing with which Gide deploys it and knows when to break it off is as much a matter of tact as anything else. That longer reading was, however, prepared by a briefer rereading of his own journal by Edouard himself, on the boat-train returning to Paris. That his own voice – that of a major, if not the principal, protagonist – prolongs the second installment of the journal read by Bernard is surely not without its relationship to the smoothness of the transition, the relatively painless immersion in the newer textual level. Emerging from it, however, is the matter of the great narrative peripeties: guilty interruptions, eavesdropping behind doors followed by dramatic entries – the stuff of melodrama which can here exceptionally be reinvented, in a non-melodramatic way, on the occasion of multi-levelled textual reflexivity. Meanwhile, once the deeper conspiratorial network is laid in place that unites all these destinies without the full knowledge of any single one of them, the more conventional chance meetings, accounts of yet further chance meetings, forecasts, projected trajectories through the city that are bound to cross other pathways we already know of, along with the finding of abandoned notes and the overhearing of secret instructions – all these well-worn devices now serve to lift and rotate the gleaming polyhedron of the new form before our eyes in ways that confirm it as a unified object and exhibit the unforeseeable glitter of its unexpected facets.

It will have thereby become clear that however film expects to achieve analogous effects, it cannot do so simply by finding and matching simple filmic equivalents to these textual ones of reading and its inner analogues. The reason has already been indicated in passing, and it is not a consequence of the deficiencies of film as a medium but rather of its superiority to narrative language in any number of representational ways. Winner loses: what makes up the plenitude of the filmic image at any instant in its narrative trajectory also secures in advance, without any supplementary work, the sheer fact of transition. The novel, and language itself – the fundamental property of which is lack and a deployment of essentially absent objects – had to do a great deal of energetic footwork to crosswire its plots in a plausible yet properly unexpected manner. Mesmerized by the shift to a new series of filmic images, no less full and absorbing than the preceding ones, the viewer of film is only feebly tempted to raise the ever fainter question of the motivation for such transitions. Difference here in the visual and in film only too effortlessly relates: but form has to be felt as the solution to an intractable form-problem. Indeed, Eisenstein's theory and practice of montage can be instructively estranged and reread, not as a solution to certain already existing problems of filmic narration, but as a stubborn attempt to produce the problems as such in all their aesthetic and ontological severity – problems for which his own conception of montage was then only too ready and willing to provide a henceforth satisfying 'solution'.

Terrorizer achieves, or reinvents, something of this by way of unique temporal overlaps that reach their climax at the end of the film, like vibrations separated from each other in time that gradually become simultaneous. The overlaps are then fastened together, one does not want to say with Lacanian tacking nails exactly, but by recurrent leitmotifs for which this term, redolent of Wagner or Thomas Mann, is also a little too modernist-traditional; let's call these,

Terrorizer

which look like images but serve as crossroads and roundhouses of various kinds, reversible signifiers. Two of these signifiers – the gas tank and the barking dog – become inscribed in the opening sequence (but like all true repetition, do not take on their functionality, their dreary sense of only too predictable familiarity, until that second time, which, for repetition as a phenomenon, is really always a first).

The shoot-out, as we have said, is not important in itself, but rather serves as a detonator for the other plot lines. What is more significant is that it takes place at first light, that first vacancy of the city in early morning which will gradually be filled in by characters, business, and routines of all kinds. Violent death first thing in the morning; we don't know whose the body is, except that it is the pretext for the young photographer to look for a scoop, and the occasion for him to glimpse the White Chick as she climbs out a balcony window and injures her leg. At that point, as the camera sets off to follow her flight, we reach another reversible signifier, a somehow less reified one, since it enfolds relationships rather than a static thing in a recurrent static place. This is the zebra crossing at which she collapses, but which will then accompany a shot of her legs at various stages of her recovery, framed by crutches, and then healed again and jaunty, ready to go about her predatory business.

The sirens may include the ambulance that takes her away, but they certainly include the police vans, which give us a glimpse of Taipei's morning rush hour at high tide, and also intersect another plot line as their wail rises to the apartment in which the doctor, Li Li-chung, can be observed about his stretching exercises on the balcony. (In another moment, we will see him also driving to work in the morning traffic, perhaps passing the police-car carrying his childhood friend away from the incident, perhaps crossing the Eurasian girl's ambulance on

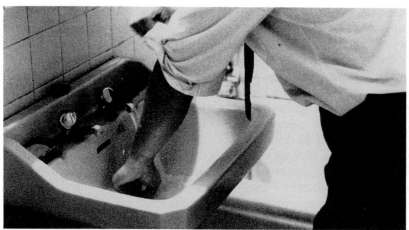

Terrorizer

its way to the hospital.) The doctor's immediate superior has just died; he stands in line for advancement and is full of high hopes, particularly since he has taken the trouble to denounce the malpractice of his only rival (otherwise or hitherto, a friend and colleague). He also has marital problems; his wife's writing block (of which we have spoken) makes life at home unpleasant, as she wonders whether she should not go back to work at her old job in the publishing house (run by a former lover, with whom she promptly renews the affair) and, indeed, whether she should not leave her husband altogether (something she does later on that same day).

Meanwhile, something of Li Li-chung's character is conveyed by yet another signifier, the motif of his compulsive handwashing, which is accomplished in well-nigh surgical fashion (scrubbing all the way up the lower arm) and only gradually, with repetition, transformed into a mania re-enacted with every new entry into an interior space (his own apartment, that of others, hotel rooms, workplace), betokening his extraordinary inner insecurity or 'inferiority complex'. The handwashing thus comes to stand for the problematic balance between public and private (career and marriage, job and home) and will eventually participate in something even more dramatic, as we shall see.

The hour of repetition meanwhile sounds for the scene of the crime, when the would-be paparazzo, time weighing heavily on his hands, decides to rent and inhabit the now-empty murder apartment. Now we see the gas-tank in all its splendor (a well-known Taipei eyesore about whose dangerous emplacement in the midst of a heavily residential area there has been much public debate).[7] Everything stylistically extraordinary about *Terrorizer* is already concentrated in this initial geographical move and choice of urban setting – the brilliant color of a dramatic shape which is also a depressing sign of urban squalor, a science-fictional profile associated with the humdrum misery of lower middle-class life. Something like a structural inversion of magic realism is to be found here, in this utterly non-magical and unsurrealistic photographic transformation of urban detail into solid colors whose stunning combinations are somehow chilled by the perfection of the technological apparatus and strike the viewer with that distance and coldness already mentioned.

Here also, the barking dog: in Taiwan, city dogs are often kept in cages, which makes for something of an auditory leitmotif. This one binds us into a recurrent space (it will later on be visited by the novelist as a result of her 'anonymous phone call') and, at least subliminally, begins to sensitize us to the situation of imprisonment, which will undergo a remarkable phenomenological transformation in the course of this particular film. Indeed, it has already begun to do its work of identification and association (the interiors of dwellings are the same as prison cells) in the motive for the move itself. For another domestic quarrel, first thing in the morning, is also virtually simultaneous with the shoot-out and Li Li-chung's exercises – it is the breakup of the photographer and his girlfriend, who appreciates the photos of the Eurasian girl even less than the early morning sorties after fire engines and the like. The older apartment is sealed within blowing curtains; the boyfriend's films and stills are trashed (as in earlier representation of the medias); she throws him out and tries to commit suicide, being rushed to a hospital in a way that does not particularly generate sympathy for her, but raises all kinds of *nouveau-roman* questions – is it the same hospital that Li Li-chung himself works in; was the White Chick treated here as well; what is the meaning of this kind of urban simultaneity in the multinational system today, in which it evidently has a rather different effect than

Terrorizer

the great village network constructed by the paths of Joyce's characters through familiar downtown sites in *Ulysses*?

As for the photographer, it should be noted that he shares with all the other characters what may be described as a time of dead transition, a temporality, not so much of waiting as of dully sitting it out. The doctor waiting for his promotion, his writer-spouse waiting for inspiration, or else to change her life completely, the White Chick waiting for her leg to heal and the cast to come off – such characters are peculiarly condemned to a marking of time that lacks joyousness or eager anticipation, because (paradoxically in the first two cases) the outcome is not particularly appetizing, something assuredly also the case for the young photographer since he is merely waiting to do his military service. All this for him is mere interim, a peculiar furlough from life; and his emotional life is thereby equally affected, as witness the whim of a fantasy-life in the drug dealer's apartment, or even the passion for the White Chick herself, whose enormously enlarged photographic image is hung in segments on the apartment wall, in the hermetically sealed space of what is used as a darkroom, beyond the world and beyond Taipei.

At this point, then, what begins to focus our attention and our curiosity is no longer the simultaneity of the four independent plot strands (the doctor, the writer, the photographer, the Eurasian girl), so much as how they can eventually be expected to intersect and intertwine in that tying up of knots which is fully as much an implicit formal expectation of this practice of multiple plots as is their significantly named *dénouement*. In *Terrorizer*, however, what may be called the event of the narrative *vinculum* is repeated on two levels virtually simultaneously, in a superposition that makes it realist and modernist all at once: rehearsing the great realist trope of authorial omniscience (what we see along with the author while the characters

Terrorizer

themselves remain ignorant) and then trumping it with the auto-reflexivity characteristic of the modernist period as one of its obsessive thematic and formal mannerisms. For the Eurasian girl in her literal confinement (the mother locks her in when she goes out at night to work) begins to make phone calls with greater and greater abandon, picking names out of the phone book and inventing nasty stories to tell the unknown people who pick up on the other end. Presumably, for Edward Yang, this media equivalent of the poison-pen letter (dear to the classical English detective story and a kind of symbol of what most unerringly undermines the calm of tribal or village social relations) entitles her to the eponymous characterization more strongly than anything associated with garden-variety prostitution or murder. It marks a peculiar intensity of *ressentiment* which is surely not unrelated to her socially marginal status and to the exclusion of half-breeds from traditional Chinese society (as from most other traditional societies). In the present context, however, it is just as significant that the genes mark the presence of American servicemen and the American empire in this hitherto Japanese colony, only recently recolonized by the mainland KMT. That side of colonization has been extensively dramatized by Hou Hsaio-hsien, particularly in *A City of Sadness*, while the US's residual effects have been more openly registered in Edward Yang's work, particularly in the recent, and significantly titled (after Elvis), *A Brighter Summer Day*.

One of these venomous, but anonymous, fictional shafts strikes the writer Chou Yufen, who thinks she has learned about her husband's adulteries, and feels herself thereby all the more empowered to go about her own independent life. Indeed, as in a peculiarly reversible toxin, this one also liberates her from her writer's block and sets her working again. Finally, the interrupted phone call had advised her, for further information, to visit an address which is none other than the murder apartment. Here, as we know, the photographer has now taken up abode, and here the White Chick will also slowly make her way, since she still has the key and is feverish and desperate after the catastrophic outcome of her attempt at free-lance prostitution (undertaken when her leg is healed and she can finally escape her mother's jail sentence).

What kicks these interesting coincidences up another level into a more reflexive kind of story-telling discourse – as I have already indicated, their equivalents can be traced all the way back to the Greek novel, via *Tom Jones* and any number of other classical adventure or picaresque texts – is obviously the redoubling of the narrative in written form, *en abysme*, as my references to Gide will already have begun to foretell. The reader will indeed scarcely be surprised to learn that the story Chou Yufen has finally been freed to write is a kind of modified alternate world in which her husband has an affair with someone not terribly unlike the White Chick herself, and in which a wife, who is a writer, is thereby freed to write another story, one which in real life wins her a prize and catapults her onto the cultural page of the major newspapers, not to speak of the television screen. But this puts a very different face on narrative coincidence, which it now refashions, as from over a great distance, into patterns and shapes as abstract as the traces of mound-builders' culture seen from a satellite or the Himalayas seen from the moon. From an intention to reunite and reassemble, which can at best be attributed to Providence (when such a concept is available), the narrative intersections become reformed into demiurgic games played by the aesthetic great Other of Romantic Irony (aesthetics now here, for the moderns as well as the Romantics, coming to replace fate, chance, and ethics). Equally clearly, however, this quintessentially modernist turn and flavor is all the more identifiable as such because it brings into the postmodern context an old-fashioned note, which can be charming or jarring indifferently, depending on whether the ambitions of modern form bring some relief from postmodern frivolity, or on the other hand, whether the implacable ideological stress of the modern on the aestheticality of life and on the implicit but inescapable role of the individual genius are now felt by us to be relatively intolerable. (Later on, however, I will show that yet a third reading or interpretation of *Terrorizer* is conceivable, which can be called on to dispel the modernist appearance in its turn and reaffirm the film's post-contemporaneous relevance, if not exactly its postmodernity.)

Even if for a moment we retain the modernist framework that Chou Yufen's novella establishes, it should be added that its transmission by way of the medium of film seriously problematizes the modernist effects that should accompany it, or at the very least renders them optional in what we will later on see to be a postmodern way. Nothing is more alien to this particular film, indeed, than the mystical-modernist overtones of the theme of inspiration from without, as when, in Cocteau's film of the same name, Orpheus copies down his poetry from enigmatic messages transmitted over the car radio like Resistance code broadcasts ('les carottes sont cuites, trois fois!') Nor is the book itself (of which, in its previous incarnation, we have only heard a few vapid samples of nature lyricism) anything like an *I Ching*, which, as in Dick's *Man in the High Castle*, one consults for forecasts of individual and collective history alike. For one thing it is not clear who in the film has actually read this prize-winning production: the photographer and the girlfriend (with whom he is eventually reunited) hear about it on television and then read a summary in the newspaper. As for her most important reader (or so one would have thought), the husband doesn't read in the first place – something of an index to his general mentality, as the following snatch of dialogue suggests:

Hospital Director (with some suspicion): What does your wife do exactly? What are these things she writes anyway?
Li Li-chung (evasively): Oh, I don't know. I don't read novels.

The novel thereby comes before us, not as an object or an alternate world or narrative, but rather as a peculiarly disembodied effect, with all the reality and objectivity of sheer appearance. It is Error made real and become flesh; it is, as it were, the image-for-the-other, the simulacrum or at least someone else's simulacrum, since the viewer never apprehends it directly but only by way of the judgments of the other characters (in this case the photographer, who recognizes the writer's picture as his mysterious visitor and suddenly grasps all this as the machinations of his equally mysterious Eurasian acquaintance). If now, however, we reposition this particular effect within what we might as well call the Hansen-Bordwell hypothesis,[8] writing at once takes on the status of one medium among others, competing for power and prestige with the more modern technologies of photography, of sound transmission (here the telephone, although more normally the radio), and finally of film itself. It should be evident that though Yang's movie camera retains the ultimate priority over all the other media – if only by virtue of the fact that they are necessarily represented within it – it nonetheless plays fair, and endows each of them with a specific power not ordinarily thought to be consistent with cinema as such.

For photography within film seems to retain what Benjamin might have called an archaic aura, a dimly threatening primitive power, as when stills of the murder victims silently circulate among the police team, who thereby *see* and are present in ways denied the movie-goer

Orphée

Terrorizer

even when the still is flashed on the screen for us in passing. In *Terrorizer*, to be sure, the photographer proves to be an idle rich youth with a hobby, and the emphasis is placed as much on the cash-value of his various cameras as on the quality of his images – save for the one mesmerizing shot of the White Chick peering fearfully around a corner, unaware that she is in the process of being seen and recorded. This is then the magnified image, three times greater than life and developed in segments of glossy prints, that will greet her eyes as she returns to the murder room: an allegory of film itself? Perhaps: but if so, only because, like the punctum in the fatal photographs in Antonioni's *Blow-up*, and unlike Rimbaud's magical flowers or Lacan's signifiers, this one does not look back at you. Here the wind that blows through the great trees in Antonioni's park only mildly lifts and ruffles the segments of the portrait. Photography's prestige here is to be equal to the simulacrum and more interesting than the reality, but otherwise little more than a way of killing time.[9]

Perhaps we need to drive a wedge more dramatically between the senses after the great synaesthesias of the modern period, and to restore some of the liberating freshness and horror of the auditory image in a society that has become one immense collection of visual spectacles.[10] Is this then finally perhaps the deeper meaning of the

141

The Parallax View

sequence whereby *Blow-up*'s postmodern sequels – De Palma's *Blow Out* (1981) and Coppola's *The Conversation* (1974) – transfer the visible clue to the realm of sound: the unconscious, Utopian longing to be awakened from the spell of images, and to be awakened by sounds as piercing as shots or whispers? The White Chick is at any rate a good deal more threatening on the phone than in her image; and the spider's nest of anonymous phone calls all over the city has rarely offered so vivid a figure for urban simultaneity, but also for the misery of confinement and powerlessness. Like Stalin or Hitler in their offices, it is hard to tell supreme power from house arrest; and something of the mystery of the definitive embodiment of psychic resources in technology – what was human reality like before the telephone, before the photograph, before the mirror? – is here recovered from the forgetfulness into which the triumph of these media plunges Being itself. But telephonic relief also returns us to the specific form of organization of this particular city, as we shall see in conclusion.

As for literature, it surely fares least well of all modes we have come to recognize as mediatic. Wrong on all counts, a vehicle for narcissism and self-pity, and for the shabby pride of commercialized prizes, it is a pitiful cultural alibi in the destiny of this most ancient of all literate civilizations on its way to televisuality like everybody else. Significantly, here alone television rears its garish competing likenesses. In this rivalry between the arts and media (which film is in any case slated to win in advance), it is important that the small screen humiliate high culture, but not enter into too distracting a juxtaposition with film, whose brilliant capacities are here so extraordinarily rehearsed. (In the era of video, someone once remarked, film recovers that aura which Benjamin had denied it in the era of its undisputed technological mastery. Is this not to say that there is something slightly old-fashioned today about the exercise of bravura cinematography, which is here in any case, as I've already observed, an icy mastery?)

All of which marks something like the content of the form; and it is important, in my opinion, to be clear about the competing interpretations that force their way through even to this level and persist in their struggle for it. The features we have just evoked, which reach their thematic climax with the novella and its relationship to a world already structured by the other media, can all be read in conjunction as a vivid contemporary replay of that modern-romantic topos of art and life, fiction and reality, the dream world, illusion and what it transfigures. Indeed, *Terrorizer* would helpfully bring all that up to date and place such topics back on a post-contemporary agenda. Yet such a reading turns the film back into a set of conceptual 'themes' or meanings, into a vehicle for certain thoughts or reflections, or for a kind of philosophy of life — rather old-fashioned commodities in the

Blow-Up

universal sway of positivism and 'cynical reason', and of the 'end' of just such 'ideologies'. To this technocratization of philosophy then corresponds the transformation of the genres into the media, along with the emergence of readings such as the one alternately sketched above (in which the deeper subject of the film allegedly consists in its articulated rivalry with competing media). It is a Gestalt alternation we will observe on other levels (and in particular on that of the 'form of the content'), about which it is perhaps most productive to use it for a degree of historical self-knowledge, and to observe the plausibility with which each option comes before us. The deeper 'meaning' of the film, in that case, would not lie in either interpretation but in our hesitation between both.

As for the psychic content of the work, that constructed effect – that 'unspeakable' narrative or filmic 'sentence' whereby a structure of synchronous monadic simultaneities seems to demand embodiment in someone's experience, if only in that of God himself – is now, with the final looping of the knots, ever more suggestively passed off as this or that subjective experience. The shock we may attribute to the Eurasian girl is just such a formal 'objective correlative': for it releases the multitudinous occult traditions of the *Doppelgänger* and its putative terrors – myself striding forth to meet me at midday! – at the same time that it mobilizes a whole contemporary philosophy of the Look (from Sartre on down) and endows me with an external being that is alien to me, but to which I am also condemned. The association of these motifs with narrative – and not only with narrative, but with a reflexive positing of narrative, in which, in writers like Gide, it is less important to produce a plot than to produce the Idea of plot itself, as an object in its own right that, absent totality, gradually disengages itself from all its local manifestations and hovers above the completed work as its visionary mirror-image in the realm of objective spirit – now has the advantage of dispelling philosophical or theosophic connotations. For the experience is as simple as it is unsettling: others have been thinking about me whose existences I was not even aware of! At the level of urban simultaneities on which we now find ourselves, this – what are you doing with my picture? – is a virtual *cogito*, the punctual other end of all those mutually exclusive synchronicities. It is a paradox that will then, from now until the final image, continue to be turned inside out ceaselessly like Benjamin's famous socks.[11] Its sharpness is intensified by Chou Yufen's blissful ignorance of the origins in other, unknown people of the story she believes to be autographical; while Li Li-chung's knowledge (the photographer 'puts him in the picture' and shows him the photos) is as numbing a form of distraction as his other worries and as unproductive, leading to what may be called externalized or 'foreclosed'[12] impersonal hallucinations, rather than to any shocked presentiment of unexpected worlds beyond his own.

144

Terrorizer

It is to be sure about Li Li-chung's experience and about his psyche that *Terrorizer* raises the most durable questions. In this polyvocal film without a hero, nonetheless a certain priority seems to be afforded gradually to this figure, whose destiny promises to hold the key to interpretation most reliably as the action draws to a close. But it may be a broken promise: to be sure, Li Li-chung loses out on his promotion, as we might have guessed; and as we know, he loses his wife as well. In both cases he tries aimlessly to salvage the situation, with clumsy efforts that confirm our initial impression of this character as the quintessential loser – something we can tell virtually from his very first appearance, doing exercises on his balcony (although I would be hard put to say why or how). I've suggested that we can have little personal sympathy for him (a remark about which there can be nothing 'personal', since it also holds for all the other characters as well). Yet his destiny can awaken a certain impersonal sadness, and it is this which marks, I believe, the allegorical investment in the figure of Li Li-chung who, more than any of the other characters (the traditional policeman, the Western-style modernist writer, specimens of a timeless *jeunesse dorée*, lumpens who have their equivalent in every urban center on the globe), can best serve as evidence for an unconscious (and collective) meditation on dependency, that is to say, on the positioning of the national entity within the new world system of late capitalism.

As a technocrat and a bureaucratized professional indeed, Li Li-chung is well-placed to offer figuration to the 'national allegory'[13] of a post-Third-World country that can never really join the First World (in the sense of capital export and of becoming a new center of the world system, its destiny conceivable only as a structural satellite of Japan or the US). His 'brilliant career' is significantly accompanied, not by dramatic and tragic failures, but by prospects which, even if successful, are not likely to modify the dreariness of his current prosperity in any marked qualitative way. One does not, in other words, foresee a more gratifying continuation of his marriage, nor, if the other bureaucrats are any indication, would the coveted promotion be likely to transform him, in a thunder-clap, in his very being. This – the joylessness of good fortune in the global bureaucratic system – is perhaps the new face of a dependency most often dramatized in terms of tendential impoverishment and the 'development of underdevelopment'. This is, as it were, the gentrified dimension of a postmodernity whose flip side is neo-poverty and 'homelessness' and a whole new attitude towards urban space also registered in this film in original ways.

From the class standpoint indeed, in a developing or underdeveloped country, the fate of the petty bourgeoisie (in this stage, a new petty bourgeoisie or professional-managerial segment of bureaucrats and formerly independent professionals) seems to be more generally emblematic of the fate of the nation or the collectivity, at least in the popular imagination. Balzac, who wrote in a roughly comparable period of France's development, often projects his petty bourgeois figures in this way, as allegories of the national misery. It is as though the rich and successful (in our time, multinational success stories) are lucky in some private and non-generalizable way; while the poor – particularly agricultural and manual workers – are already universally exploited anyway and can scarcely be allegorical of anything save of the perennity of class struggle itself. In some situations, to be sure, *lumpens* – as in the picaros of the Spanish Golden Age – can also be allegorical of the nation; while the sadness we have attributed to the figure of Li Li-chung can be thought to include all the mixed feelings attributable to the developing Third World. He could not be allegorical of Taiwan exactly as such, for there are many other unique determinants of that special situation that are omitted from his story, but it may at least be permitted to see his fate as a figural acting out of fantasies about the limits to Taiwanese development in a world system. What such an interpretation does to the potential universality of such a narrative, and in particular to its relevance for and reception by First-World audiences, will be the topic of a concluding reflection.

But it would be a mistake to assimilate 'national allegory' in this new postmodern sense to the traditional or stereotypical view of this structure as a supremely static and mechanical one, in which cut-and-dried meanings are paired off one by one with equally cut-and-dried features or aspects of the narrative situation and its components. There is in post-contemporary allegory a kind of inner self-transcending dynamic for which even the older word 'reflexive' is too weak. It is rather a self-regulating transformation of such organisms under their own momentum, in which initial figures are ceaselessly and dialectically modified by virtue of the very fact that in them the

Terrorizer

problem of representation is itself already thematized, and must therefore produce and re-produce itself in a variety of new guises and levels.

So here the seemingly colorless drama of Li Li-chung develops in unforeseeably dramatic ways which would seem to have little enough to do with the revelation of the story within a story, the anonymous interventions and self-reflexive modernist and conspiratorial rewritings, that were the burden of his wife's narrative line. Those come only to compound the doctor's general confusion and to separate him, in his dejection, even more completely from real life. There follows what is surely one of the most astonishing scenes in recent cinema, in which Li Li-chung revisits his childhood friend the policeman and makes a remarkable announcement. Beaming with joy, he explains that he has finally won his promotion; and that he has also been able to come to terms successfully with his wife's departure and to realize that he is better off without her; that he is a happy man at last – successful, at peace with himself, fulfilled. The gestural and physiognomic euphoria with which these falsehoods are conveyed transcends the usual signs or tics of mendacity or simple lying (if only because we can see no point to the deception, so that our own confusion washes back over the effect to intensify it). It is difficult to convey the terrible joy, the radiantly false happiness, that streams in effulgence from the ghastly smile of a character who has rarely smiled before and with whom we have come to associate the furrowed brow of an essentially plodding man meeting his difficulties with uniform perplexity and without skill. The heightened expression, not registered in close-up, is projected off the screen in a way only comparable (although the content is altogether different) to that supreme *oeillade* in *Mr Arkadin* (Welles, 1955), in which the zoom shot of the bearded

Welles' sharp return look shows that he knows, and that he knows we know, and so forth: *supreme* being indeed the climactic word one wants for this kind of thing in which the event pulls itself up by its own pigtail onto a higher, formally transcendent level.

As for Li Li-chung's 'supreme' happiness, however, modernist readings can still be imagined for it, as in the Nietzschean-fictional suggestion that under certain circumstances the acting out of alternative, unrealized possibilities – sealed by my celebration with the 'elder brother,' the ritual of festive eating and drinking, enjoyment of my new esteem, having lived up to expectations at last – might be as satisfying, perhaps more fully satisfying, than the reality. The interpretation in terms of life and art would here continue to find corroboration and plausibility, but should be complemented by its own alternative possibility in a reading of what I will only for convenience's sake call a relatively more postmodern type. After all, in retrospect, one of the fundamental signs and symptoms of an impending change in our mode of thinking consisted in the increasing dissatisfaction with what I have elsewhere called the 'depth model'[14] – in this case, the opposition between life and fiction modelled roughly on some notion of a reality behind or opposed to an appearance. What took the place of that appearance-and-reality model was something variously characterized in terms of textuality or of practices, a conception of the succession of various surfaces none of which was somehow metaphysically or ontologically privileged over the other. But that Li Li-chung's fictional or unreal alternate life can also be seen and read in this second way a remarkable series of multiple and mutually exclusive *dénouements* will now show.

For in another early-morning sequence, after their late-night celebration, the husband-physician awakens in the policeman's house and removes the sleeping man's revolver; assassinates the hospital director on his way to work; and then, breaking into his wife's lover's apartment, shoots the latter in gruesome execution style. Unable to

Terrorizer

Terrorizer

do the same for his wife, he stations himself instead in the crowded downtown area in which we have seen the White Chick pick up her victims, and waits for her, presumably because he has seen her photograph and has decided to hold her responsible for all his troubles. But by now we know that both of these hitherto absolutely unrelated characters are very dangerous indeed. The final plot loop, whether involving sexual intercourse or murder, is a putative climax of great tension and instability, whose narrative satisfactions, even granting the tying up of the last remaining threads, are no longer clear. But now time runs more swiftly: the policeman wakes suddenly; the pimp who in classical fashion follows the couple down the hotel corridor unexpectedly finds himself locked out of the room; the police come pounding down the hall; and at the same moment we observe the protagonist characteristically, preparatory to anything else, begin to wash his hands extensively one final time. But this time the motif has been activated: the liquid splashing out of the faucet coincides with the splintering of the hotel-room door as the police break in. What results however is the splattering of blood and brain tissue over a different wall, in a different space, as Li Li-chung shoots himself in the early morning in the bathhouse of his friend's building; at which point the wife suddenly wakes up in her lover's flat, staring with wide eyes at an unidentified premonition.

It will have been obvious, from all the conventional aesthetic signals we well as from whatever vantage-point common sense itself decides to take the thing, that the preceding sequence was a fantasy or wish-fulfillment of some kind. Nor do I mean to argue against the obvious; but rather, to urge the return of a certain indecidability to the sequence itself, whose remarkable loop – the water faucet reappearing with all the portentous formal significance of Freud's *Nach-*

träglichkeit (retroactivation or 'deferred action', the childhood trauma activated by puberty) – arrests us in its own right by its striking narrative temporality, without our being able to determine the presence of any specific content or message. It is rather a kind of prestidigitation in which we watch the abstract fillip of the form itself, and are thereby distracted from the content, and in particular released from the tiresome (realistic) obligation of deciding whether it is supposed to be real or just another dream sequence.

Indeed, this multiple ending is in my opinion very delicately balanced, carefully arranged so that such decisions can be eluded, if not avoided altogether. Its skillfulness cannot really be appreciated unless we are willing to acknowledge how tiresome the interpolation form of the flash-back or the fantasy has become in recent years. They were staples of the older cinema, and knew a kind of Indian Summer in the era of film noir, immediately after World War II (and immediately before the wide screen, the end of Hollywood, and the senescence of realism itself). The framed narrative has always carried the message of fate, of sealed destinies, of events now gone irredeemably into the past. The interpolated filmic (and less often, literary) daydream also probably served to reinforce the sense of imprisonment in a current situation; indeed, if Bierce's 'Occurrence at Owl Creek Bridge' (filmed by Robert Enrico, 1962) can be taken as the fusion and synthesis of both, their symbolic value – in the instants before a capital execution – becomes dramatically explicit. Stylized revivals of the technique – as in Gilliam's *Brazil* (1985) – would seem even more explicitly to enlist the unreal interpolated narrative segment in order to drive home the collective imprisonment of a *1984*-type society. But for post-contemporary viewers, the traditional frame, which asks us to leave the present, to which predictably we will return only at the end of the film – as, for example, in *Le Jour se lève* (Marcel Carné, 1939) – is evidently irritating in direct proportion to our systemic commitment to a postmodern present; while the Hollywood fantasy narrative vainly tries to substitute alternate reality satisfactions in ways that make us equally impatient.

The alternate endings of *Terrorizer*, however, do not require heavy subjectification. The film is over too fast, and its polyphony, the multiplicity of protagonists, leave it entangled with their destinies in ways impossible to sort out (our last view of the Eurasian girl is *within* the fantasy-sequence, for example, which thereby continues to carry a certain informational authority). Meanwhile, if it was fantasy, the embarrassing question arises insistently as to whose fantasy it will finally have been? The argument can indeed equally forcefully be made[15] that it is Chou Yufen's fantasy rather than the husband's daydream filled with passionate exhalations of revenge (as we have seen, he is not a particularly passionate character, while the details of the White Chick's modus operandi cannot have been known to him either). What this marks is the modernist interpretive temptation, the urge to tie up the threads by locking it all back into identifiable subjectivities and points of view. The 'postmodern' alternative that immediately proposes itself is then clearly what springs into view when subjects are abolished as meaningful categories (or if you prefer, when the hold of philosophies of the subject are significantly weakened). This alternative is the aesthetic of textuality or of interminable segmentation, in which we are at equal distance from all successive sequences, and the whole begins to offer itself as an immense set of variations or recombinations, as in the *nouveau roman* or Robbe-Grillet's accompanying filmic production. But this temptation has been carefully conjured as well. If a certain period aestheticism clung to the modernist (and Gidean) theme of the *mise en abysme* of the story within a story, a far more contemporary but still relatively archaic 60s aestheticism surely informs this kind of permutational free play, and it is evidently not at all the note we wished for in conclusion to this particular film.

What we must admire, therefore, is the way in which the filmmaker has arranged for these two powerful interpretive temptations – the modern and the postmodern, subjectivity and textuality – to neutralize each other, to hold each other in one long suspension in such a way that the film can exploit and draw on the benefits of both, without having to commit itself to either as some definitive reading, or as some definitive formal and stylistic category. Besides Edward Yang's evident personal mastery, the possibility of this kind of mutually reinforcing suspension may owe something to the situation of Third-World cinema itself, in traditions in which neither modernist nor postmodern impulses are internally generated, so that both arrive in the field of production with a certain chronological simultaneity in full post-war modernization. *Terrorizer* thereby enjoys the freedom of a certain distance from both, the advantages of which, indeed, it has been the burden of this chapter to explore.

But in conclusion it is worth taking this alternation and co-existence of readings and competing interpretations even further, and attempting to appreciate the way everything changes if, for the masculine pathos of Li Li-chung's story, we substitute the rather different drama of the women figures as the film's fundamental center of gravity. To see this as a film about women's destinies – whether it can be argued to be a properly feminist film I cannot judge – is to assert a certain postmodernity about it, to the degree that the women's situations here are grasped and articulated as fundamentally spatial. The male figures – doctor and photographer alike – are wrapped up in their temporal destinies. Success or failure still hang over them like the category of the future itself, some immense moon that can still make you happy or miserable. Meanwhile, as males, they are spatially more mobile, and can also console themselves with public areas,

Terrorizer

whether the police station, the hospital or the streets themselves.

But the women's spaces are essentially spaces of confinement: the one form of public space open to the novelist is the television screen itself, scarcely a space to stretch or relax in. Archetypal here is, of course, the confinement of the Eurasian girl, locked up in her mother's apartment, as though it were not bad enough to be condemned to crutches. Indeed, even more intolerable for this adolescent is the way in which, in the apartment, she is imprisoned in her mother's 50s' past, a past in which the mother is herself equally imprisoned, to the tune of 'Smoke Gets in Your Eyes'. Our significant first view of the girl had been her desperate escape from the confinement of the murder apartment; while, equally significant, her time of greatest physical mobility is a frustrating night-long bus ride back and forth across Taipei in a feverish state of exhaustion and collapse. Nor does it, finally, seem inappropriate to observe that her principal work-place, as it were, is not a public one, as with the men, but rather the quintessential anonymous hotel room, always the same, in which the self-same drama of theft, violence and blackmail is played out over and over again.

But this is not a unique situation in this particular film, as witness the photographer's girlfriend, equally imprisoned in something which remains *his* room and *his* apartment, even after he removes his pictures, the blowing curtains sealing off this now abandoned space from the street and the out-of-doors in what is a virtual minor leit-motif.

Nor is it clear that the writer's far more sumptuous apartment is any less constricting: 'my world is shrinking', she literally tells her former lover. The semi-traditional rugs and furniture are to be sure wonderful occasions for catching the change of light, one of the fundamental concerns of this intensely visual and photographic film. Meanwhile, the bathroom, in which notoriously her doctor-husband washes his hands on his return from work, is suffused with a yellow glow virtually marked out as his symbolic color. (We meet it again in a stunning sequence in the hospital as he mounts the stairs into a sea of yellow light; it may therefore be taken as an essentially artificial color, associated with modernization.) But the far more open and airlit space of the rest of the apartment, associated with Chou Yufen – a kind of yuppie or professional space, not unrelated to the even more expensive family villa of the young photographer (with pool and maid) – is not a great deal more positive. It is a kind of dead space, filled with elegant unused furniture which is there primarily to be turned into images. And from it, just as clearly as the Eurasian girl from her locked apartment, Chou Yufen is equally necessarily driven to escape.

That modernism is temporal and postmodernism spatial has often been affirmed, while the spatiality of *Terrorizer* and its images is inescapable. But I would like to insist on a unique feature of the spatiality of this film: the insistent relationship it establishes between the individual space and the city as a whole. The women's dramas are thus spatial, not only because they are somehow postmodern (although the characterization of postmodernity in terms of the new social movements in general and of feminism in particular is a widespread one), but also and above all because they are urban, and even more because they are articulated within this particular city.

Terrorizer is indeed very much a film about urban space in general, and offers something like an anthology of enclosed dwellings, whether apartments or individual rooms. It is these that predominate, and that are reconfirmed by the punctuation of an occasional street scene which always tends to return us to the aerial perspective, the view from above, the glance down from the balcony, and thus implicitly the confinement to the apartment on the upper storey. The zero degree of this dwelling space would then be constituted by the murder room, as it is sealed off into darkness by the photographer: the act thereby betraying the essential characteristic of all these dwelling spaces, which function as cubicles that open onto the city and the street in one way or another, and which are somehow incomplete and spatially parasitic upon it. Only the hotel room of the Eurasian girl is somehow buried away in space, beyond the city somewhere; while the underworld, redolent of the 'mystères' of the classical nineteenth-century cities and melodramas, finds itself here reduced to a housing unit that gets repaired and repainted and only coincidentally re-

rented to someone who remembers what happened in it.

Taipei is thus mapped and configured as a superimposed set of boxed dwelling spaces in which the characters are all in one way or another confined. The film thereby acknowledges what seems to distinguish it from both traditional and modern Chinese cities on the mainland, as well as from the cultural and historical styles of other cities in East Asia – a rapid construction of buildings along both sides of great linear arteries which are somehow its central formal category. The apartments do not imply the formal centrality of a single building to which they belong (as belatedly and extraordinarily in Perec's novel *La vie: mode d'emploi*, about an apartment house). Nor do they offer the kind of panorama one experiences in Jesus Diaz' film, *Lejania*: interiors into which Miami is projected by way of home movies and videotapes; a roof-top from which Havana as a whole is viewed spread out around us; and finally the real streets into which the protagonist, on the point of asphyxiation, manages to escape (but in this Second-World film, the streets are still a genuinely public space, the space of the collective social project).

The dominant First-World experience of the post-contemporary city is surely that of gentrification, and of dead monuments about which it is no longer clear that they can be called public, but which are just as surely no longer private either; while what lies outside the gentrified zones is coming to be acknowledged as a new Third-World space within the First-World city. As for properly Third-World urban representations, all that can be conjectured as a minimal generalization is perhaps the now conventional form of the peasant as witness, the narrative point of view of the villager seeing the metropolis for the first time.

None of which seems to me comparable to this inscription of Taipei, which is also, as has already been observed, dialectically distinct from Hou Hsaio-hsien's images of the Taiwanese countryside. A foreigner and an outsider may be permitted to wonder whether this way of looking at urban experience does not have something to do with the 'representation of totality' of a small island which is also a non-national nation state. The enclosed spaces in their range and variety thereby figure or embody the unevenness or inequality of the world system: from the most *traditional* kind of space – paradoxically or not, that is the barracks apartment of the policeman (and it cannot be without significance that the protagonist, after washing his hands in so many modern and anonymous Western-style bathrooms, should kill himself in what is a very traditional-looking hot bath and hot-tub-sauna type area) – all the way to the *national* space of the hospital, the *multinational* space of the publisher's office (the media, surely of a global range, now housed in a great glass high-rise) and what I am tempted to call the equally *transnational* anonymity of the hotel corridor with its identical bedrooms.

The allegorical comment being made here on Taipei itself is one that engages a kind of Third-World situation we have rarely until now included in that (rather traditional) category: namely, the developing Third World or the newly industrializing First-World tier of the Third World or Pacific Rim (excluding Japan). Taiwan is somehow within the world system as its citizens are in their city boxes: prosperity and constriction all at once; the loss of nature (which is only observed twice, in a park close-up, and in the policeman's backyard, if one excludes the manicured pool and lawn of the student's villa); the failure of the classically urban to constitute itself standing in some intimate relationship and counterpoint to the failure of the classical psychic subject to constitute itself. What is grand and exhilarating, light itself, the hours of the day, is nonetheless here embedded in the routine of the city and locked into the pores of its stone or smeared on its glass: light also being postmodern, and a mere adjunct to the making of reproducible images.

I want to conclude by stressing the point that in the postmodern, the relations between universal and particular, if they persist at all, must be conceived in an utterly different way from those that obtained in previous social formations, and just as surely from what characterized the modern moment of our own. For the local – we used to say, in a more modernist or modernizing language, the provincial – meaning I have found in this work from a 'semi-peripheral' country is precisely not local in any traditional sense, but is rather what makes this work universal in its aesthetic value (to use an equally old-fashioned language). It is because in late capitalism and in its world system even the center is marginalized that powerful expressions of the marginally uneven and the unevenly developed issuing from a recent experience of capitalism are often more intense and powerful, more expressive, and above all more deeply symptomatic and meaningful than anything the enfeebled center still finds itself able to say.

Notes

1. London: Routledge and Kegan Paul, 1982.
2. It is safe to say that Hou Hsiao-hsien is Taiwan's leading film-maker today, and the first – after the liberalization of 1987, when for the first time the history of Taiwan since World War II could publicly be discussed – to launch into the construction of an ambitious historical epic, *A City of Sadness* (1979). His social material – drawn from youth and the countryside – is quite distinct from that of Edward Yang, and the spirit of his fine works – a kind of populist pathos or sentimentalism – is also distinctive (see below).
3. Renata Salecl has described such nationalisms (at work in the Yugoslavian context) in terms of a most suggestive Lacanian analysis, in her 'Struggle for

Hegemony in Post-Socialist Yugoslavia', in Ernesto Laclau (ed.), *On Identity* (London: Verso, forthcoming).

4. See, for further on this, my *Postmodernism, Or, The Cultural Logic of Late Capitalism* (Durham, NC: Duke University Press, 1990), pp. 20–1.

5. I am indebted to Michael Denning for the observation that the Italian setting of *Godfather III* finds its deeper function in allowing Coppola to avoid issues of race and drugs which would have fatally reimposed themselves within the frame of the superstate itself.

6. Alessandro Manzoni, *The Betrothed*, translated by Bruce Penman (London: Penguin, 1972), pp. 223–4.

7. This is the moment to express my gratitude to Shu-chen Chiang for her commentary on an earlier version of this chapter, and for the indispensable information about the Taiwanese setting of the film, and the local or vernacular connotations of some of its features. I have also benefited greatly from the chance to read Yingjin Zhang's 'The Idyllic Country and the (Post) modern City: Cinematic Configurations of Family in *Osmanthus Alley* and *Terrorizer*', (forthcoming in Wimal Disanayake (ed.), *The Family in Third World Film Today*).

8. See above, Part One, note 19.

9. Clearly, this treatment demands comparison with the role and function of the deaf-and-dumb photographer in *A City of Sadness*: he is the youngest son, something like an excluded witness, and, with his equally excluded Japanese wife, our most privileged 'point of view'. For that very reason, in Hou Hsiao-hsien's film, this character would seem to provide the technical means for estrangement in its classic, Russian-Formalist, sense (such as, for example, the child's point of view in Ambrose Bierce's 'Chickamauga').

10. Proust's pages on the telephone are to be found in *Le Côté de Guermantes, Part I* (Editions de la Pléiade, 1988), Vol. II, pp. 431–6; this technological mediation is immediately followed by an ocular inspection of Marcel's dying grandmother conveyed in terms of the technology of photography (pp. 438–9). In 'Modernism and Repetition: Kafka's Literary Technologies', *Journal of the Kafka Society of America* 1990, pp. 59–63, James Rolleston draws our attention to Kafka's representation of the telephone in the posthumously published sketch, 'Der Nachbar', valuably suggesting that we reckon it back into Benjamin's forms of technological reproduction as well; but see also *his* version – 'Der Telefon' – in *Berliner Kindheit, Gesammelte Schriften* (Frankfurt: Suhrkamp, 1981) vol. IV, pp. 242–3).

11. In his 'Berlin Childhood' (*Gesammelte Schriften*, p. 284, in 'Schränke'), translated as a separate unit in Shierry Weber Nicholson's English version of the Paris edition:

> The first cabinet that opened when I wanted it to was the bureau. I had only to pull on the knob and the door clicked open for me. Among the underclothing stored there was the thing that made the bureau an adventure. I had to make a path to the farthest corner; there I found my stockings piled, rolled up in the old-fashioned way. Each pair looked like a small pouch. Nothing gave me more pleasure than plunging my hand as deep as possible into the inside of that pouch. I did not do so for the sake of the warmth. It was 'The Dowry', which I held in my hand in the rolled-up interior, that drew me into its depths. When I had got my hand around it and confirmed my possession of the soft woollen mass to the best of my ability, the second part of the game, which brought the revelation, began. For now I began working 'The Dowry' out of its woollen pouch. I drew it closer and closer to me until the amazing event occurred: I had extricated 'The Dowry', but 'The Pouch' in which it had lain no longer existed. I could not test this process often enough. It taught me that form and

content, the veil and what it hides, are one and the same. It led me to extricate the truth from literature as cautiously as the child's hand brought the stocking out of 'The Pouch'.

And see also sentences like this: 'Methodological relationship between the metaphysical investigation and the historical one: a stocking turned inside out' (*Gesammelte Schriften* vol. I, p. 918).

12. Lacan uses the term 'forclusion' for the way in which, in psychosis, where language or the Symbolic Order is not available to organize such impulses, the sufferer's thoughts return as it were from the outside, in the form of disembodied voices, for example. (See 'On a question preliminary to any treatment of psychoses', in *Ecrits* (Paris: Seuil, 1967).)

13. See again Introduction, note 1.

14. See *Postmodernism*, p. 12ff.

15. I am grateful to Tang Xiao-bing for this suggestion.

Chapter 3
High-Tech Collectives in Late Godard

If the separation of the genres – or better still, of the discourses, or the modes – still meant anything, then shuffling them might offer a path to defamiliarization, and thereby to fresh enlightenment. In that case, we might want to shade out the fictional parts of *Passion* (1981), and read it as an essay-film, an experiment in a kind of provisional theoretical criticism, even, if you like, a statement on the canon, but in some non-canonical, cannibalizing form: the aesthetics of quotation, film considered as one of the fine arts but also as a rival to elegant artbook publishing and high quality photographic reproduction.

This would be to take it at its word or letter as a contribution to art history: the same art history that fascinated the hero of *Pierrot le fou* (1965) in his bathtub, and which here resurfaces in Laszlo's extended lesson on Delacroix's notebooks. Books about pictures rather than the pictures themselves – let's not at first draw all this back towards properly filmic theories and problems, not even by way of the interesting video experiments, or the experimental instruction on lighting and effects of depths and breaks. The theory of painting is certainly related across all those things to film itself, but by way of what is most general or universal in it (optics, perspective, theory of colors, and the like). Here, rather, what we first need to do is to set some distance between them: I would propose the kind of radical difference that has always maintained between film and the theater. The tableaux of the visual masterpieces are in that sense not unlike stage plays that have to be rehearsed and directed, and around which the camera moves and takes its distances. But film – as though it were a living organism – has always sensed the threat of spoken drama as such, and has most often tried to deal with it by incorporating it and imposing its own viewpoint. One thinks of everything from Renoir's *Nana* (1926) to the well-nigh dual system in Bergman's *Naked Night* (1953), in which the circus people are introduced as a counterfoil to the theater people.

Indeed, we have already at several points in the preceding chapters[1] confronted the more general principle that, whenever other arts are foregrounded within a film – and, generally visual, those can range

Passion

from video to cuneiform, or, as here, from theater to painting – what is at stake is always some implicit formal proposition as to the superiority of film itself as a medium over these disparate competitors. There would thus be a kind of built-in auto-referentiality in the very cinematographic medium, which, without having read Wagner, instinctively proposes itself as the fulfillment for the ideals of the *Gesamtkunstwerk*, an affirmation triggered at moments of danger when the medium's instinct for self-preservation comes into play. However this may be as a general interpretive hypothesis, it certainly seems appropriate for this particular film, if not for Godard in general, where the possibilities of cinema are ceaselessly ruminated and reinterrogated. Godard's strategy is to pose the strongest objections to the medium – to foreground its most urgent problems and crises, beginning with that of financing itself, omnipresent in these late films and above all here – in order the more triumphantly to surmount them. Appropriately enough, Jacob's struggle with the angel is the allegory of this process – which is to say the moment in which the exasperated Jerzy, dismissing the protests of his actors and crew, confronts a very large and muscular extra in an angel's costume who tries to retain him physically for one long moment.

What this does for us, in the present formal context, is to enact an extraordinary and as it were post-canonical reinvention and resurrection of the classical 'masterworks' of the museum or the picture gallery. The reinvention moves from Goya to Ingres, from Rubens to El Greco, from the traditional landscape of the medieval Italian hilltown (passed off as Jerusalem in the Western icon-tradition) to the

Passion

night-time streets of the heroic Dutch city-state in Rembrandt's
Nightwatch, of which we are told that its gleams and faint illuminations, the glints of the weapons and the very volume of the torches
themselves, betoken the horizontal rays, not of the setting, but of the
rising sun. For human actors, with real flesh-tones, to take their
places in these grandly restaged paintings is comparable only to the
theatrical re-enactment of printed scripts of the most richly suggestive
extant dramatic writings: and to gaze at the shadows in the folds of
the no longer painted togas and draperies, is to recover an extraordinary experience of visuality, which has probably been lost since the
completion of the experimental exploration of perspective in the late
Renaissance. What is the condition of possibility of this historical
resurrection that defies all the laws of gravity of historicism itself, let
alone of late capitalism and the postmodern (in which the past has
become a dead letter no longer susceptible to reanimation)?

In this sense, Godard's tableaux redramatize the historicist

160

question of the possibility of a contemporary or post-contemporary access to some original visual text as vividly, or perhaps even more vividly, than current questions of authentic instrumentation and performance in the temporal arts. Yet in both registers, the dialectical nature of the question is inescapable. It does not arise as such until we have reached the high-tech stage of either sonorous or ocular reproduction, or in other words, a stage of machine technology from whose standpoint any illusions about the natural conditions of perception in the past are dissipated (and the same would hold good, *mutatis mutandis*, for the technology of reading). Now, in other words, the 'classics' can be reached only through and by way of the most advanced reproductive technology; that is to say, by way of a capital investment and a plant inconceivable in earlier periods, and very specifically in the immediately preceding high modernist one, whose factories were the envy of less developed cultural regions but seem only antiquated period pieces and industrial museums from our own perspective. This latter perspective is very specifically the historical and technological space of *Passion*, whose characters tell us that its studio (like Godard's own real-life one) is the most advanced in Europe. Meanwhile the director himself, in the extraordinary *Scénario de Passion* – which, made in the following year, should rather be considered an independent work in its own right, and something of an aesthetically autonomous satellite to *Passion*, rather than some mere accompanying document – virtually inhabits such high-technological space like an astronaut.

Passion

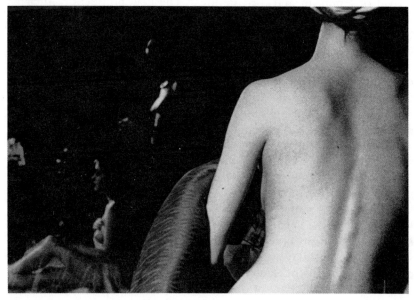

It is important to add to this particular discussion that the question of the classical canon is not limited to the visual arts. Indeed, this particular film of Godard's rediscovers and virtually reinvents, in all its splendor, Dvořák's *G Minor Piano Concerto*, which has been built into the visual structure, from which it is now inseparable, above all in that moment in which the piano's insistent reassertion of its primacy over the orchestra coincides with the hooves of the Crusaders' horses as they invest the miniature city and search out their hostage. (It may also be worth observing here how the initial images are all those of state power – whether Rembrandt's night police or the executioners of the anti-Napoleonic Spanish guerrillas. Later, this selection principle seems to modulate through sexuality and prostitution – the odalisques – into more delirious proto-religious visions, which, via St Caecilia, return us to the matter of music itself).

'La musique – c'est mon Antigone,' Godard himself prophetically intones in the most sublime moment of the accompanying *Scénario*. But one may be forgiven the speculation as to whether – in late Godard – it is not more fundamentally a question of what Adorno thought it was detestable to call 'classical music', that is to say, what it may in another age altogether be equally detestable to refer to as the question of the canon itself. I have to feel that classical music returns with a more obsessive emphasis, and thereby a modified symbolic significance, in what we may call Godard's works 'after the break'; after the commercial silence of the political period; after the end, both of the so-called major period (this expression being itself an example of canonical thinking and canonical language), and of the Dziga Vertov Brigade, the 60s, world revolution, political art, and after the arrival of feminism and 'private life'.[2] The new production, then – virtually by definition and in advance it comes to be called 'late Godard', rather as one imagines Beethoven one day deciding to change his style and finally to write 'late Beethoven' – seems to be constitutively tormented by canonical questions, such as what it means to have been turned into a classic, and also those – in which the apparent issue of the classic hides, harbors and conceals the more fundamental issue of the modern, and of an extinct high modernism proper – turning on the formal problems of the closure of the work and of how the centrifugal levels and elements of the filmic as such – sound, color, and the like, which differentiate *ad infinitum* and produce new agglomerations of ever greater and more minute complexity, could ever be thought to add up to some complete thing.

For Godard – surely as postmodern *avant la lettre* as one might have wished in the heyday of auteurist high modernism – has today in full postmodernism become the ultimate survivor of the modern as such. Who else today would reaffirm – by way of that unexpected permutation of his otherwise grotesque self-mockery (the invalid of *Carmen* [1982], the Fool of *King Lear* [1987], the Prince Myshkin of

Soigne ta droite [1987]) into the ultimate seer and prophetic figure of the *Scénario de Passion* – the conception of the Romantic genius and creator in the strongest and most unseasonable expression it has found in our own time? But the essential modernism of these late works – better to call it a survivor's modernism, the high modernist remnant of the last Neanderthals or dinosaurs, rather than some more placid *late modernism* of the Jencks coinage – does not consist in the reinvention of the autonomous work of art, or in the achievement of major or significant form, or any of those other things that, as we have been told, characterize those masterworks of the high modern we have been taught to consider classics. But of course they never really did so characterize these works in the first place, and it would be preferable to think of all such modernist classics as failures of variously monumental kinds, to persuade ourselves that *Ulysses* is not a unity and never could have been (not to speak of the *Cantos*), that in Proust there remains, forever unsolved and out of reach, the gap between intention and realization, between the idea of the book and the pages themselves, no matter how numerously piled up. The benefit of such a way of thinking is not merely to ward off the relentlessness of reification into which these by-products and after-effects gradually and fatally congeal like so much cold grease; it is also to keep them alive as efforts and experiments, that fall into the world and the past when they succeed, but stand out with something of their agency still warm and palpable in them in their very failure. Above all, it is to emphasize the modernist ideal of formal totality by way of the impossibility of achieving it. What makes a work modernist, then, in this sense is not its ultimate monadic self-enclosure like a scripture, which enveloping the entire world folds it all back upon itself, ('everything,' in Mallarmé's famous saying, 'existing to end up in a Book in the first place'), but rather precisely its longing for such monadic closure, about which the postmodern text could care less.

Still, *Passion* in particular and late Godard in general also seem to have little enough in common with the residual modernism we have tried to identify in Edward Yang's *Terrorizer* in the preceding chapter (but much more in common, oddly enough, with Third World naif or 'tourist' art, as we shall see in the following and concluding chapter). In *Terrorizer*, reflexivity became itself the object of representation, like the foreign body it may well be in the context of import-substitution. Here in Godard the impulse is convulsively acted out among the tangled reels of film themselves, as though the German Romantics had dreamed their fantasies only yesterday, and the distinction between kitsch and classicism was historically abolished in their sense and fashion, rather than in ours. For reflexivity to remain alive, however – indeed, for modernism itself (along with whatever modernist rereading of its putative Romantic precursor) – the problem of representation must be perpetuated as a throbbing pain

163

that won't go away, rather than as an X-ray plate.

'Il me faut une histoire,' bellows *Passion*'s Italian backer, and what is modernist about this film is not the way in which it finds its narrative – story and history all wrapped up in one – if indeed it ever does, but rather its obsessive search for one, its lucid awareness of what it lacks, the convulsive effort of so many broken pieces to add up to something ('a film missing its center has to move heaven and earth'). Whether *Passion* ever finds its center or its 'histoire' is undecidable ('je cherche une ouverture,' observes the protagonist in one of its more obscene moments). But as has been suggested, it would be preferable to decide that it never really does so, because only then can it be grasped for what it really is, namely, an experimental laboratory in which we examine the various things that having a story or narrative might mean; grasped, if you prefer, as an instrument or a geiger counter for detecting narratability and narrativity, narrativization and anec-dotality out from among the various pre-fabricated materials of late capitalist life and society. This then finally is also pre-eminently high modern, this sense of the work of art as a machine and an instrument for exploration (rather than as an inert object or monument). Le Corbusier described the house as a 'machine for living', and few enough of the other high moderns, from the painters and musicians to the poets, novelists and film-makers, have not thus similarly thought of their productions: not as a commodity to be consumed by a public and in a pinch to change and modify its views and actions, but rather as a vehicle for revealing new zones of being and for churning up the sedimented levels of the world itself, whether social or natural. As has been suggested, such a trans-aesthetic vocation – in which the work of art wants to be much more than a mere work of art, but rather to replace philosophy itself (an august Hegelian and anti-Hegelian vo-cation and a better way of putting it than the time-honored notion of spilt religion for an age in which religion may be even more meaning-less than philosophy anyway) – is not shared at all by the postmodern, in which something of the perhaps far older and precapitalist vocation of decoration and ornament has been reborn. But Godard's films are that as well, tapestries of the contingent, complacent textualizations of 'alles, was der Fall ist,' superficialities as depthless as the silver screen itself, if not of the video band. And what then becomes interesting is our own fundamental and indispensable decision, faced with these Gestalt objects, as to whether we prefer to read and to re-form them in a modernist or a postmodernist spirit.

Everything turns, then, on whether the film is coherent in some modernist (if not traditional) sense, or whether it is not precisely some new kind of incoherence which the spectator relishes and which therefore constitutes a kind of postmodern *jouissance*, a revelling in loose ends, the desire called chaos or contingency. It will be observed that the critic's work is greater and more demanding in the first

Passion

instance than in the second. For the first requires more active analysis, whereas the postmodern option would seem to involve little more than sitting back to watch it all hang out. Still, this second option ought to commit one to the job of constructing a description of a new kind, though now not of the individual film itself, but rather of the new perceptual processes at work in postmodern pleasure and reception. But maybe these two paths, like Proust's two 'ways' going in opposite directions, nonetheless eventually and miraculously meet somewhere and unexpectedly become one.

Let's begin with the first path, that of a search for some principle of narrative coherence, which can itself be read in several different ways whose multiplicity scarcely inspires confidence. Indeed, the various readings suggest redoubled but incompatible efforts to endow a set of materials with this or that significance after the fact, even the various versions of the plot I am about to propose approaching the status of interpretive themes. At any rate, here is how Godard himself (at the end of *Scénario*, and in the subtitler's translation) describes the *fabula* he has finally managed to come up with:

> A factory girl is sacked by her boss. She falls in love with a foreigner come to make a film. Then the boss's wife also falls in love with the foreigner. He for his part cannot find a subject for his film, although there are dozens around him.

As with any number of remarkable observations contributed by the author/auteur in *Scénario*, this one must be received with vigilance and a priori suspicion. No one is more adept than this particular author in cooking up ex post facto interpretations of his own works (we will try to evaluate the quality of his mind and thought in a moment); and in any case there is no particularly binding reason to prefer his impressions and reactions to our own. These last – at least for me – involve a sense of collective action and team play, multiple plots and Dickensian or Altmanian narrative intricacies, which Godard's sober four-sentence summary signally fails to convey. Its greatest failing, indeed, is the suggestion and the implication that this is something like a plot with old-fashioned individual characters and protagonists, the triangle (to which we will return) being then emblematically rendered by Titian's *Bacchus and Ariadne*. Even here, a significant Gestalt shift is effected depending on whether we foreground the male protagonist as the central character, or the two women: that will also be examined in a moment. But we do not have to do any of this. Indeed I believe it is aesthetically (if not even morally) wrong to posit any 'central characters' at all; wrong to see Jerzy as the 'hero'; wrong to extract the women's two subplots from what is a very tangled web indeed, full of any number of other story lines – such as the electrician and his wife ('dis ta phrase!'), the violent jealousy drama between Laszlo and the two assistants, and even the acrobat-contortionist (a potential plot-line frequently in Godard being marked by static and grotesque characterology, which holds its place, as it were). As in Balzac's constellated system of novels and tales, the most minimal shift in the film's perspective might well have foregrounded any of these, around which the illusion of centrality would immediately begin to develop, relegating Jerzy and his two loves into the background as extras and supplementary material. It would therefore seem wise as well as prudent to formulate a new kind of ad hoc or experimental imperative, at least for the reading of this particular film – namely, not to think of Jerzy as the central figure, but whenever and wherever he appears always to treat him as a means rather than an end, and as one more character among many, all in principle of equal value and significance.

If we can do that, then what emerges is the stunning dynamic of a collective social machine without a center, a bewilderingly rich choreography of incidents and necessarily decentered subjects, new features and details of which are disclosed at every new viewing. This truly inexhaustible text is then one of the few recent aesthetic responses to the 'schizophrenic' line on decentering the subject. That way, via Wenders and Handke and Herzog, led not into some 'joyous' Deleuzian Nietzscheanism, but into a fantasmagoria of the perceptual fragmented present no less somber and insulated than the classical solipsism and anomie reserved for the traditional individualistic centered subject. The alternative was always much less extensively covered by the media, but collective life and existence is no less fundamentally 'decentering' in its effects on the individual subject than is ideal or postmodern schizophrenia, and perhaps somewhat more satisfying in the long run. At any rate, the film-maker is well placed to grasp these structures of collectivity, since as with theater, but unlike the other arts or media, film is already in its very nature a form of collective praxis, straining, as with Marx's view of co-operative labor processes within a business owned by a single individual, to rupture its signed and individualized integument and appear as such, in its true social appearance. *Passion* works energetically at the democratization of all this, by the rotating structure of its collective Gestalt repeatedly and insistently suggesting the momentary centrality of any of its numerous cast (any one of whom, as Andy Warhol might have put it, will in this Utopia be the main character for a good deal less than fifteen minutes). *Scénario* on the other hand recalls us to the more depressing realities of a social and business world in which this revolution has not yet taken place. For it is there, in the documentary, but not in the film proper, that Godard characterizes the extras as cannon-fodder in the service of those great generals who are the directors and the auteurs. It is there also that, with a certain sadness (utterly uncolored, it is true, by arrogance), he deplores the structural lack of imagination of his production team, who can only grasp the reified and finished image, and not its emergence and its nature as a process – something reserved for the modernist seer and creator alone. But perhaps in that respect, *Scénario*, which must be seen as an

Passion

dependent work of art in its own right (and which I will examine for itself later on), can be said to be the modernist work, and *Passion* its relatively more postmodern variant.

At any rate, the seething dynamic of collective relations is in *Passion* registered with a formal intensity comparable only (with a very few intervening exceptions) to that of Jean Renoir's *La Règle du jeu* (1939), which then becomes its great predecessor, as *Passion* equally becomes the latter's great completion and reinvention in our own period. Notions either of influence or of intertextuality seem to me very feeble in conveying the exchange of energies between these two extraordinary works, which reinvent for the ambitious art-film of the sound period something of that collective primal soup of the earliest silent comic chase scenes and the chaos of the Mack Sennett farces. I would indeed very much dislike having to describe Jerzy's stabbing as a mere 'allusion' to the disintegrating fancy dress ball in Renoir, through which the game warden pursues his adulterous rival, meanwhile terrorizing the high society guests with repeated pistol shots. But I suppose it is 'significant' in some portentous sense that the maniac in Godard's film is a relatively anonymous little man who has been done out of his 'check' by the boss. Perhaps Godard's title, which I have never understood, is an ironic commentary on how far passion in corporate society has come from Renoir's doomed *ancien régime*. Perhaps indeed the two titles should be switched, for passion, of a relatively stupid kind it is true, is a better description of Renoir's aviator, whom Godard, at least, allows to go home alive and scarcely

Passion

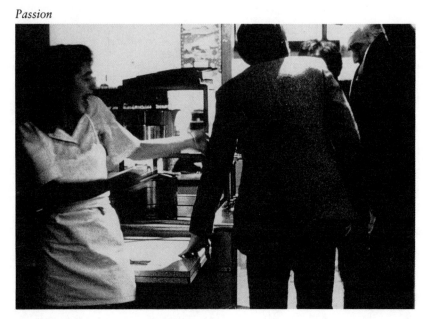

Passion

even disabused. Yet even though rehearsals are a grand theme in Renoir (think above all of *French Cancan* [1955]!), chaos, in *La Règle du jeu*, only happens once, and climactically. But in *Passion*, in keeping with the plot's dimensional structure, which we will examine in a moment, the chase scene is repeated several times: once in the factory, where the boss and various police-persons desperately pursue the stubborn Isabelle; and once, *mise en abysme*, within one of the visual works of art itself, the Delacroix *Conquest of Constantinople*, in which a fleeing and ultimately naked victim is pursued through the miniature medieval city by the Crusaders' horse guards, who seize her and carry her off to the sound of the percussive and triumphant rhythms of the piano and full orchestra in Dvořák's concerto. How these echoes work, presumably somehow repetitions rather than rehearsals, we will probably not begin to understand until the intricate theorization of *Scénario*, which characterizes this film as the meeting place between metaphor and its real. But the nature of the tripartite space in question here will become clear in a moment, even if its structure remains tantalizingly complex and obscure, and avid for its own theorization.

Meanwhile something more now needs to be said about the representation of collectivity on another level. I have indeed in another place[3] found myself able to suggest that in our time the referent – the world system – is a being of such enormous complexity that it can only be mapped and modelled indirectly, by way of a simpler object that stands as its allegorical interpretant, that object being most often in postmodernism itself a media phenomenon. In the film I was discussing then, that interposed object (following Sartre I called it the *analogon*) turned out to be the star system itself, whose hierarchy conveyed the film's deeper social content more effectively – that is to

169

Passion

say, articulated it and made it more readily available for an operative reading – than the ostensible realistic story or plot itself. It seems important to affirm something like this here, in a film which like Renoir's 1939 production is also a vision of transnational European space. In Renoir it was an older pan-European culture on the point of eclipse and doom, here it is a rich and complacent Europe on the point of imminent post-1992 transmogrification (by prophetic accident, Godard even foresees the impending incorporation of the East as well). But Renoir's more classical star system transmits and mediates all this by way of a stellar French repertory cast that includes a single foreign representative (not even, I believe, an actress, but an aristocrat whose Austrian culture conveniently masks the German reality, and thus concentrates Renoir's model of Europe on that essential cultural resolution of the Franco-German tension).

Godard's cast is that of something like an international or at least pan-European art-film or *nouvelle-vague* star system, all wearing their own real-life first names and marked by a specific speech disorder: frequent coughing, stuttering, mutism, the gift of tongues, or on the other hand a foreign accent, or finally the simple pigheaded refusal to say anything ('Dis ta phrase!'). Thematically, we know that for Godard language is pre-eminently the place of lies and the visual pre-eminently the place of truth. You're only free before you have to finish your sentence, Jerzy says here somewhere, while the very title of *Prénom Carmen* evokes some well-nigh Lacanian indeterminate space before the tyranny of the name and its destinies. Whether these various organs of Europe's *corps morcelé* are thereby envisioned as coming together in some healed and transfigured post-1992 body, the various local speech impediments all somehow miraculously cancelling each other out, cannot here be decided. But it is pertinent to recall Karatani Kojin's observation about the way in which contemporary European thought unconsciously and perhaps uneasily works at mapping its own geographical future: nowhere so luminously as in Deleuze's return to Leibniz, where the monadology offers a more substantial philosophical solution than all the various current ideologies of pluralism. *Passion* is also just such a monadology, in convulsive and constellative, permanently provisional emergence – set emblematically in Switzerland, with some ultimate mission further to the East.

So *Passion* can first be seen as a representation of the collective which, rehearsing and repeating bits and pieces of its script, finally erupts in the great forms – the strike, the theatrical representation, even the political deliberation of a group – only to be 'set in motion' as a kind of vibrant collective chaos by the farcical chase scenes, followed by a gradual cooling, in which the individual members of the collective slowly peel off again, going their various ways, abandoning the emptying field of the Event (or the carnival, if you prefer a different theoretical language).

But all this can now be reformulated in a somewhat different way

Passion

La Règle du jeu

which raises the classic *Ulysses*-question: does anything really happen on Bloomsday? Is this not merely sheer iteration and repetition, 'encore une journée!' as Flaubert's Saint Antoine puts it; or does it mark a decisive, although minute and scarcely visible, change? Godard's 'event' is in any case given to us as exceptional rather than as quotidian. To make a film (in some metaphysical sense), to assemble all these distinct and separate subjects (drawing them together with the literal or Greek form of Freud's Eros), instituting the collective itself for one long provisional and fading moment – unlike Joycean or Proustian modernism, this emphatically does not happen every day.

The fundamental changes may therefore seem superfluous in this form, and a remnant of some older narrative aesthetic. The boss, Michel, decides to sell his factory; the film-maker Jerzy decides to chuck his project and to go back home to martial-law Poland. But one cannot feel, even retroactively, that these decisions are substantively motivated by the action of the film: that is to say, as in some ordinary psychological narrative, one cannot particularly feel that decisions of this kind then return upon the whole trajectory of the previously narrated experiences in order to lend them the weight of an evidence and a destiny. But the strike was relatively pitiful (it is Godard's way of keeping faith with the political while acknowledging the reality principle); and Jerzy's financial and technological problems can surely not come as any surprise to him, if he has the background Godard attributes to him in the first place.

Nor is this the Shakespearian side of Godard, the serene, magisterial impatience with which he scatters his characters, kills them off perfunctorily in great heaps of unreal corpses (where we occasionally find gentlemen in armchairs calmly enjoying their newspaper in the middle of the shoot-out). (In any case, in my opinion, the only true presence of death in Godard – save perhaps those fantasmatically attributed to the influence of women, as in *A Bout de souffle* [1959] – is to be found in *Le Petit soldat* [1960], where history and torture intervene to fill out the masks and shed real blood.)

The symmetry of the two relatively gratuitous decisions of Michel and Jerzy is thus not particularly meaningful in any traditionally realist or realistic way. It serves to block out the great spatial opposition in *Passion* between the film studio and the factory, between superstructure and base, the image of the thing and the thing itself,

Passion

Prénom Carmen

reproduction and production, aesthetics and political economy, the technology of the postmodern period and the older assembly-line technology of the previous (or monopoly) stage. Clearly, then, the very existence of these two alternate spaces – which, complementing each other, complete the film's world and save it from the sheer idealism of a meditation on film-making or indeed a meditation on labor either – open up the possibilities of a well-nigh infinite process of interpretation, in which a provisional meaning of one of the two spaces sends us back to the other to invent for it a new meaning or thematics. One must also mention what this allows in the way of an interspace, that shabby, brightly painted zone of cars and superhighways and gas stations that seems to attract Godard's deepest predilections: a space outside of the real world itself (as Chandler once said about police stations), in which a different kind of violence always threatens, the violence between things, and above all between automobiles, which dent each other, strike stray passers-by, and finally open up into the ultimate steaming and bloody Apocalypse of *Weekend*, in which the world comes to an end in a traffic jam. On the other hand, the gas station is also the home of the Mary of Godard's annunciation; and it is the place of the first long look and *coup de foudre* between Jerzy and Hannah in *Passion*. Nothing is indeed in Godard quite so touching as the human accommodation to these anonymous spaces of a plastic no man's land, in which nonetheless 'affect' is able to continue, whether in violence or in the spark of the look. All one can say is that it would not have been possible in the modern proper, where such spaces are radically inauthentic from the outset.

Finally, however, these two great antithetical signifying spaces of the shooting stage or film studio (one never sees it from the outside or manages to place it in the landscape) and of the textile factory – these turn out not to exhaust the spaces of the film after all. They are themselves strangely decentered by a third kind of positive space (as opposed to the interspace of the automobile). This is the space of the hotel, and it belongs to the woman (the wife of the patron), reawakening all our deeper fears about these structuring oppositions, which now seem on the point of folding back into public versus private and male versus female. But Hannah's hotel is about as private and intimate as the gas station; and although children are intermittently present here, as elsewhere in Godard, I think we can take it as axiomatic with him that in late capitalism private space and private life as such have been abolished, turned inside out onto the standardized and mass-produced universe of the urban (which by the same token is no longer a real public space any longer either).

The hotel, then, simply functions to disturb the symmetry of base and superstructure, work and art – to prevent that from freezing over into something symbolic, something too meaningful. The modern longed to forge that kind of symbolic meaning out of the detritus of nascent modernization, to heal the intolerable disintegration of Weberian tradition by reinventing a transaesthetic third term. As a consequence the present finds itself littered with the broken remnants of all these modernist symbols, which (as Barthes said of the full signification of advertising photographs) inspire a nausea in their own right, the repugnance one feels for what has cheated on the contingent and claimed to transcend and subsume it in some higher meaning. The contingent, therefore, the messy, the inauthentic, the mass-produced – what is neither beautiful nor ugly but simply junk or kitsch – this will alone validate the new kind of work and present the credentials of some new kind of reality that we can no longer call authenticity. These credentials are honored when you reach the point of no longer being able to absorb all this detail into a meaningful interpretation. There is an incompatibility, Barthes also said, between meaning and the real – but it is not clear whether that was not still a lesson he learned from existentialism, rather than an anticipation of the very different lesson of the postmodern, where the contingent is no longer nature, the tree root, the human body, but rather the man-made itself, the gas pump, or the horrible mass-produced lampshade.

Yet the multiplication of such spaces – and the sudden reduplication of the women themselves (into Jerzy's two lovers, whom it would be just as well not too rapidly to assimilate to the fair and dark heroines of traditional romanticism) – may well begin to alert us to the gradual exhaustion of this line of thematic interpretation. The feeling can only be strengthened by the dawning realization that here the category of the individual character as such is also outmoded, as outmoded as that of the nation state (the comparison, meanwhile, very much including the fact that both these things still exist). We are once again in that remarkable world of microscopic realities and tropisms so memorably evoked in a famous letter by D. H. Lawrence, in which he proposes to abandon the old 'stable ego' for the radium effects and chemical interactions within and between subjects.[4] This is precisely what Godard's camera – which masks out the long view or the perspective of old-fashioned action – now achieves; nor is what results a diminution of psychic politics, but rather an intensification. As in Lawrence himself, gender relations are now magnified and become visible in a non-psychological way, which equally excludes the various sexist or essentialist mythologies of the male and the female.

We must therefore now abandon the attempt to read *Passion* as a larger form or Aristotelian narrative, with stable characters and named events, and turn now to that other interpretive possibility which used to be called thematics. But this confronts us, as I promised, with the interesting issue of Godard's thought itself, from the brilliance of which the clowning of the persona should not be allowed to distract us. Yet it is a thinking that has been systematically redirected away from system altogether (if not from philosophy), and, as befits someone for whom the image is more reliable than the sentence, towards a certain kind of reification – that of the remark, the boutade, the saying, the proverb, whatever these sometimes maniacal characters write down in the little notebooks they carry around with them. Meanwhile, in a situation in which the persona has replaced the personality, and in which the 'old stable ego' or centered subject is gone, it will not make much sense to try to recombine Godard's 'themes' into some coherent mythic world-view as the older thematics taught us to do for the moderns. Perhaps, on the contrary, it is the formal language of Benjamin and Adorno that ought to be evoked here, a language of constellations and of twelve-tone rows:[5] Godard's themes, in other words, only distantly resembling ideas, and serving as the various lights that strike his aesthetic object in rotation, tinting it, highlighting a relief, flooding another side or aspect, and then plunging the collective substance – the totality of the film's relationships – back into the chiaroscuro of a Rembrandt.

Nonetheless one can begin to enumerate some of these thematic perspectives. One can above all say which are the least convincing and most untrustworthy, as Godard allows his 'secondary elaborations', his 'folie d'interprétation', his instant philosophical rationali-

Passion

zations, to be swept on towards a metaphysics which the film will certainly end up earning, but not because of its profundity of thought. We must therefore from the outset exclude the religious invocations,[6] and in particular the various mumblings about grace and 'la grâce' and 'grâce à vous', which in any case are somewhat distanced by their appearance in the most obscene part of the film (on anal intercourse). Nor is this sham religiosity without its relationship to the sham or opportunistic politics, the equally vacuous invocation of Solidarity, which seems to boil down to a few puns and far-fetched analogies (as when the filmic image is described, pertinently enough, as a 'solidarité dans les idées', by which he seems to mean that relationship between the various dimensions, above all sight and sound, to which we will return later on). Isabelle's affiliation with a Catholic rather than a Communist workers' movement is obviously a way to go on talking about the labor movement without having to mention the unnameable and seemingly defunct Marxism in the new and demarxified postmodern France of the Parti Socialiste (PS). But both these topics are in reality covers and disguises for something else. No serious assessment of Solidarity and its politics is to be sought here: the slogan simply drapes a topical and pseudo-philosophical veil over the far realer matter of collectivity already touched on. As for religion, and in particular the matter of 'grace', we will not really be able to identify it until the *Scénario de Passion*, at which point its true significance is revealed to be the coming into being of the film or the work of art itself (what used to be called 'inspiration').

The other themes are omnipresent in Godard and organize themselves around the ec-centric three-fold space we have just outlined.
They cluster around the question of what a film is, to be sure – 'juste
une image', the matter of language, the video of Hannah's facial
expressions, 'solidarity in the ideas', and so forth. Indeed, I would go
so far as to suggest that this whole redoubled tortuous meditation on
what cinema is and how it functions finds its ultimate focus in the
matter of synchronization, which may then be thought to be the final
form, Godard's or the postmodern's version of the more classical
synesthesia, already shrewdly seized on and rehearsed by Baudelaire.
It is here, rather than in any visual tricks (bravura movements of the
camera seem rather the mark of the preceding generation of modernist auteurs, like Hitchcock), that the deepest technical innovations of
Godard may be found: in the political meeting, for example, where,
as the strike is planned, the voices of the participants are oddly
matched to other, non-speaking listeners (the true organizing *punctum* of this scene being the presence of a transvestite, so that a deep
male voice wanders across all these women's faces looking for a
body). Or then again in the great love scene with Hannah (if one may
put that that way!), where it is not only a question of taping her face
and her most minute reactions to Jerzy's whispered remarks, so that,
as in some high-tech far future bordello, both characters can then
watch each other, not in mirrors but on the video screen playback;
but also of their high-cultural version of *karaoke*, in which Hannah is
called upon to mime the glorious operatic voices choiring all around
her. This now projects the matter of rehearsal from the purely visual
dynamics of the film within a film onto the technology of instant-
playback video and the mysteries of multidimensionality, of the identity and difference between sight and sound, the image and the text,
the face and the voice.

The other two great themes are of course work and love, or rather
the mirror-relationship between them, which is not exhausted by the
permutations of the slogan itself: the love of work, the work of love.
Implicit here is the deeper preoccupation with pornography. Why,
Isabelle asks, do films never show work as such; why are the gestures
of the labor process banned from the camera? But the point is not
only that neither work nor sex is represented directly, in and for itself,
but that neither can be, and that there is a way in which such representation only becomes minimally possible by way of analogy with
the other. To compare the physical movements involved in factory
work with those involved in sexual intercourse is to begin somehow,
in the voyeuristic mind's eye, to see both of them a little more sharply.
To pun back and forth, as when one of the strikers puzzles over the
need to issue a strike 'declaration' – 'c'est comme une déclaration
d'amour?' – is to sharpen our thought in a somewhat different way,
perhaps, than the classical mode of defamiliarization: mutual refami-

liarization, perhaps – a structural question which will return again in the musings of *Scénario* on the relations between metaphor and the real.

Beyond factory work of course lies money itself, one of the other great obsessions in Godard, and very much part of a sexual metaphorics in which the theme of prostitution replaces that of pornography, this last being less strong in *Passion* than in some of his other films. Here, I think, the omnipresent worries about financing, backers, the Europeans versus the Americans, and so forth, are less a theme than an element that pervades everything in this social world, on the factory side too ('Mon chèque!'), and well into the running of the hotel, Hannah's fur coat, her 'japonaise' (dented by offensive bourgeois drivers), and so on. This reality – something like the very exchange value of the image itself, which accompanies it as its price tag at every moment – then rejoins the grander (or more philosophico-aesthetic, more metaphysical) question of story or narrative with which we began: 'Il me faut une histoire!' Is success here the unity of the image? Is it rather Jerzy's finding a center, to his personal life and his film alike (and thereby becoming the more traditional protagonist or hero of a story-telling film)? Is it what will play in Peoria, or maybe Cannes, or is it the Lukácsean symptom or signal that life has again become coherent? Or then again is it only the overcoming of the modern, with its plotless élite poetic texts, and the return to the story that signals the magical reunification of high and low culture in the postmodern, but under the latter's aegis and its cost-accounting?

With the theme of nature, finally, we touch the point at which what looks most modern in Godard in fact reveals its postmodernity, rejoining other peculiar survivals that turn out to be just as peculiarly postmodern, such as the autodidact's fondness for cultural and canonical 'masterworks' already touched on: but in the age of the specialist, presumably only the autodidact is non-bureaucratic anyway. In any case, the interpolated quartet (in *Prénom Carmen* [1982]) is a rather different signifier than the poetry books Lemmy Caution carried around in the 1965 *Alphaville* (whose message was at best as trivial as that of *Fahrenheit 451* [1967]). In late Godard, I'm tempted to say, nature is not culture but high culture; and vice versa. It is perhaps clearer in the *Carmen* film than in *Passion*, since the former 'has' a plot (and a high-cultural plot at that), so that its heterogeneous materials are not drawn in the same way by the central magnet of the theme of plot construction. In the later film, indeed, the themes or 'great ideas' have been reduced, more properly, to great sentences, taken down by a nurse who follows the great man (Godard himself) around. That is to say that they are already verbal objects of some kind, reified, and no longer available to subsume particulars. What the mind tries to hold together is disparate kinds of items: nature, in the form of the sea churning over rocks; classical music, in the form of

179

the Beethoven quartet practiced throughout, linked to the main plot by way of the young violinist who tries to find her protégé (it is never really clear if it is Don José, in another avatar) a suitable job of some kind, and then finally performed in the grand hotel in time for the concluding kidnap sequence; young bodies whose sexual relationship is peculiarly unpornographic, with an innocence perhaps 'signifying nature' but equally possibly designating the reproductive apparatus of the camera and its glossy products; the settings finally, the inexplicable shift from Boulogne to Paris, and from an empty luxury apartment on the sea to a grand hotel full of prefabricated furnishings, from the chandelier being cleaned throughout to the anonymous furniture (under whose cushions, as one character puts it, they never clean, so that the guns can be stowed there handily). *Carmen*, then, in retrospect seems to be something like a meditation on these different kinds of visual objects, some natural, some artificial, but all somehow glossy and neutralized. The sea here is a beautiful photographic reproduction of the sea; while the chandelier, expensive cutlery and flower vases are not enhanced by the elegance of their reproduction. On the contrary, they are if anything diminished by it, and reduced to something second-hand and ordered in bulk from outfits that furnish large hotels of a particular status or level.

At that point, the deeper motivation for Godard's scatology becomes clear: it is somehow, desperately, to soil all this and to break through the sealed closure of its reproductive technology – as it were, from either end. The repeated discussions of shit and assholes are then echoed by the slob in the freeway gas station rest room, watching the lovers urinate while he scrapes the last smear of flavored yoghurt from its plastic container and stuffs it into his mouth. As for the blood on the parquet floor next to the bodies of the robbery victims, it is effortlessly mopped away 'without a trace'[7] by the after-hours cleaning lady. Nothing *takes* on this surface, nothing can soil the splendor of late capitalism, either in its urban or its natural forms. No doubt the clown-like nature of Godard's own persona, living in an immaculate hospital and trying to catch a fever, is also a response to this dilemma. He succeeds in being the most disreputable component of the film, but mainly because he is a has-been and a survivor from the distant (modernist?) past. The apparatus itself reigns supreme and cannot be subverted; disorder and chaos are all alike to it; exotic stories from the classical past are grist for its mill and at once become late-capitalist postmodern.

Can we still even posit some allegorical relationship between form and content, such that the girl herself – a truly mesmerizing life form – re-enacts the dynamics of the reproductive technology itself, with her motto (borrowed from an old American film noir): if I fall in love with you, too bad for you! Too bad for reality, then; too bad for nature itself, above all, which is here appropriated with more exploitative violence than anything in Walt Disney, yet somehow – mysteriously, in a trick of which only Godard seems to have the secret – retains a 'critical' note, such that its very beauty gives off a corrupt signal and, smothered under advertising imagery, resonates a genuinely tragic poignancy, beauty no longer convulsive but merely twitching with a barely perceptible shudder of life not yet extinct, even though the very longing for such natural beauty has become the most inauthentic Flaubertian cliché, instilled from the outside by all the most elaborate Madison Avenue methods and techniques.

I do not want to end, however, on the deeper social and formal realism of a film that engages, as *Passion* does, all the great issues and questions: modern love, modern work, money, even art itself in the age of its technological reproducibility. Rather we must do Godard the justice of rising to the occasion of the sublime itself, which he is one of the very rare artists in our time to attain for fleeting instants (and is not the sublime always a matter of the fleeting instant, an intensity of transcendental affect – o altitudo! – that cannot ever be borne or sustained for long?). The classical music was surely that, the challenge and the rivalry – to do something with the camera that matches ecstatic moments only music was supposed to achieve, and that language, as in Proust, can only describe after the fact. Nor were the great paintings really in the running, for whatever they ultimately achieved depended on the three-fold background support of music to begin with (the Dvořák concerto), then the camera that 'set them in

Prénom Carmen

motion'; and the deeper pornographic substance, finally, of the human body itself as it subtends the visual and lends it warmth.

And over against all that, the opening shot of *Passion*: the sun itself racing ecstatically across the heavens, gleaming like a Baroque monstrance, caught in leaves as a sign of its kinship with earth; the sun filmed from a car at high speed, marriage of nature and late or high technology, sublimity of the reproducible image. This new Nature is thereby historical as well, the nature of late capitalism (which has as we know abolished nature in all the older senses). It is an abolition then figured in the new free-floating autonomy of the natural image itself in *Passion*, against whose scenic backdrop seasons change without warning, passing from high summer to heavy snowfall overnight, without any magic realism and in so unselfconscious a fashion that it takes the most alert and forewarned viewer to notice it at all (so absorbed as we are in following the intricacies of the human plots).

But this sublime is not exclusively visual: indeed one would want to make the case that it can never be purely visual at all in that sense. And this is why Godard seems to have felt the need, exceptionally, to complete his already 'completed' film (about an incomplete filming) with something else, something more, something insufficiently expressed or visually rendered – indeed with that oxymoron which is the filmed scenario of the preceding film itself (which surely never had a scenario to begin with). This postscript is then remarkably verbal, its *mots justes* following one another in a corruscating brilliance that ends up, whatever its linguistic suspicions, in multiple puns, but also in the ultimate visionary ecstasy, the beatific vision itself: *voici la lumière ... voici le cinéma ....*

Passion

Passion

Faire le plein d'histoires: fill 'er up, fill 'er up with stories and narratives. But *Scénario* is remarkably the story of that proliferation of stories. Unique in the literature of descriptions of the so-called creative process, it rivalizes with the most daring and thoroughgoing structural, genetic, and dialectical analyses of individual texts – whose components emerge one by one before our eyes in successive projects that loop back upon each other and finally come together in the thing itself, about which it only remains unclear whether it is not itself its own visible 'scenario': not a world, but the possibility of a world, or at least the probability of that possibility. From the initial glimpse of a bouquet of flowers to the flower-painting of Delacroix in his old age – such is the trajectory of this emergence, which includes a remarkable variety of different psychological phenomena. We begin by needing an arrival (abstract narrative form); then Godard projects himself (or his role as producer-director) onto various characters (more properly, psychological forms of identification); the puns then open up a properly Ricardolian or Simonian dimension in which Mallarmé's 'page blanche' – the screen! – leads to a 'plage blanche', a beach, which is also, in old-fashioned French, a 'grève', a word that means 'strike' – so that at once the dimension of labor militancy and of the factory is given in the initial starting-point of modernist silence and the autonomy of the work of art. Finally the scenario generates its own meta-dimension in the return upon the reality of the image itself as the image of reality, and that extraordinary zone suddenly appears which is, as has been mentioned, the joining of metaphor with the real – the great galleon in full nature and on dry land, the characters in costumes, recalling the older story-book figures who wandered through the woods in *Weekend* (1967).

A metaphor in the real:[8] this peculiar object, calculated to mesmerize Lacanian theorization at its most hyperintellectual, is not without some structural similarity to the inner form of *Passion* itself – its love-work analogy projected onto the aesthetics of the visual, with gaps and distances for which, for the moment, we still only have the term 'allegorical' as the sign of a theory yet to be constructed. This is now the task with which *Passion* confronts us, as a peculiar signifying artifact of a wholly new sort, which nonetheless, like a meteorite fallen from outer space, bears within it the promise and the suggestion that grasping its structure – were that really ever possible! – would also lead to grasping the structure of the modern age itself.

Notes

1. See above, Part One, note 19.
2. In *Jean-Luc Godard, par Jean-Luc Godard* (Paris: Editions de l'Etoile, 1985), the periods are characterized as follows: les années Cahiers (1950–1959), les années Karina (1960–1967), les années Mao (1968–1974), les années video (1975–1980), les années quatre-vingt (1980–1985).
3. See my *Signatures of the Visible* (New York: Routledge, 1990), Part One, chapter 2: 'Class and Allegory in Contemporary Mass Culture'; along with the closing pages of my *Postmodernism, Or, The Cultural Logic of Late Capitalism* (Durham, NC: Duke University Press, 1990), pp. 413–18; and now the first part of the present volume.
4. 'There is another *ego*, according to which the individual is unrecognizable, and passes through, as it were, allotropic states which it needs a deeper sense than any we've been used to exercise, to discover are states of the same radically unchanged element ...' Letter to Edward Garnett, June 5 1914, in Harry T. Moore (ed.), D. H. Lawrence, *Collected Letters* (New York: Viking, 1962).
5. See, on the constellation and the twelve-tone system, my *Late Marxism: T. W. Adorno or the Persistence of the Dialectic* (London: Verso, 1990), pp. 49–62.
6. That is to say, I will exclude: for nothing excludes the possibility that Godard himself may take these religious motifs more seriously than I do, or that the combination of religion and Solidarnosc may well, for other postmoderns, mark a significant philosophical theme or development. Both are, however, in

my opinion, to be subsumed under the dawning theme of a new (post-Marx and post-socialist) Europe referred to above. Meanwhile, Colin MacC: correctly suggests that the film includes at least one serious political com/ ment (not at all unrelated to the European matter), namely, Jerzy's principlea refusal to go to the US to make movies.

7. The trace: one can never be sure whether the momentary obsessions in Godard are to be taken decoratively or conceptually; this one appears at a moment in *Passion* in which (after the scatology) one would think the 'trace' might mean pregnancy. But the horror of the trace was always a modern and indeed Sartrean matter – being afraid you would be marked once and for all, that things were definitive or better still irrevocable. It makes sense then that the wish not to leave any traces could in a pinch characterize a postmodernism, which, ultimate form of American optimism, thinks everything can be solved, changed, rebuilt, in the absence of ground or consequences.

8. This metaphor 'in the real' is perhaps to be compared to Ernst Bloch's notion of the *Realsymbol*: 'one whose level of meaning remains shrouded for itself in the real object and not merely for human intuition. It is thus at one and the same time an expression for what has not yet become manifest in the object, but is nonetheless signified in and through it. The human symbolic picture is only a replication and a substitute for it', etc. See *Das Prinzip Hoffnung* (Frankfurt: Suhrkamp Verlag, 1959), p. 188.

Chapter 4

'Art Naïf' and the Admixture of Worlds

Just as surely as *The Perfumed Nightmare* (1977) is scarcely to be thought of as paradigmatic of Third-World film in general, so also Third-World cinema itself is rarely today defended as a space in which models for alternate cinema are to be sought. Indeed the very term Third World seems to have become an embarrassment in a period in which the realities of the economic have seemed to supplant the possibilities of collective struggle, in which human agency and politics seem to have been dissolved by the global corporate institutions we call late capitalism.[1] The promise of alternate forms in the cinema of that now distant period we call the 60s (but which covered the 70s as well, in chronological retrospect), included the promise of alternate ways of life, alternate collective and communal structures, that were expected to emerge from a variety of struggles against economic, military, and cultural imperialism (and in some cases, those of China, Cuba and Vietnam, for example, this promise overlapped with the Second-World project of the construction of socialism). Meanwhile, for many of us, a degree of fantasy invested the hope, then called Third-Worldism, that precapitalist societies who came to modernization only in relatively recent times would somehow be able to overleap everything crippling for the industrial West in its experience of capitalism and to move into the future with a measure of cultural originality, drawing on the existence of precapitalist and collective social relations for the invention of historically new, non-Western and non-individualistic, postcapitalistic kinds.

The scenario was not a new one, and had already been played through in the nineteenth century. Marx was himself interested in the collective possibilities of the Russian *mir*,[2] but those who placed their hopes in dialectically uneven development were opposed by the more orthodox Mensheviks, for whom capitalism, and the commodification of labor power, had to be complete before socialism could be considered a practical possibility. Something of the same set of oppositions now seems on the agenda for late capitalism and the new world system, where the autarchy of the socialist countries and the cultural and social possibilities of Third-World or post-colonial areas have seemed to evaporate under the dreary requirements of modernization and the balanced budget (or the Debt). Third-World 'culture', however, in the narrow sense, has been gratefully absorbed by the international entertainment industry, and has seemed to furnish vibrant but politically acceptable images of social pluralism for the late capitalist big city.

Under these circumstances, clearly, Third-World film – technically modified in its evolution out of a militantly 'imperfect cinema' (García Espinosa) – no longer makes the same kinds of symbolic claims on us as its great predecessors in the formal inventiveness and the political ferment of the 60s, when form was also an extra-aesthetic issue, and what you did to movies and movie-making was also expected to have its impact on changing the world. But these were claims that also asked to be validated in terms of the originality of the form itself; and the effort was thus menaced by two kinds of failure. It could be crushed politically, as universally in the Latin America of the 1970s; or the filmic experiment itself could fail to take, or could be reabsorbed and co-opted by an enlarged and more ecumenical mainstream (or classic Hollywood) cinema. It is therefore a symptomatic moment, and something like the symbolic end of an era, when in 1985 David Bordwell and Janet Staiger publicly review the 'alternate modes of film practice' and conclude that none of them have ultimately fulfilled their promise:

> apart from the dominant and long-lived Hollywood style, only a few other general modes of film practice have existed. ... Because of the world-wide imitation of Hollywood's successful mode of production ... oppositional practices have generally not been launched on an industry-wide basis. No absolute, pure alternative to Hollywood exists.[2]

The argument is richly detailed and persuasive; but as a political or historical symptom, it is of a piece with current market rhetoric in which, also, alternatives to Western economy are pronounced flawed, contradictory, failures or non-existent. Ultimately, what is at stake in both these (properly postmodern) positions is a feeling about daily life or the life world itself: that after all is said and done, this particular life world is somehow *natural*, that efforts to live in other ways are misguided (or occasions for a properly Utopian violence); that our social values demand a 'representational realism' (of the Hollywood or market type) which is a disabused acknowledgment of the perennity of the status quo. (Equivalents to these aesthetic, economic and social positions can meanwhile be found on all the other levels of contemporary social life, such as the psychic and the sexual, or the penal, or the institutional.) The so-called crisis of Marxism turns out rather to have involved the death of anarchism and its Utopian spirit. It is not revived, of course, by complaints, or by the taking of a thought; the preceding remarks rather attempt to characterize features of the intellectual atmosphere in which we all live today, with a view towards determining our 'current situation'.

That is the situation, indeed, in which we need to invent some new questions to ask of Third-World cinema, and of the Third World generally, as the last surviving social space from which alternatives to corporate capitalist daily life and social relations are to be sought. The fear is, to be sure, that the West will have been so successful in destroying radical political movements in the Third World as to leave only the sterile passions of nationalism and religious fundamentalism (and this is the sense in which, as I've argued elsewhere,[4] these last may also ironically be counted among the current forms of the post-modern). 'Otherness', meanwhile, is a peculiarly booby-trapped and self-defeating concept; and the slogan of 'difference', while politically impeccable in all the obvious senses, is formalistic and empty of concrete social and historical specification – where it does not, indeed, relax and lend itself to the usual late capitalist celebration of multi-cultural pluralism. (It has, in short, all the ambiguity of an essentially liberal, rather than radical, value.)

My own feeling is that new forms of political art – if not a post-modern political art, then at least a political art within postmodernity – are so far to be felt dimly stirring in the general area of the didactic. By weakening the older forms of aesthetic autonomy, by breaking down the barriers, not merely between high and low culture, but also between literary language and other kinds of discourse, by dissolving the fictional into a whole immense world of representations and image-spectacles which are henceforth as real as any referent, the postmodern situation has, perhaps unwittingly, released new possibilities, and in particular enabled new and different uses of the art object, owing to the heterogeneity of its contents – some 'intrinsic' in the older aestheticizing sense, some 'extrinsic' in ways that go well beyond the older conceptions of collage, montage, ciné vérité or newspaper novel. As an astute observer noted, we are not averse to learning things (facts, recipes, history) out of postmodern books and even out of postmodern novels, in a readerly impurity hitherto taboo and excluded from the practice of the high modernist classics. Reading having been redrawn in contemporary theory, perhaps it is now time to restructure our conception of learning itself. If fantasy is epistemological, as Deleuze has argued in the *Anti-Oedipus*, indeed if narrative is itself a form of cognition, then an obvious next step lies in the systematic harnessing of the energies of those hitherto irrational activities for cognitive purposes. The conception of cognitive mapping I have proposed elsewhere[5] was intended to include that possibility as well, and to be prescriptive as well as descriptive. The idea has, at least on my view, the advantage of involving concrete content (imperialism, the world system, subalternity, dependency and hegemony), while necessarily involving a program of formal analysis of a new kind (since it is centrally defined by the dilemma of representation itself). Even as an exclusively retrospective and analytical instrument – critical and historical rather than speculative and productive – 'cognitive mapping' in this sense can be judged on its results and findings. But since it has been affirmed as an activity of individual and collective subjects in general (I have tried to associate it closely with Althusser's classic redefinition of ideology), it is obviously encouraging to find the concept of mapping validated by conscious artistic production, and to come upon this or that new work, which, like a straw in the wind, independently seems to have conceived of the vocation of art itself as that of inventing new geotopical cartographies.

Such is therefore the interest of *The Perfumed Nightmare* (which subsumes its many other varied and rich interests): that cartography and circumnavigation have a special meaning for this film-maker is documented by his most recent project (as far as I know, unfinished at present writing), which takes as its theme the very fact and invention of circumnavigation itself. *Magellan's Slave* (alternately entitled *Memories of Overdevelopment*, a title that as we shall see would hold good equally well for all of Kidlat's films[6]) is reconstructed from the hypothesis of contemporary historians that the slave, whom Magellan purchased in Seville but who was captured in the Indonesian archipelago, seems to have spoken a language not unrelated to

The Perfumed Nightmare

The Perfumed Nightmare

present-day Tagalog; if so, presumably he originated in what are today the Philippines. But since Magellan died on Mactan island in the Archipelago, his slave was the first human being to circumnavigate the globe. Needless to say, he is played by Kidlat himself.

Tahimik is first and foremost a clown: something rare enough, which marks his filmic kinship with Chaplin or with Jacques Tati, and underscores his essential distance from all contemporary filmmaking, whether Third World or Hollywood alike. Philippine cinema has a vibrant tradition of social realism; the late Lino Brocka was only the most well-known of any number of film-makers who can draw on the unique resources of this national situation, in which a quintessential urban agglomeration finds itself internally and externally related to an idyllic tropical countryside in which older forms of village life persist. Their production is then subtended by a long and durable tradition of revolt and guerrilla warfare. Whatever its overt politics and its specific messages, the co-existence of artistic production and political struggle cannot but be stimulating and fertile for the former (and perhaps for the latter as well).

In *The Perfumed Nightmare*, Kidlat plays a jeepney driver – jeepnies being rebuilt and brightly painted jeeps that serve as buses, and in this case as the transport linking the village to the metropolis – who, in his enthusiasm for the US moon landing, has organized a Werner von Braun fan club among the village children. When he eventually wins a trip to Paris to see modernization for himself, he finds older markets being supplanted and destroyed by hideous concrete supermarkets, not without a certain resemblance to atomic power-stations.

At length, he renounces his enthusiasm for Western technology, and returning home, rememorates the martyrdom of his father, who was killed by American soldiers during their occupation of the Philippines. But this account endows a series of episodes and gags (reminiscent of Eisenstein's original conception of the'montage of attractions') with a misleading semblance of narrative unity.

As for politics, the film, assembled almost a decade before the collapse of the dictatorship, contains only a handful of tactful and discreet allusions to state power, in the shape of police or army uniforms at the outskirts of the image. Indeed, I will want to argue shortly that the relevance of Tahimik's production for the contemporary (or post-contemporary) situation lies precisely in the way in which he eschews the political for the economic, and the thematics of power for that of reification. Nonetheless, there remains in this film a fundamental substitute and 'place-holder' (*tenant-lieu*) for the absent dictator and his regime; something like the ultimate reference itself, which, in a peculiar allegorical reversal, is now called upon to stand in for the signifier and, by taking its place, somehow to represent a phenomenon which was its own effect and secondary expression (indeed, we have argued elsewhere in this book, particularly in Part One, that the force of allegory seems to depend on just such indirection and systematic displacement from one level to another). In the present instance, the allegorical 'substitute' is in fact American imperialism (itself the cause and origin of the Marcos regime), inscribed mythically, as I will show later on, in the person of the murdered

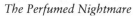

The Perfumed Nightmare

father. But this peculiarly involuted and self-referential allegorical reversal enables the film's crucial move from imperialism as outright political domination and gunboat power to imperialism as cultural domination in a far more contemporary media sense. What is significant about this move is that it makes a link – or 'bridge', to use the film's own symbolic language (see below) – between power and culture without assimilating either to the other in the ontological fashion of First-World theory, which somehow always feels compelled to 'decide' which comes first and where the fundamental or dominant instance is to be located. In Tahimik's episodic rhythms, these two realities remain autonomous, and are simply juxtaposed, side by side or in sequence, without any particular priority being assigned by the form itself or suggested by narrative or causal perspectives.

As for Kidlat's more basic political credentials, they are secured, or so one would have thought, by his second film, *Turumba* (1983), which offers a virtual textbook demonstration of the penetration of capital into a traditional village, and the transformation of collective relations by the market and money relationships. It is a process symbolized by the impact of the 'cash nexus' on the religious ritual designated by the title, and turns on the change visited by production for the market on the musician-performer traditionally responsible for this annual event. It is a festival in which what are separated in modern societies as culture and religion have not yet been dissociated, and whose beauty the tourist-spectators who are this film's Western public can still distantly glimpse and reconstruct from behind the interposed medium of the camera and its travelogue language. Here already, therefore, formal elements that we will find more ambitiously deployed and developed in *The Perfumed Nightmare* can be enumerated: a secondary symbolism marked as such, and the co-optation of co-optation involved in admitting and ostentatiously foregrounding the inauthenticity of the Western spectator and of the travelogue spectacle. Here handicraft is the vehicle for what never changes and is yet changed irrevocably, beyond all recognition. A German tourist-businesswoman likes some of the decorations used in the festival and orders more. Family and then village itself must be enlisted in the gradual mass-production of these items, which eventually destroy the cyclical or ritual time of the village and prevent the organizer from wasting any more of it on the festival which was the source of the objects in question in the first place. Even the crudeness of the final irony – as their reward the manufacturer and his son are given a trip to Europe, to the Munich Olympics of 1972, the Third World visiting the First at the very moment in which the latter is about to be violently impacted by the former – is consistent with Kidlat's aesthetic, in which a gesture toward language and representation (which must therefore designate itself as such) is preferable to the thing seemingly achieved and thereby mistaken for the real.

192

What remains real in the later film is the historic fact of the destructive effects of a new money economy. It is a fact that more 'modern' societies have once lived, long ago, and have now forgotten, save in the form of empty slogans ('the penetration of capital') that stereotype themselves by living on without experiential meaning. But *Turumba* does not try to reinvent that, or to put us as subjects imaginatively back into a concrete situation of otherness in which we might fleetingly recapture this historically unique event. It does not even make an appeal to historical pathos; nor is its essential gaiety a frivolous or restorative matter either, but the face of an essential indifference, the icy disdain of farce for the fates of individual subjects, the joyous mask that covers a stoic refusal of complicity with the ego's life and death. What *Turumba* does, therefore, is not to commemorate the ancient catastrophe in any Benjaminian or historicist way, nor to represent it with the immediacy of the historical novel, but rather merely to designate its simple existence as a fact: you forgot it, you don't remember what it was like, or even that it happened, but it is still here, somewhere, still happening in one form or another, whether you remember it or not! This peculiar deixis – here is a phenomenon, in the richest philosophic sense of the word; it doesn't matter what you think of it, it is simply here – proves to have unusual pedagogical or didactic potentialities of what we may perhaps term a post-Brechtian kind. And it includes a paradoxical relationship to the public and the spectator by virtue of its very indifference to them.

The incisiveness and simplicity of *Turumba*'s demonstration, however, preclude the richness of *The Perfumed Nightmare*, in which we

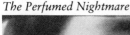

The Perfumed Nightmare

Playtime

not only get to Europe, but wander through the Third-World metropolis itself. Significantly, Kidlat is absent from his second, more completely rural film, something which must have disappointed viewers of the first, in which the epistemological properties of the clown were fully mobilized and put to work in the appropriate environment. As a film of this kind makes clear, the setting in motion of that object-world demands a certain resistance; its tactile exteriors lend themselves to exploration and articulation by way of the elasticity of the clown's body. Chaplin's big city, and even more dramatically the virtually already postmodern Paris, the *société-de-consommation* Gaullist Paris of Tati's *Playtime* (1967), in which the ungainliness of the protagonist elicits, like two surfaces slowly beginning to lean towards each other, the inhuman unloveliness of the glass walls and

194

The Perfumed Nightmare

decor – these already begin to suggest the elective affinities between the modern clown and urban modernization itself: Kidlat's machines, and above all his jeepney, but also the modernizing Europe of NATO and the Common Market – urbanizations spreading from Manila out into the villages, but also from the former European nation states out over new multinational customs unions and trade zones. That particular story, one feels like saying, no European or First-World writer or film-maker could tell, because it too fatally resembles the modernizing stories of an earlier and now old-fashioned era, the commodifications clumsily detected by the naturalist libidinal apparatus, the consumers' goods, the peasants, the prostitutes shifted back and forth through the narratives of Dreiser or Zola. Polls, sociological treatises, documentaries and economic forecasts are the genre in which such materials are now transmitted. Elegant representationnns of the more expensive television kind would fatally transform such *examples* into the expectation of a thesis whose second shoe waits to drop, thereby unsettling an already uncomfortable viewing public. Only a mode of representation which is not uncomfortable with clumsiness could accommodate such social developments. Kidlat's home-made movies handle them very well indeed, as a bonus or by-product allowing us to reflect on our own generic discomfort much as Brecht thought his audience should spend some time mulling over the meaning of the actions represented in the play.

The Perfumed Nightmare

The same is true for the conceptual or philosophical content of this work, which one could imagine 'resolved' in very different ways from this, according to the respective aesthetic. 'Mediation', for example, is here symbolically designated by the picture of a bridge, and specifically of the little hump-backed stone bridges of the village, over which real and toy vehicles laboriously pass. As a 'concept', it has something to do with the relationship between cultural stages (Third and First Worlds); between the 'levels' of social life itself, not excluding the episodic heterogeneity of this film, which passes abruptly from technology to work, art to politics, anthropology to gentrification without smoothing over the traces or making the 'transitions' (the bridges) any less bumpy; between the past and the future, as well, and between confinement and freedom. In a representational work, all these awkward transitions would have to be concealed by a plausibly constructed plot along with mesmerizingly naturalized camerawork. In Eisenstein, their intersections, rebaptized montage in all of its senses, would be transformed, by violence and by fiat, into powerful slogans and statements, concrete relationships prestidigitated into 'dialectical' models. In Godard, meanwhile, who will here and throughout serve as the most enlightening First-World co-ordinate for rethinking Kidlat, the specific mediation would be projected onto the screen as an open problem – image and text side by side and incommensurable, unresolvable, but also irrepressible, and the pretext for nagging returns to antinomies which, repeated often enough, seem to turn into 'themes' of an old-fashioned literary type.

The Perfumed Nightmare

But Tahimik's 'bridges' also look like themes in the more old-fashioned sense of symbols (rather than the theoretical motifs that stud Godard's essay-films). The very archaic nature of these figures is in fact what saves them, for here, as in naif art generally, the gap between the image and the intended meaning lies open as innocently as in a child's or a schizophrenic drawing. This kind of symbol is therefore so pre-representational as to rejoin all of the most post-modern and poststructural strictures on the arbitrariness of the sign and the essentially allegorical nature of the symbol, the ineradicable gap between figuration and meaning, the impossibility of achieved representation, the generation of more and more text out of the unsynchronizable syncopation between the signifier and its signified. Here then the picture postcard of the bridge leads us further on into sheer space: the space of the village, and then the space of the bridge or transport between the village and Manila – figured by the jeepney that conveys passengers back and forth. At length, in a larger open-ing, this is not merely the bridge between the earth and the moon (along with the Werner von Braun fan clubs that celebrate it), but that more tangible bridge which the protagonist will at length cross lead-ing from Asia to Europe, from Third World to First and back, from Manila to Paris (and from Paris to the Rhine), and from a Philippino present to a traditional Parisian past itself in the process of being obliterated by its own Common Market future. All of these spaces are then in constant decomposition and modernization, including each other heterogeneously, in such a way that narrative progression becomes unthinkable, except as a bus ride, and we learn to substitute for it the discontinuous series of spatial exhibits that might be offered by a collection of snapshots, or by the old variety show implicit in the form of the clown's gags – that vaudeville 'montage of attractions' from which, as I've already mentioned, Eisenstein's own theory and practice ultimately derived in its own very different and distinctive way. There is, I think, a fable buried in this particular collection of episodes: it is the movement of disillusion that leads from the first enthusiasm for Western technologies – the conquest of the moon, the fan clubs – to their ultimate renunciation, after the experience of the real First World itself. But the meaning of this renunciation is ambiguous, as I will argue in a moment.

Yet the heterogeneous form of the sequence is itself as different from that celebrated by First-World radical cinema as Latin American magic realism is from its European surrealist predecessor: and for the same reason, namely, that here heterogeneity is inscribed ahead of time in the very content itself. In First-World cinema (in Godard, for instance) it was programmed to happen to the form, not merely by way of transformation of realities into their own representations, so that we are no longer looking at a Bazinian person but rather at a photograph or image of that person; but also very much by way of that incommensurability between the different representations or texts which the West always seems to live in terms of this or that crisis of relativism. But Western relativisms – however internally jarring and contradictory – have always seemed to take place within some essential class homogeneity: the most dramatic eruptions of otherness – as in race or gender – always ultimately seeming to fold back into conflicts on the inside of a sphere whose true other or exterior eluded representation altogether. And that virtually by definition, since in the very moment in which a thought or impulse from that unrepresentable Outside enters the field of thought or discourse, it will already have been represented, and, henceforth belonging to 'us', can no longer be truly other or noumenal.

It is a dilemma that all consequent First-World artists must face in their own unique and distinctive ways, but which Godard's Maoism can serve at least to dramatize in a consequent manner, which has the advantage of including the formal plane within itself. For his obsession with the opposition between images and words is surely itself already, if not a replay, then at least a pre-play of the dialectic of inside and outside that Maoism will at least for a time be invoked to resolve. 'Juste une image': the famous reversal, accompanied by an oddly defensive insistence on the unlikely proposition that images cannot lie, suggests at the very least a multiple strategy, in which a nostalgia for a solid visual world cleansed of the ambiguities of language can co-exist with the possibility of interrupting the visual and its illusions with multiple languages external to it that ceaselessly problematize its messages and symbolically re-enact an outside threatening at every point to penetrate the security of the visual monad.

Godard's 'method' is then to stage his heterogeneities statically – within the image, rather than, as in Kidlat, between the narrative segments – in such a way as to pry the auditory image away from the iconic ones. This is done, not in order to reveal some more 'natural' reality behind those formal planes, which is the strategy of eighteenth-century bourgeois revolution; nor even to transform their incommensurability into a new kind of history lesson, as in Brecht; but rather in order to exacerbate a kind of negative dialectic, an intensified and frustrated consciousness of the simulacra within which we find ourselves immobilized and bewitched. 'Maoism' cannot be the same kind of answer to this dilemma, nor can it generate the same kind of dialectical lesson, as the Great Method of Me-ti which enables the provisional pause, the provisional ending, for Brecht's didactic plays. The moment Maoism appears as such in Godard (in *La Chinoise* [1967]) it is immediately degraded to the status of a new kind of image in its own right and releases a new flood of degenerate iconographies. As for the larger global horizon it once promised and designated within the First World, this bourgeoisie reverting to barbarism and cannibalism scarcely has the leisure to hear its distant accents, save in those moments in which an inner Third World appears in flesh and blood in the person of migrant workers – as with the famous African garbage collectors of *Weekend*, who recite Lenin and Fanon to the bemused white middle-class refugees from a world on its way to Apocalypse.

Kidlat's grotesque Europeans are apparently all Filipinos in disguise, acting out American imperialists or German businesswomen with comic gusto: something surely more cathartic for them than for Godard's Africans or Palestinians. For the fundamental lesson of this comparison must surely lie in the radical dissymmetry between these two situations, which are not mere inversions of one another. What the First World thinks and dreams about the Third can have nothing whatsoever in common, formally or epistemologically, with what the Third World has to know every day about the First. Subalternity carries the possibility of knowledge with it, domination that of forgetfulness and repression – but knowledge is not just the opposite of forgetfulness, nor is domination the opposite of oppression.

In the same way, the village, as it extends outwards to include Manila, and then Paris and Europe itself, is a very different kind of space from that – exactly coterminous and identically superimposable on the same map – which stretches out from Paris and Europe to envelop the Philippines, Manila and ultimately the village itself. Alejo Carpentier implied as much in his fundamental definition of the 'real maravilloso' (magic realism) years ago, when he observed that surrealism expressed a First-World subjective craving for heterogeneity and de-reification, whereas that superficially similar trend in Latin American literature called magic realism sprang from the objective fact of uneven development in the post-colonial object-world itself. In the latter, the co-existence of layers of social time, from the most modernized to the most ancient peasant customs and thought modes, all persist side by side within the Latin American present, their chaotic juxtaposition at once detectable on the recording surfaces, where uncommodified experience spills out more richly than the twice commodified data of a more completely standardized and uniform late capitalist reality – which has already been processed in daily life before being processed a second time by the media that control its representations.

Meanwhile, both these kinds of social reality have their absent other in what it may be abusive to name with the same word, that is, 'the body,' since even this pole of the organization of experience is radically different in the two economies and the two cultures. In both, to be sure, the body is what guarantees individual experience as its most apparently concrete form, a ballast of the social imaginary, that ultimate individuality that nails in place the layers of the general and the abstract, the universal or the collective. But in the West, the corporate impoverishment of experience determines a kind of frenzy and desperation in which the promises of the last bodily layer are sought after with a well-nigh pathological single-mindedness. It is

The Perfumed Nightmare

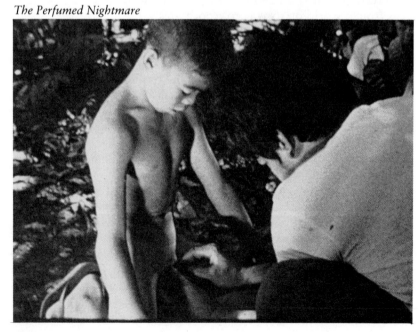

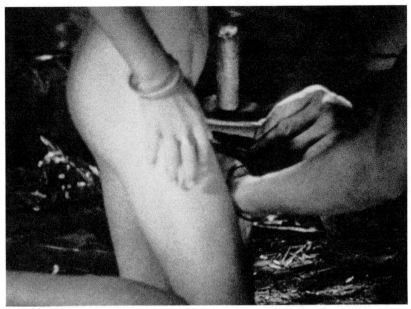

The Perfumed Nightmare

what can be called the reduction to the body and observed in its more symptomatic forms in pornography and violence porn, provided these are not greeted with a simple-minded moralizing but rather acknowledged historically as deeper truths of our social experience, and as primordially characteristic of our socially specific relationship to Being. Godard's pointless explosions of violence and scandal – from the dentings and bashings of cars all the way to the cannibalism of *Weekend*, and in the seemingly gratuitous incidence of prostitution throughout, which, in the fashion of Baudelaire, Simmel and Karl Kraus, he systematically links up with art, acting and exhibitionism, and the infinite thirst for financial backers – these attempt, if not to master, then at least to inscribe this function of the bodily substratum.

Whether or not Third-World culture is in general more reticent about bodily experience – perhaps it would be better to say that it does not seem to put the same premium on the consumption of simulacra of the corporeal and the physiological – it is certain that *The Perfumed Nightmare*, having concentrated this kind of libidinal investment in the figure of the clown himself, is not concerned in the same obsessive way with surfaces and textures, and with the microrepresentation of the pores of being. It is therefore all the more significant to locate the body's inscription here in a very different place, namely, that of ritual. How else indeed to account for the gratuitous and scandalous irruption of the two shocking episodes of circumcision and of childbirth

201

that oddly and arbitrarily punctuate this otherwise humorous text with all the jarring incoherence of Stendhal's pistol shots at a concert? But in Stendhal (and in the very period of Napoleon's dictum that politics is destiny) those were the incursions of the political into the realm of the social and of what was apparently private life: these mark a similar intersection, where the collective, however, invests the great biological rhythms as they cut across individual lives.

It does not, indeed, seem to be an accident that what is widely considered to be the first African novel in French, the *Batouala* of the Caribbean writer René Maran, which won the Prix Goncourt in 1921, also turns centrally on a gruesome ritual of circumcision. Clearly, Kidlat Tahimik cannot have the same justification of a kind of realism and the representation of social customs still extant, nor can his fantasy circumcision even be thought to reflect elements of the style of some indigenous culture on the point of eclipse. This non-existential bodily violence may be thought to be something like the mask both works turn with a certain ironic *ressentiment* towards the voyeuristic public of the First World, of the Prix Goncourt or of the film festivals, as it avidly receives these presumably authentic specimens of geotopic otherness.

That is a reading which is not inconsistent with another one, however: namely, the sense that in otherness of this kind – in the styles that conjure up ethnicity, that nourish stereotypes and quicken the various racisms fully as much as the various celebrations of collective identity – it is somehow the fantasy of religious otherness that is the ultimately determining instance. Religion on this view is grasped as little more than some central point of otherness in the collective relations – the mirages and optical illusions – between the various groups. Religion then, here deeper than the individual body itself, is what is unclean in the other *ethnie*; but as a fantasmatic property or essence it can only be grasped by way of their outlandish practices and rituals. At some deepest unconscious level then, all foreign cultures are somehow fantasized as so many religions, as specific types of abomination and superstition. Yet by the same token, when I come to attempt to reaffirm my own imaginary cultural identity, only the rags and trappings of 'religion' are available, trappings which it takes a certain fanaticism to talk myself into for any extended period of time.

These features of *The Perfumed Nightmare* are, to be sure, divested of their more alarming implications by the episodic structure of the narrative. But they nonetheless ultimately connect, however weakly, with that interpretive temptation of a kind of cultural nationalism which we will evaluate in conclusion. Otherwise, these two gratuitous episodes of bodily pain merely serve to anchor or ground the sequence of gags, which, as in all classical farce, since it ultimately concerns the body itself, must insist in passing on the thump of the fall, the stab of the gouty toe, the biting of the trained fleas, or the smarting of the paddle.

It is time, therefore, to look more closely at the form itself and the contents that determine it: something that can initially best be approached negatively. For all generic law is as much concerned with warding off the wrong or inappropriate reactions, questions, readings, and receptive attitudes, as it is to produce the 'right' ones. In the present instance, it seems clear that *The Perfumed Nightmare* faces at least one fundamental generic dilemma: that is, how its segments are to be prevented from degenerating into that travelogue which is just as surely its other generic pole and the content of its form. For the film is our travelogue on the Philippines and includes Kidlat's travelogue on Europe; and in order for the images not simply to fold back into their own stereotypes, and for them to affirm themselves as realities, a gap must be kept open between the contents and what displays them. This last must ceaselessly be designated as an arbitrary form in its own right, must point to itself, and the fact of the travelogue as form must itself become part of the film's content, included in the subject-matter.

Meanwhile, if the decline into travelogue menaces this work from one end, its disintegration into outright farce and comic gags await it at the other. The persona of the clown, and the concomitant vaudeville structure of discontinuous numbers, motivate the willed and necessarily episodic structure of the film, but this motivation must remain weak. Tati's project (in *Playtime*) can accommodate an infinite series of humorous situations; but here the laughter must somehow remain within the film, as is the case with the hilarity of the members of the Werner von Braun fan club, village children whom the Kidlat character has assembled around himself as a supporting cast and to justify his application in the international contest for the best slogan describing the moon shot. The narcissistic sentimentalism of the Kidlat persona is clearly one of the ways in which this formal tension is defused: we are free to attribute our amusement to the 'objective situation' or to the absurdity of its protagonist indifferently. Yet another solution is also present in the regrounding of the travelogue itself into something like a family photo, with our conviction that the shots of the village and the villagers will be shown to the latter for their analysis and appreciation, and received according to the norms of naive realism. Thus Kidlat's sheepish passport photo is remodelled by the village children in the form of a smiling dog. Meanwhile, the shots of the 'West' will also presumably be rescreened in the village, where Kidlat's presence in that exotic scenery can be presumed to have been greeted by equally appreciative hoots. The film, in other words, includes its spectator (or narratee) within itself. Palpably made for a First-World (or film festival) public, it also requires its First-World audience to look over the shoulder of a Third-

The Perfumed Nightmare

World public at the same time, or through their 'implied' point of view, without any irony in the Western sense. Travelogue is here rescued and transformed, not by metamorphosis into the great Western spatial image (as, say, in Antonioni's notorious documentary on China), but rather by regression to some first and more primal level of the first forms of photography, the family snapshot or the home movie, the wonderment of sheer reproduction and recognition. The First-World/Third-World dialectic is thereby inscribed within the film, in its very form and the structure of its viewing; at the same time that Kidlat's aesthetic rejoins a whole range of Western avant-garde or experimental projects in which the home movie, the non-professional, non-institutional use of the camera, symbolically becomes the Utopian escape from commercial reification.

The difference is, as I began to suggest above, that this particular film has a message and seeks to transmit an ideological lesson of a type embarrassing if not inconceivable for First-World (realistic) film-makers. Just as *Turumba* sets out to illustrate the ravages of a money economy, so also *The Perfumed Nightmare* may be read as a virtual textbook illustration of the classical account: 'constant revolutioning of production, uninterrupted disturbance of all social conditions, everlasting uncertainty and agitation distinguish the bourgeois epoch from all earlier ones ... all that is solid melts into air' (Marx and Engels, *The Communist Manifesto*).

What is paradoxical about the illustration – and what distinguishes the procedure here from the aesthetic of Kidlat's second, more openly didactic film – is that the proposition is demonstrated on the First World rather than on the Third. The lesson is learned in Paris rather than in Manila, and the political or pedagogical pathos that might have been expected to be aroused in the service of a properly postcolonial militancy is here displaced and redirected back to the source, and exercised on behalf of the very metropolis that under other circumstances would have been denounced as the subject of the imperial domination and the agent of commodification and of the destruction of the old ways. What Kidlat observes and dwells on is rather the destruction of the older *quartiers* of Paris itself, the sweeping away of a traditional petty bourgeoisie of small shops and shopkeepers by the new chains of supermarkets, the bureaucratic control of space itself, the late capitalist onslaught on the classical capitalist city, something like the dialectical self-destruction of the First World and its own internal social relations. Meanwhile, across the Rhine, the decline in handicraft is also dramatically and spatially registered, in the episode of the setting in place of the last hand-crafted *Zwiebelturm*, distinctive emblem of a specifically German culture which is also in the process of homogeneization and stan-dardization.

This paradoxical redirection, this substitution of referents, does not merely recall attempts of the New Criticism to characterize what is unique and specific to poetic language and its effects in paradox itself and in reversals of all kinds. It also makes one think of what must be among the very first texts in this genre, in which, in 1859, the passing of the classical city and its mutilation by technology, modernization and the new, are lamented – *The Swan* of Baudelaire, in which the destructive effects on Paris of that earlier state of modernization symbolized by the name of Haussmann are unexpectedly evoked by way of the memory of a classical reading (Virgil) and the hopeless situations of Third-World exiles and prisoners: by way, that is to say,

The Perfumed Nightmare

The Perfumed Nightmare

of the deep past and the violence of European domination (itself then reinscribed, but classically, 'aesthetically', within the Virgilian text); as though the intersection of both these co-ordinates were necessary in order to allegorize the fate of a few old buildings and to project the fate of the city itself as an emblematic destiny.

Kidlat's travelogues shake similar perceptions free by way of the transformation of distant superhuman fantasies of the space program, transmitted by satellite into the village, into the ugly poured-concrete masses of the new supermarkets that fall into traditional *arrondissements* like meteorites from the future. Even so, the message is by no means as simple as the feeling, and it is to imprint the latter with the former that, in Baudelaire fully as much as in *The Perfumed Nightmare*, the indirections and substitutions already mentioned have been deployed: for the perception must be prevented from implying or transmitting any simple denunciation of modernization as such. The lesson's classical text is itself here the model, and conveys the additional lesson that the dialectic necessarily posits mixed feelings. For Marx, the ceaseless destruction of the old by the new is as positive as it is negative; the archaic needed to be given a shove (as Nietzsche put it), everything that is tragic about its disappearance is also to be welcomed. I'm tempted to say that in Baudelaire what is positive about the destruction of Paris is the excuse it offers for the deployment of that new content called *spleen* and the occasion it provides for the new (modernist) poetic and formal production the latter now demands. It is therefore language that is here the beneficiary, *its* modernization is the productive face of the wanton bureaucratic efficiency of Haussmann's baleful embellishment of the city.

The Perfumed Nightmare, however, would seem to be threatened with a different set of impossible alternatives. For in a Third World classically fixated on the dualism between the Old and the New, between tradition and Westernization, culture and science, religion and secularization, the critique of modernization risks tipping the

206

scales, in a situation in which neither alternative can really be satisfactory. It is an ideological message that is ready to transmit itself, simply by the removal or suspension of its opposite. Thus, something like cultural nationalism is implicitly revealed when the option of advanced technology is taken away, whether or not the author or film-maker has thought it through and really means to endorse this reversal and this essentially political position. Kidlat's film, however, goes further than this, for its concluding sections really do seem to conjure up a whole discursive world of visionary legend that fleshes out and gives content to the cultural-nationalist alternative, which despite the images of the village and the countryside had not yet fully taken shape. But this is also the moment in which politics, and the historical fact of imperialism, enter the picture far more vividly, and in which the American conquest and the American occupation, the murder of the father, inscribe power and history openly, as themes, and with none of the tactful indirections of the sparse allusions to the internal political situation.

Yet it is a politics conjoined with another kind of raw material which had not yet been pressed into service in the film's series of vaudeville numbers: that is, myth itself, in the form of the great wind or typhoon which is set in place at the film's climax, and which is called upon to symbolize the will to revolt, the archaic or natural power of the great Third-World revolutions. It is what the New Critics would have called an 'unearned' ending, little enough in this

The Perfumed Nightmare

The Perfumed Nightmare

film justifying the banner of revolt raised in its concluding moments. On the other hand, the New Critics worked with organic conceptions of the work of art and of the concrete universal; their conception of a full motivation is unseasonable here, in a form which is deliberately disjointed and heterogeneous. It is precisely that heterogeneity which also frees this unearned ending, and allows the inscription of the force of revolt, but only as a specific figure in this particular film, and not as any generalizable political or cultural program that can be transferred elsewhere. The beauty of the resolution on this particular level – the way in which the image of a butterfly that enfolds the sun in its wings unites the gentleness of the Kidlat persona with the violence of revolutionary rage itself – is marked as a fragile figure by the very nature of its content. The image itself, which we here manhandle with clumsy fingers, has all the brittle delicacy of the butterfly's wings, no matter what may be the ultimate destiny of this figure – from tattoo to historical force of nature. This is perhaps to say that the cultural-nationalist alternative – a politics which draws on indigenous cultural traditions in order to summon the force and will to dislodge the invader – is here inscribed as an impulse rather than a program, as an aesthetics of revolt rather than its concrete politics. It is, as in the Sartrean concept of derealization, a message transmitted by the quality of the image, rather than its structural implications. Above all, it is a message transmitted by the unreal or derealized quality of the image, which consists in very precisely that unreality and that provisional aestheticism.

But that message has also been transmitted outside the image itself,

The Perfumed Nightmare

by the very unevenness of its figural context. The great typhoon, the butterfly, must in fact compete with the 'bridge', with the jeepnies, with the *Zwiebelturm* and the supermarket, the airplane and the man in the moon, a competition in which it proves to have a kind of resilience which is not merely aestheticist or *fin-de-siècle*. By the same token, the interpretation in terms of cultural nationalism must itself compete with other readings, which I have withheld until now. For First-World modernization and advanced technology is not in fact, in *The Perfumed Nightmare*, simply one term in a dualism or binary opposition: a third term comes to join those familiar ones of the West and of mythic traditional or native culture.

This third term is the moment of industrial production within an otherwise agricultural context (for even the Parisians in this film sell agricultural produce); nor does it turn on the nostalgic essentialization of the vanishing moment of artisanal labor and craft, as we see it for one last time in the final *Zwiebelturm*. Rather, it consists in the building, the unbuilding, the rebuilding, of the jeepnies – bricolage if there ever was, a scavenging for spare parts and home-made ad hoc solutions – the constant re-functioning (Brecht's *Unfunktionierung*) of the new into the old, and the old into the new, the reconstruction of military machinery into painted traditional artifacts, and the dismemberment of those artifacts for the handicraft assemblage of the jeepnies. This is not merely the auto-referentiality of the *naïf* film itself, whose aesthetic consists precisely in this unremitting collection of miscellaneous footage that you put together at your pleasure. It also in and of itself immediately blasts apart the sterile opposition

The Perfumed Nightmare

between the old and the new, the traditional and the Western, and allows its former components themselves to be cannibalized and conceptually resoldered. Unlike the 'natural' or mythic appearances of traditional agricultural society, but equally unlike the disembodied machinic forces of late capitalist high technology, which seem, at the other end of time, equally innocent of any human agency or individual or collective praxis, the jeepney factory is a space of human labor which does not know the structural oppression of the assembly line or Taylorization, which is permanently provisional, thereby liberating its subjects from the tyrannies of form and of the pre-programmed. In it aesthetics and production are again at one, and painting the product is an integral part of its manufacture. Nor finally is this space in any bourgeois sense humanist or a golden mean, since spiritual or material proprietorship is excluded, and inventiveness has taken the place of genius, collective co-operation the place of managerial or demiurgic dictatorship.

It is, indeed, instructive to juxtapose this particular factory space, tossed in as yet another vaudeville number or travelogue segment, with earlier places of production in this book. The optical fitting-room and business convention of *Videodrome* were clearly outposts of distribution, while Pakula's newspaper office – notwithstanding Joyce's Cave of the Winds – was less plausible as a workplace than those journeys into the bowels of the infrastructure we were able to glimpse in *Three Days of the Condor* or in *The Conversation*. But Hitchcock's Seagram Building is yet another place of management

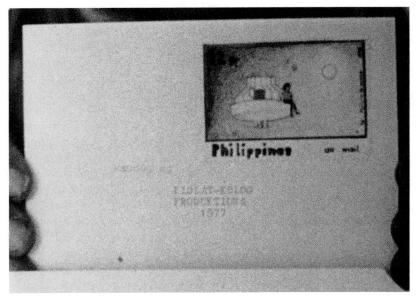

The Perfumed Nightmare

rather than of production, one we see from the outside at that, and from the point of view of an advertising agency executive. Only the Europeans seem willing to make their way back onto the shop floor: but Sokurov's documentary sequence (on 'the building trades' in Central Asia) is spliced into his fiction film as though to make the point about the vanity of all human labor and the impossibility for Soviet people to attain the reliable and efficiently planned and produced object-world of the West. Appropriately enough, then, Godard's Swiss factory seems far more high tech, but also to betray a kind of Western or First-World mesmerization with human interactions and social relations exclusively (how do you show labor, Godard's characters ask; can you make a film about work – isn't it something like pornography?) This is the context in which Kidlat's jeepnies mark the place of a properly Third-World way with production which is neither the ceaseless destruction and replacement of new and larger industrial units (together with their waste by-products and their garbage), nor a doomed and nostalgic retrenchment in traditional agriculture, but a kind of Brechtian delight with the bad new things that anybody can hammer together for their pleasure and utility if they have a mind to. Kidlat's film is then itself just such another jeepney, an omnibus and omnipurpose object that ferries its way back and forth between First and Third Worlds with dignified hilarity.

It is also an excellent provisional ending to this selective anthology of movies from the current world system. It is well to be able to take as one's text and for one's lesson a work so inimitable, for it is unlikely that *The Perfumed Nightmare* will mislead by serving as an immutable model of anything, just as it is improbable that Kidlat should found a school or movement. What is instructive for the new political culture to come is the way in which here the economic dimension has come to take precedence over a political one which is not left out or repressed, certainly, but which (in the person of the father and the butterfly, and the doomed revolt against the army of occupation) is for the moment assigned a subordinate position and role. In *The Political Unconscious*,[7] I suggested that from the point of view of content or raw material we have some interest in distinguishing between three distinct categories or levels: the immediately political, in the sense of the contingencies and reversals of punctual events themselves; the conjunctural, or the realm of social class, in the sense of the larger collective and ideological forces at work all around us, coming to articulation and retreating again into a world of blurred contours and mystified obfuscation, only occasionally, in supreme moments, finding the stark definition of the outright class conflict itself; the economic, finally, in the larger sense of the history of modes of production, the great patterning systems that imprint the daily lives of producing and consuming subjects, forming their habits and their psyches in the process, and only occasionally entering into crisis as they are challenged with forms of the new, with new collective structures and new human relations (if not indeed with the sometimes equally problematizing recurrence and revival of much more ancient ones). Each of these three dimensions – which always co-exist – has its own logic, so that in politics as much as in art it is advisable to sort them out for openers, it being understood that you may well want to recombine them (explosively or architectonically) later on.

One's sense, in the present conjuncture, sometimes called the onset of postmodernity or late capitalism, is that our most urgent task will be tirelessly to denounce the economic forms that have come for the moment to reign supreme and unchallenged. This is to say, for example, that those doctrines of reification and commodification which played a secondary role in the traditional or classical Marxian heritage, are now likely to come into their own and become the dominant instruments of analysis and struggle. In other words, a cultural politics, a politics of daily life, which emerged in earlier decades but as something of an adjunct and a poor relative, a supplement, to 'politics' itself, must now – at least in the First World – be the primary space of struggle. This is indeed precisely what Kidlat's film teaches us: that the other levels must be inscribed – from the sheerly eventful or punctual (as in the Munich Olympics) to the great class warfare of the national liberation struggle – but that today as never before we must focus on a reification and a commodifcation that have become so universalized as to seem well-nigh natural and organic entities and forms. We must retain the visibility of these

artificial entities, and attempt, through a long night of unive
domination, to maintain a flickering self-consciousness of their or
presence; inscribing them tirelessly on the form of the work as I
ka's lieutenant had his sentence carved over and over again on his
own back (or Kidlat's character, his tattoo), in hopes that this second
nature can again, by dint of concentration, reveal itself as historical
and as the result of human actions, and thereby once again 'lead us to
take pleasure in the possibility of change in all things'.[8]

Notes

1. I take it that the slogan 'Third Cinema' is an attempt to square this circle and
   to retain the formal strengths of Third-World political cinema in a period in
   which its content has necessarily been modified beyond recognition. See on
   this the excellent collection edited by Jim Pines and Paul Willemen, *Questions
   of Third Cinema* (BFI, 1989).
2. See Teodor Shanin (ed.), *Late Marx and the Russian Road* (New York:
   Monthly Review, 1983), in particular the drafts of Marx's letter to Vera
   Zasulich and Haruli Wada's illuminating commentary. Marx's discussion, on
   forms of a transition from communism to capitalism in Russia, is unexpectedly suggestive for the present conjuncture as well.
3. David Bordwell, Janet Staiger, Kristin Thompson, *The Classical Hollywood
   Cinema* (Columbia University Press, 1985), pp. 381–5. But see also the
   articles by Teshome Gabriel (in *Questions*) for an attempt to redefine just such
   an alternative.
4. See my *Postmodernism, Or, The Cultural Logic of Late Capitalism* (Durham,
   NC: Duke University Press, 1990), pp. 386–91.
5. *Postmodernism*, pp. 50–4, and 409–17.
6. Kidlat exhibited some rushes from the project at the 'Challenge of Third
   World culture', a conference held in September 1986, at Duke University and
   organized by Charles Bergquist, Ariel Dorfman and Masao Miyoshi. See also
   the interview with Kidlat by Loris Mirella, in *Polygraph* 1 (1987), pp. 57–66
   (including a valuable article by Mirella on *The Perfumed Nightmare*).
   Tahimik has apparently completed two other films since this conference:
   Yan-ki and *I am Furious, Yellow*, which I have not been able to see. The
   distinguished Filipino film critic, Isagani R. Cruz, was able to find only two
   brief references to Kidlat (as an 'experimental' film-maker) in recent Filipino
   film criticism, which seems to be mainly oriented around the analysis of
   national commercial production. But if Tahimik remains unknown to the
   general public in the Philippines, he is admired by younger intellectuals 'as a
   model of what can be done alone and without national recognition' (Cruz, in
   private correspondence).
7. Fredric Jameson, *The Political Unconscious* (Cornell University Press, 1981),
   pp. 75–100.
8. Bertolt Brecht, *A Short Organon for the Theater*, in John Willet (ed.), *Brecht
   on Theater* (New York: Hill and Wang, 1964), p. 202.

Index

Cocteau, Jean, 32, 128, 139
cognitive mapping, 3, 10, 25, 49, 58, 79, 88, 188, 189
Cold War, 3
collective, the, 3–5, 9, 10, 14, 29, 59, 60, 63, 103, 109, 127, 146, 150, 154, 166, 167, 168, 171, 172, 176, 177, 186, 189, 192, 200, 202, 212; and assassination narrative, 47, 64, 66; and cultural repression, 119; and the detective story, 33, 37–41, 46; and history, 139; and praxis, 210; and the unconscious, 145
collective imaginary, 119
collective Other, 3
Color of Pomegranates (Paradjanov), 111
commercialization, 25, 87, 100
commodification, 5, 25, 131, 186, 205, 212
communism, 58, 109
conditions of possibility, 4, 73, 106
Conrad, Joseph, 128
conspiracy, 10, 15–17, 19, 23, 27, 29, 31, 32, 34, 35, 39, 45, 46, 55, 56, 58–61, 64–9, 79, 82, 88, 129; as allegory, 9; figuration of, 1; film, 3; and social totality, 63
Conversation, The (Coppola), 20, 142, 210
Coppola, Francis Ford, 20, 142, 156
Cornford, F. M., 50, 83
Counterfeiters, The (Gide), 121, 123, 127, 128, 130
Cronenberg, David, 22, 24, 30
Crying of Lot 49, The (Pynchon), 16, 21, 82
Cuba, 50, 186
Cuban missile crisis, 49
cyberpunk, 77
cynical reason, 28, 130, 144

Dante, 15
Days of Eclipse (Sokurov), 1, 87, 89, 90, 92, 101, 110, 112
De Palma, Brian, 142
Dead Zone, The (Cronenberg), 48
Definitely Maybe (Strugatsky Brothers), 111
Delacroix, Eugène, 158, 169, 183
Deleuze, Gilles, 171, 188
demography, 2, 4
Desnois, Edmundo, 50
Despair (Fassbinder), 98, 122
Desperation (Zhou Xiao-wen), 118–20, 138, 200
Diaz, Jesus, 154
Dick, Philip K., 14, 23, 27, 30, 35, 90, 93, 139
difference, 35, 39, 40, 43, 122, 130, 131, 133, 158, 178, 188, 204
Dispatches (Herr), 43

Doblin, Alfred, 123
Dos Passos, John, 34, 123
Dostoyevsky, Fyodor, 24
Dr. Strangelove (Kubrick), 50
Dreiser, Theodore, 195
Dust in the Wind (Hou Hsaio-hsien), 120
Dvorak, Antonin, 162, 169, 181
dystopia, 32

Eisenstein, Sergei, 100, 133, 191, 196, 198
El Greco, 159
El Salvador, 45
Elvis, 138
Epic of Asdiwal, The (Lévi-Strauss), 14
Escape from New York (Carpenter), 83
Escher, M. C., 76
Espinosa, Garcia, 187
ethnicity, 38, 117, 127, 202
Europe, 3, 5, 12, 120, 161, 170, 171, 190, 192, 194, 195, 197, 199, 203
Exorcist, The (Friedkin), 13

Fail-Safe (Lumet), 48
Fanon, Frantz, 199
fascism, 62, 108
Fassbinder, Werner, 122
Faulkner, William, 21
feminism, 66, 130, 131, 153, 162
feudalism, 108
figuration, 1, 2, 31, 56, 91, 145, 197
film noir, 119, 150, 180
First World, 1, 50, 93, 109, 111, 145, 146, 154, 155, 192, 195, 196, 198–200, 202–5, 209, 211, 212
Flag for Sunrise (R. Stone), 43
Flaubert, Gustave, 9, 172
Fonda, Jane, 52
Fonseca, Carlos, 40
Forster, E. M., 132
Fort Apache, the Bronx (Petrie), 83
Foucault, Michel, 66
Frears, Stephen, 119
French Cancan (Renoir), 169
Freud, Sigmund, 149, 172

genre films, 5
geopolitical unconscious, 3
Gherman, Alexei, 100
Gide, André, 121–32, 138, 144
Gilliam, Terry, 150
Godard, Jean-Luc, 1, 23, 70, 71, 121, 159–68, 170, 172–6, 178, 179–85, 196–9, 201, 211
Godfather III (Coppola), 156
Goffman, Erving, 15, 101
Goya, Francisco, 159
Greimas, A. J., 33
Grifters, The (Frears), 119
Guthrie, Woody, 57

Handke, Peter, 166

217

218